D0340427

THROUGH BLOOD & FIRE

*This Congressional Medal of Honor
was awarded to Joshua L. Chamberlain
for his service during the Battle of Gettysburg.*
SPECIAL COLLECTIONS, BOWDOIN COLLEGE LIBRARY

THROUGH BLOOD & FIRE

Selected Civil War Papers of
Major General Joshua Chamberlain

Mark Nesbitt

STACKPOLE
BOOKS

Copyright © 1996 by Mark Nesbitt

Published by
STACKPOLE BOOKS
5067 Ritter Road
Mechanicsburg, PA 17055

All rights reserved, including the right to reproduce this book or portions thereof in any form or by any means, electronic or mechanical, including photocopying, recording, or by any information storage and retrieval system, without permission in writing from the publisher. All inquiries should be addressed to Stackpole Books, 5067 Ritter Road, Mechanicsburg, PA 17055.

Printed in the United States of America

First edition

10 9 8 7 6 5 4 3 2

Library of Congress Cataloging-in-Publication Data

Chamberlain, Joshua Lawrence, 1828–1914.
    Through blood and fire. : selected Civil War papers of Major General Joshua
L. Chamberlain / [edited, with commentary by] Mark Nesbitt.
        p.   cm.
    Includes bibliographical references (p.) and index.
    ISBN 0-8117-1750-X
    1. Chamberlain, Joshua Lawrence, 1828–1914. 2. United States—History—
Civil War, 1861–1865—Personal narratives. 3. United States—History—Civil
War, 1861–1865—Campaigns. 4. United States. Army. Maine Infantry
Regiment, 20th (1862–1865). 5. Generals—United States—Bibliography.
I. Nesbitt, Mark. II. Title.
E467.1.C47A25   1996
974.1'041'092—dc20
[B]   95-25430
                                                                                          CIP

To the memory of
Anna Pasko and Mary F. Ryan,
my grandmothers who lived in Chamberlain's time.

*"We pass now quickly from each other's sight;
but I know full well that where beyond these passing scenes
you shall be, there will be heaven!"*

—Joshua L. Chamberlain

☞ CONTENTS ☜

⊶ ACKNOWLEDGMENTS ⊷

To a writer there are numerous people who are absolutely indispensable in the research and writing of a book.

Julia Colvin Oehmig, Curator of the Pejepscot Historical Society in Brunswick, Maine, nurtured this project along from its inception. From talking initially to the Board of Trustees of the Pejepscot Historical Society to lobby for my permission to use their vast archives, to the final historical editing of the manuscript, Julia worked out of a deep love for history and a sincere appreciation and remarkable knowledge of the life of Joshua L. Chamberlain. She guided me through the Society's files, paved the way to other collections and pertinent individuals, and provided crucial historical details for key parts of this book. I cannot thank her enough. Many thanks also to Mark Cutler at the Pejepscot Historical Society.

Rosamond Allen, of St. Petersburg, Florida, granddaughter of Joshua L. Chamberlain, through Mrs. Jacquelyn M. Beard gave me permission to publish the vast number of personal letters of Chamberlain, without which the fabric of this book would have been greatly diminished. Chamberlain was a man as well as a soldier, and his letters to his wife, sister, parents, brothers, and children exhibit that fact in this book, thanks to Miss Allen.

Others in Maine contributed to the production of this work by easing my path through the often labyrinthine search through various repositories.

Susan Ravdin, Assistant Curator, Special Collections, Bowdoin College, Brunswick, Maine, was incredibly helpful, first in permitting access to the original Chamberlain documents preserved in the college's collection, and second by allowing me to use photographs of Chamberlain as a Bowdoin professor and of the Medal of Honor won by Chamberlain at Gettysburg, now resting in their collection.

Tom Desjardin, of Lewiston, Maine, and the University of Maine, Orono, got wind of my writing a book on Chamberlain and went out of his way to help me. His book on the 20th Maine at Gettysburg, *Stand Firm Ye Boys from Maine,* should be in every Civil War library.

Sylvia Sherman, at the Maine State Archives, was a great help and provided me with all the pertinent documents from the institution's collection.

Holly Hurd-Forsyth, at the Maine Historical Society, Portland, procured a copy of the June 18, 1864, letter, "lines before Petersburg."

Muriel A. Sanford, head of the Special Collections Department, Raymond H. Fogler Library, University of Maine, Orono, was prompt and helpful in answering my queries.

Erik C. Jorgensen, Executive Director at the Pejepscot Historical Society, was always helpful when I needed assistance.

James Talbot, of Turner, Maine, provided fresh information on the fate of the Chamberlain papers after the sale of Chamberlain's house.

Mr. and Mrs. Abbot Spear were kind enough to allow me to use some of Ellis Spear's account of Gettysburg. Mr. Spear's book on his ancestor's papers is being published by the University of Maine and should provide much additional information on the role of the 20th Maine throughout the war.

Deb Beale, of Augusta, Maine, gave me information on how to get around that section of Maine while I was researching.

Christine Weidmen, Archivist of Manuscripts and Archives, Yale University Library, New Haven, Connecticut, was kind enough to review the library's Chamberlain holdings for me. Nan Card, of the Rutherford B. Hayes Presidential Center in Fremont, Ohio, supplied information on that institution's collection. Eva Moseley, of the Schlesinger Library at Radcliffe College, Cambridge, Massachusetts, was helpful in answering my inquiries.

Chris Calkins, historian at Petersburg National Battlefield, Petersburg, Virginia, unselfishly shared his immense knowledge of the battlegrounds there and helped me practically pinpoint where Chamberlain took his wound in that action. As well, his tours of Five Forks and the battles leading up to the fight there were remarkable.

D. Scott Hartwig and Eric Campbell, at Gettysburg National Military Park, have always been helpful in sharing new information and in gleaning old files for relevant documents.

Stan Clark, of Stan Clark Military Books in Gettysburg, gave permission for me to document the two letters in private hands that he published in *"Bayonet! Forward,"* his collection of Chamberlain's Civil War reminiscences. Stan deserves thanks for publishing and reprinting a number of books on Chamberlain, all well worth reading.

I also thank my friends in Gettysburg, Cindy and David Wright, for their endless hospitality, and Cindy's brother, Dr. Roger Timperlake, for explaining Chamberlain's wounds in medical detail. It would have been impossible to write about them without understanding their severity.

To Ron Wilson, my former mentor at Gettysburg and currently Chief Historian at Appomattox Court House National Historic Park, I am indebted. I always seem to just show up and ask him questions, and he then spends weeks finding the answers. He walked me in Chamberlain's footsteps during the general's brief but climactic visit to Appomattox and what the general recorded about the changes he saw. History, as anyone who has spent much time studying it knows, is not static but fluid, as new information is continually uncovered (Like a river—always the same but always different and new). During my last visit, Ron said the most honest thing any historian has ever told me about a piece of history he had just uncovered and documented: "That is how it happened as far as I know right now. Ask me in another week or a year, and things may have changed." All historians should be so wise.

Though I never met her, I must recognize Alice Rains Trulock for her magnificent biography of Chamberlain, *In the Hands of Providence.* She and her husband, James, put together a virtual day-by-day account of Chamberlain's life during the war. I relied heavily on the Trulock's work to provide an itinerary of Chamberlain's military career.

John Pullen's classic, *The 20th Maine,* and Willard Wallace's *Soul of the Lion* I must mention as seminal to my interest of Chamberlain as well as supplementary to this book in helping me understand the details of some of the smaller battles fought by Chamberlain.

Thanks also to the many people with whom I've spoken who gave me a small clue as to where to find a bit of trivia on Joshua L. Chamberlain, or who encouraged me over the several years it took to research and write this book. You share in this as well.

✤ EDITORIAL METHODS ✤

A NUMBER OF graduate students in history during the 1950s took on projects to edit various historical manuscripts. Sadly, they understood editing to mean cutting down of the manuscripts so that nonhistorians would not have any trouble understanding them.

It has always been my editorial style to leave everything in the original document, including misspellings (which sometimes give clues to colloquial pronunciation by the writer), grammatical errors (which show the individual's education or mastery of writing skills), and quirks unique to individual documents. In other words, I do not change or cut anything from the original. I merely add clarification and my own interpretations as a historian to the documents.

This does two things: First, it leaves the original documents and all their information intact for future historians who may be looking for something completely different from what I seek. And second, it allows others to disagree with my interpretations.

In fact, one of the stipulations of the Pejepscot Historical Society, which oversees most of the Chamberlain papers, was that I not cut anything from the documents—that I reprint them verbatim. This I did.

If something has been added within the body of the letter to clarify the meaning to the reader, it is enclosed in brackets. Anything emphasized by Chamberlain by underlining has been underlined here. If a proper name is spelled one way in one letter and another way in a different letter, I have not corrected it.

I was often working from photocopies of photocopies of photocopies. Sometimes the originals are not available even to serious scholars. Small marks like periods or commas in the original sometimes do not show on the copy. Regardless, though a small punctuation mark might be missing from a letter in this book, the meaning and tenor of the document remains for posterity.

Sometimes ink ran, as when Chamberlain was writing in his smoky tent and his eyes were tearing. Where a word or letter was illegible, I have so indicated thus: [ill.]. Julia Oehmig of the Pejepscot Historical Society helped immensely in deciphering much of Chamberlain's handwriting. Where a word was obviously omitted, I have inserted it in brackets. When obvious mistakes were made by Chamberlain or somewhat confusing words or phrases were used, I left them and have indicated them with [*sic*].

A very few pieces of Chamberlain's correspondence extant are merely military forms that he filled out, for the most part on a quarterly schedule, to report expenses or receipt of supplies. When all he did was fill in numbers or a few words, I have omitted the form. Perhaps the most significant thing that emerges from the forms, however, appears on an account form dated from June 1 to August 31, 1864, wherein he requests clothing and subsistence "For 2 private servants not soldiers." In the "Description of Servants," he notes one Lewis Jones and Jack [ill., possibly Williams], "Colored boys." Although it was not uncommon for Federal officers to hire locals as servants while in the Southern states, this is the first I have read anywhere that Chamberlain did so.

Copies of virtually all of Chamberlain's correspondence (as well as correspondence related to Chamberlain) are held in the Pejepscot Historical Society, in Brunswick, Maine. Alice and James Trulock donated their immense collection of copies of Chamberlain's papers to the Society after they completed their magnificent biography of Chamberlain, *In the Hands of Providence: Joshua L. Chamberlain and the American Civil War.*

The Library of Congress in Washington, D.C., houses approximately one thousand items from the life of Chamberlain, including much on his personal life both pre- and postwar. Hundreds of pages of information on the Warren Court of Inquiry, fine pencil sketches by his brother Horace, photos, regimental indexes, and originals of some orders and reports are included in the collection in eleven boxes. Most important to this work are the letters to his wife, nearly all of which were found in the Library of Congress collection. Probably most fascinating to the historian are the battlefield maps, upon which Chamberlain drew march routes and unit positions as he collected his thoughts for his postwar speeches and writings. To hold in your hands the same map over which a Civil War personage such as Chamberlain pondered, then drew positions upon from personal recollection, is an experience only a historian can understand.

Many original Chamberlain papers reside in the Bowdoin College Library in Brunswick. The Maine State Archives in Augusta contain much of Chamberlain's correspondence to state officials.

Other Chamberlain manuscripts used in this book reside at the University of Maine in Orono, the National Archives in Washington, D.C., and the Maine Historical Society in Portland.

⇥ INTRODUCTION ⇤

LYING ON THE floor of a barn that once stood behind the home of Joshua L. Chamberlain—late major general of Maine Volunteers—were soiled papers scattered and slowly soaking up the mud from boots that recently trod Maine and Potter streets in Brunswick, Maine. For years people visited the barn because stored within were antiques and furniture from the Chamberlain family for sale and for perusal. The papers were a combination of letters and notes, canceled bank checks, correspondence, perhaps a few maps and sketches of old battlefields, most of them dropped from the drawers of furniture being moved out of the barn by its new owners. Some of the documents were in piles in the barn mixed with other correspondence. More letters and documents were stored across the river at a place called the Walker Homestead in Topsham. There were "hundreds and hundreds of letters," according to one gentleman. "Many were Joshua Chamberlain's." There was a sign in the place that read, "Any Letter—$5." That was a lot of money in the late 1930s and '40s.[1]

The Walker Homestead no longer exists. The letters and documents, like the old barn that once belonged to one of Maine's—and America's—most famous sons, have also vanished.

This body of work contains all the letters of Joshua Lawrence Chamberlain that are housed in public and semipublic archives. There are a number of Chamberlain's letters in private collections that, for one reason or another, may never see the light of day. Perhaps, with the publication of this book and the recent resurgence in popularity of Chamberlain, collectors holding those unseen papers will be encouraged to place copies of them in public archives.

Still, much has been said, written, and dramatized recently about Joshua Lawrence Chamberlain, called by himself and his friends and family in Maine simply Lawrence.

Certainly Chamberlain's legacy of long public service to his country, to his state, and to his alma mater would deserve attention in any era. That he served with distinction in the American Civil War, rose from lieutenant colonel to major general, taking six wounds in numerous battles, and was chosen to oversee the official laying down of arms by the Confederate

1

Army of Northern Virginia at Appomattox would certainly qualify him as a man of great courage capable of solid judgment and heroic action.

But heroes usually emerge because of one singular event. Many modern Civil War buffs believe that for Chamberlain, this would have been an hour-and-a-half battle in which he directed his men to defend the extreme left flank of the Union line at Gettysburg against numerous Confederate assaults, receiving the Medal of Honor for his actions. In recognizing a hero for just one action, however, one can lose sight of the whole man he really was or the other men who helped him get to his place of recognized prominence. No one would have disliked this more than Chamberlain.

Chamberlain's military career lasted from August 1862 until August 1865.[2] He died on February 24, 1914, at the age of 85, and so his life as a soldier would seem but a small part of his lifetime, perhaps even inconsequential.

But war changes everything. Visiting the frightening realm of combat changes everyone engaged, in one way or another, forever. The gentle college professor who once felt the irresistible pull of patriotism would visit a number of times that inscrutable place between death and life. The experience of being there, of watching close friends around him suddenly be taken from this life, of imagining himself on that journey in the very next moment, changed him. You can see the progressive metamorphosis in his photos. That youthful friends and comrades-in-arms died at age twenty-one or twenty-two haunted him the rest of his life. If he did not necessarily feel guilt for surviving when they did not, he certainly pondered both the mysterious nature of the horrible happenstance in battle that plucks one and leaves another, and the guilt of command an officer must carry for the rest of his life. You can read of it in his book *The Passing of the Armies.*

The battle that seemed to change him the most was Gettysburg, his first as a commanding officer. "You are to hold that ground at all hazards!" were the words of Col. Strong Vincent, Chamberlain's brigade commander at Gettysburg. The meaning, to any military man, was not to leave until so ordered. Vincent died and Chamberlain held the ground at Gettysburg, and then held on to it, returning to it over and over, for the rest of his life, obeying, like the good soldier he was, Vincent's last orders to him.

But his other battles were—even if slightly less memorable to us— no less dangerous or horrifying to him. At Fredericksburg in 1862, he spent more than twenty-four hours lying behind dead bodies in front of the Confederate line at the wall of Marye's Heights listening to the grisly thump of bullets as they hit the corpses that shielded him. The living there were saved over and over by the dead—soldiers true, performing their last, most hideous duty. The June 18, 1864, charge at Petersburg almost killed Chamberlain on the spot; the effects of his brutal wounding there eventually did kill him fifty years later. And in the last few weeks of fighting at the very end of the war, he took another bullet, which wounded him in two places, deflected from his heart only by a leather case and a brass-mounted hand mirror.

At the war's end, he was chosen from among all the officers in the army to oversee the laying down of arms of the enemy. This moved him greatly, perhaps more than anything else in his whirlwind military career of three short years.

Then it was the long march home to Brunswick, Maine, and an active—and painful—half century of public life. His wound from Petersburg hurt him the whole time and affected everything from his sitting for long periods to his intimate life. His marriage, which suffered much from his absences, suffered even more. But his spirit of public duty and daily evidence of his personal courage remained strong.

Postwar, he served four terms as governor of Maine; was president of Bowdoin College; was appointed by the Hayes administration as commissioner of education representing the United States in Paris at the Universal Exposition; was president of three companies, including a railroad firm and an electric motor company; and later became surveyor of customs for the port of Portland, Maine. In spite of his Petersburg wounds, which never really healed, you can see photos of him attending Bowdoin functions in his gown and mortarboard or riding down a street astride a huge horse, his distinctive mustache white and flowing, his body as straight in the saddle as any eighteen-year-old cavalryman of the World War that was soon to break out. He was, no doubt, in pain in those photos; there are records of him suffering from simply sitting in a comfortable chair too long. He never wrote much about it, though, and he was active to the end, his passion for duty and service buoying him again and again above the physical pain.

Most modern aficionados of Chamberlain know him from the movie *Gettysburg* or the novel on which the movie was based, *The Killer Angels,* by Michael Shaara. Chamberlain was the centerpiece of both, but both were about just one battle of the many he experienced.

And both of those were works of fiction. The most basic facts were accurate, but most of the content was made up, especially the dialogue.

This collection and interpretation of Chamberlain's own letters—his words, not a fictionalization—will help the reader visualize what the Civil War was really like, through the eyes of one of its most distinguished participants. It is a guided tour of the Civil War by Lieutenant Colonel, then Colonel, then Brigadier General, then Major General Joshua Lawrence Chamberlain. It is also a guide by Lawrence.

My own interest in Chamberlain goes back much further than just the last few years since the media popularized him. While working as a park ranger at Gettysburg National Military Park in the early 1970s, I gave talks on Little Round Top to visitors. I wove the story of the 20th Maine into the tale of the gallant defense of the key terrain feature, because it was an important part of the battle. I gave directions to the monument of the 20th Maine to the very few people who asked where it was. More often than not, they would return, not having found it and I would have to lead them down the narrow, wooded path on the southern spur of the hill. Now, the paths to the monument to the 20th Maine at Gettysburg are being worn down and new ones created.

Although I studied the American Civil War for more than thirty-five years and have been a professional historian since my days with the Park Service, it was not until I began working on this book that I fully understood why the Union soldier fought.

For me, the reason the Confederates fought was easy to understand: Their very land was being invaded, their homes ransacked, their families threatened, their small-farm livelihoods in danger of being taken away, which would leave them and their dependents without food or shelter.

It was through my intensive study of Chamberlain that I finally came to comprehend why the Union soldier fought and suffered and died. The reasons came to me late, even after all the studying, because it was a concept that my experiences growing up in the cynicism of the Vietnam era didn't allow me to ponder. They were concepts that were out of date to me, alien, and will perhaps sound strange to many people studying the Civil War today.

These men of the Union were fighting for love of country. They were fighting for patriotism. They were fighting for the honor of their country's flag so that it wouldn't go down before an enemy. They continued to fight because of their ideal of manhood, which disallowed quitting once their duty was defined. They believed in these principles strongly enough to be willing to risk death and lifelong disfigurement for them. They believed in them so passionately that some even gave up—like those under the numbered tombstones in national cemeteries—not only their lives and families but also their very identities.

Over and over in the letters that make up this book, but especially in the ones to his family, Chamberlain repeats this theme. His love of country and his resolve to do his duty as long as his country needed him are paramount. He passionately explains to his governor that he will pass up a safe sabbatical in Europe to join others who would "rescue our Country from Desolation." He gently explains to his wife, "I feel that I am where duty called me," and that "Most likely I shall be hit somewhere at sometime, but all 'my times are in His hands', & I cannot die without His appointing." And to his father, who has been pressing him to resign from the army and take a safe civilian position, he writes simply, "I owe the Country three years of service." But perhaps he sums up his feelings of patriotism best in writing to his six-year-old daughter: "There has been a big battle, and we had a great many men killed or wounded. We shall try it again soon, and see if we cannot make those Rebels behave better, and stop their wicked works in trying to spoil our Country, and making us all so unhappy."

Duty. God. Manhood. Honor. Country. Always his "Country," with a capital *C*.

This book, therefore, has been a journey and an epiphany for me as well, thanks to Joshua Lawrence Chamberlain's letters.

It is both curse and blessing that people have rediscovered Chamberlain. It is a curse because they are "overvisiting" the very ground he fought for and are literally wearing it down. It is slowly losing its semblance of the terrain as he saw it on that sultry July afternoon in 1863.

It is also tempting for visitors to stand on the small plot of ground where Chamberlain once stood, where his men once fought, within the horseshoe or angle formed by the 20th Maine's line, and, having looked from end to end, say to themselves, "Now I've seen it all—where the Civil War was won." But that is untrue. You cannot quantify history; you cannot say that one place was more hallowed or more important than another. That is too simple. The battleground where Chamberlain paced and his men fought and died as heroes is just one more place on the Gettysburg battlefield, just one more place on one of the thousands of battlefields, large and small, across America, where heroes trod and bled and perished for something nobler than themselves, nobler than you or me.

But Chamberlain's rediscovery is a blessing, too, for in rediscovering a man like him and the men he associated with—and even those he fought against—perhaps we can rediscover something or things in ourselves that have been missing for a long time and have needed rediscovering. Years after Appomattox, Chamberlain described the Confederate soldiers who laid down their arms, but he could have been talking about the Union soldiers who had fought them as well: "Before us in proud humiliation stood the embodiment of manhood: men whom neither toils and sufferings, nor the fact of death, nor disaster, nor hopelessness could bend from their resolve; standing before us now, thin, worn, and famished, but erect, and with eyes looking level into ours."

Will anyone ever be able to say anything like that about us?

Chamberlain was born in Brewer, Maine, on September 8, 1828. He was named Joshua after his father and grandfather and was given the middle name Lawrence as a tribute to Commodore James Lawrence, who became famous during the War of 1812 with his dying entreaty "Don't give up the ship!"

Firstborn Lawrence grew up near the water and forests of Maine. He was soon joined by siblings Horace, Sarah (whom he called "Sadie" or "Sae"), John Calhoun, and Thomas Davee. Lawrence helped with the farm, pursued his studies, enjoyed riding horses, and especially loved sailing, commanding his younger brothers as crew. Hunting, however, was one common nineteenth-century pastime that Chamberlain never engaged in.

His mother encouraged him to study for the ministry; his father steered him toward a military career. He attended Whiting's Military and Classical School for a while but later agreed to study for the ministry. While waiting to be able to attend Bowdoin College in Brunswick, Maine, he taught school in North Milford. With the help of a friend from Whiting's, he learned Greek and Latin, and in February 1848 he entered Bowdoin.

In later life, Chamberlain would be remembered for his magnificent public speeches. As a young man, however, he stammered over words beginning with *t, p,* and *b.* With the same power of will that got him into college and that would serve him during army life and after, he tackled the problem, creating several methods of overcoming the speech impediment. After he applied himself, few could detect the problem; eventually, the condition was mastered so completely that he even won prizes in college for his oratory.

He missed a year of school because of a serious illness. When he returned, he got involved in the local church, often playing the organ as the choir sang. There, one Sunday morning, his eye paused upon Miss Frances Caroline Adams, nicknamed "Fanny"—the adopted daughter of the pastor. A relationship blossomed, and then deepened, at least on Chamberlain's part, but was interrupted by Fanny's returning to New York to study music. Meanwhile, Chamberlain focused his energies on studying and became a top scholar at Bowdoin.

After graduation, he attended Bangor Theological Seminary and studied German, Hebrew, Arabic, and Syriac. Though he and Fanny were engaged in 1852, she left for Georgia to teach music there. Chamberlain then, as later, was disappointed by her apparent dislike of letter writing. In 1855 Chamberlain graduated from the seminary and received his master's degree from Bowdoin just a week later. By the next term, Chamberlain was instructing natural theology and logic at Bowdoin. Fanny had returned from Georgia, and in December 1855 they were married.

A daughter, Grace, who would be called "Daisy," was born the next fall, and in the autumn of 1859, a son, Harold—called by his middle name, Wyllys—was born. In the spring of 1860, another daughter, Emily Stelle, was born to the couple, but the baby died in the fall. In December 1861, Chamberlain lost his brother Horace to disease.

His personal tragedies were mirrored by national catastrophe on a far greater scale. Since Abraham Lincoln's election and inauguration, eleven Southern states had seceded from the Union, and armed conflict had broken out between the Federal government and the states in rebellion, now known as the Confederacy. During 1861 and through half of 1862, Chamberlain watched Bowdoin boys, as well as thousands of others from Maine, join the Federal forces and march off to the seat of war in far-off Virginia. Within him something stirred—every bit as powerful, it would turn out, as the passion he held for Fanny. Yet there was something different

Professor Chamberlain. Special Collections,
Bowdoin College Library

about it. He would write about it many years later: "The flag of the
Nation had been insulted. The honor and authority of the Union had
been defied. The integrity and the existence of the People of the United
States had been assailed in open and bitter war."[3]

In July 1862, Chamberlain offered his services to his state.

⇥ 1862 ⇤

*The regiments passing to the front marched not between festoons of ladies' smiles
and waving handkerchiefs, thrown kisses and banner presentations. They were
looked upon sadly and in a certain awe, as those that had taken on themselves a
doom. The muster rolls on which the name and oath were written were pledges of
honor,—redeemable at the gates of death. And they who went up to them, knowing this, are on the lists of heroes.*

—Maj. Gen. Joshua L. Chamberlain, *The Passing of the Armies*

Brunswick July 14 1862.

To His Excellency Governor Washburn:

In pursuance of the offer of reinforcements for the war, I ask if
your Excellency desires and will accept my service.

Perhaps it is not quite necessary to inform your Excellency who
I am. I believe you will be satisfied with my antecedents. I am a son
of Joshua Chamberlain of Brewer. For seven years past I have been
Professor in Bowdoin College. I have always been interested in
military matters, and what I do not know in that line I know how
to learn.

Having been lately elected to a new department here, I am
expecting to have leave, at the approaching Commencement, to
spend a year or more in Europe, in the service of the College. I am
entirely unwilling, however, to accept this offer, if my Country
needs my service or example here.

Your Excellency presides over the Educational as well as the
military affairs of our State, and, I am well aware, appreciates the

9

*Israel Washburn, Jr., governor of Maine in
1861 and 1862.* MAINE STATE ARCHIVES

importance of sustaining our Institutions of Learning. You will therefore be able to decide where my influence is most needed.

But, I fear, this war, so costly of blood and treasure, will not cease until the men of the North are willing to leave good positions, and sacrifice the dearest personal interests, to rescue our Country from Desolation, and defend the National Existence against treachery at home and jeopardy abroad. This war must be ended, with a swift and strong hand; and every man ought to come forward and ask to be placed at his proper post.

Nearly a hundred of those who have been my pupils, are now officers in our army; but there are many more all over our State, who, I believe, would respond with enthusiasm, if summoned by me, and who would bring forward men enough to fill up a Regiment at once. I can not free myself from my obligations here, until the first week in August, but I do not want to be the last in the field, if it can possibly be helped.

I am sensible that I am proposing personal sacrifices, which would not probably be demanded of me; but I believe this to be my duty, and I know I can be of service to my Country in this hour of her peril.

I shall acquiesce in your decision Governor, whether I can best serve you here or in the field. I believe you will find me qualified for the latter as for the former, and I trust I may have the honor to hear a word from you, and I remain,

Yours to Command,
J. L. Chamberlain[1]
To His Excellency
The Governor

From his teaching post at Bowdoin, Chamberlain had watched large numbers of men from his state form around the national colors and march to war in Virginia. He had opportunity to hear of the defeats and humiliation of Federal forces at Fort Sumter, South Carolina, and Balls Bluff, Virginia, in 1861. The Federal defeat at Manassas, Virginia, nearly a year before was common knowledge. From the fall of Fort Donelson, Tennessee, in February 1862 emerged a new hero: Ulysses S.—"Unconditional Surrender"—Grant, and Union troops occupied Nashville. In the Eastern Theater of the war, an ironclad gunboat called the *Virginia* (or, from its former incarnation as a United States Ship, the *Merrimack*) had threatened to destroy the U.S. fleet at Norfolk and cruise up the Chesapeake Bay and attack Washington. The Federal counterpart, the *Monitor*, fought the *Virginia* to a draw at Hampton Roads just four and a half months before Chamberlain wrote his letter to the governor. Since then, Gen. George B. McClellan had begun his slow march up the Virginia peninsula formed by the York and James rivers, which led directly to Richmond.

In April 1862, a battle had been fought at Pittsburg Landing around a little country parish house called Shiloh Church near the Tennessee River. The losses, to a nation still not used to modern warfare, were appalling. Also that spring, the U.S. forces captured distant New Orleans. Confederate general Thomas J. "Stonewall" Jackson was leading troops to victory in battles in the Shenandoah Valley of Virginia. June brought word of battles near Richmond, Virginia, and Memphis, Tennessee.

Having had some military schooling, Chamberlain was no doubt interested when Confederate cavalry leader J. E. B. Stuart humiliated the

Federal army on the peninsula by riding completely around it. Stuart returned with information that helped the new commander of the Confederate army, Gen. Robert E. Lee, launch a counteroffensive against McClellan and drive him from the doorstep of Richmond in the Seven Days Battles in June and July 1862.

Though the Federal armies in the West seemed to be successful, the war in the East was going badly for the Union. Chamberlain's patriotic blood stirred, and his family's military background, as well as his own early though brief military training, encouraged him to believe he could fight as well as any other man. More than that, he was absolutely positive, because of his educational background, that what he did not know he could learn. With full recognition that he was risking personal health and wealth, he offered to persuade his students who had not yet volunteered to join in service to their country.

He was encouraged by the governor's reply and so offered to work to gather enough men for an entire regiment:

> Brunswick July 17 1862
>
> To His Excellency, Gov. Washburn
>
> I received your note of yesterday, and thank you for your favorable opinion. I shall endeavor to comply with your request, and see you tomorrow. Mean time let me say that I only want to be where I can best serve you. I do not wish to stand in the way of others— especially of our gallant men on the Potomac.
>
> I believe I can get together a thousand men in a very short time, and shall hold myself entirely at your Excellency's command in so doing.
>
> Several young graduates of the College have come to me of their own accord, and say they will go with me as privates or any way.
>
> I know my men, & know whom to pick. I think they would prefer a new Regt. but it shall all be as your Excellency sees fit.
>
> Hoping to see you tomorrow
>
> I am
>
> Yr. Ex's most obdt sevt.
>
> J. L. Chamberlain[2]

But word of his efforts at joining the army rather than taking his sabbatical got to his colleagues at Bowdoin. Several of the faculty there opposed his enlisting. Though he had recently been elected to a new department and had chosen to serve the college on sabbatical in Europe, some of his fellows began an organized campaign to discredit him.[3]

Brunswick July 22d 1862

Hon. Israel Washburn:

I beg your Excellency will understand that these mortifying reports in regard to my appointment, did not come from me in any way that I can imagine.

To Genl. Howard[4] alone, in a private conversation, I stated that though it was scarcely probable that a new Regt. would be raised, yet in case it should be, I had received the impression that you thought favorably of my having it, and I asked the Genl. what I had better do in the mean time.

To others I had, of course, every notion to maintain a discrete [*sic*] silence, as to the result of my visit to Augusta.

I hope your Excellency will not be as disturbed as I am, at these reports and contradictions which are so embarrassing and injurious to me.

I do not know any way in which I am to blame for them, and I only hope that at some time I can overcome their mortifying effect by actual service in the field.

I am persecuted with applications and propositions, but I urge all I see to enlist at once in the first Regt. they can find.

We had a good meeting Saturday, and the effects of it are very evident in this slow town.[5]

Very truly
Your Excellency's obdt. servt.
J. L. Chamberlain[6]

Brunswick July 23d 1862

To whom it may concern,

I take pleasure in commending Mr. Charles Bennett of the Sophomore class of Bowdoin College, to the favor of any to whom he may address himself. He has made up his mind to go into the Army.

He is a young man of capacity & energy, and of the right spirit

& stamp for the business. I hope he will be successful in his application, as I am confident he will make a true soldier, & do himself honor & his country good service.

J. L. Chamberlain[7]

While Chamberlain could help secure appointments to the army for his students, he was still having problems with some of the faculty at Bowdoin.

Brunswick Aug. 8th 1862

Governor Washburn,
My dear Sir,

I find I have to encounter an unexpected degree of opposition in the Faculty of the College. They are unwilling to give me any sort of countenance in the matter. But I feel that I must go, & I trust that the representations that they propose to make to induce you to withhold my commission, will have no more weight with you than with me. I feel it to be my duty to serve my Country. Your call to a post of honorable service finds me as a good citizen to come forward without delay & without excuse. I regret that I am obliged to act against the wishes of my colleagues, but I feel that I can make no other decision.

One or two matters of note to mention.

Would another company be accepted from Brunswick? Our quota is not half filled, and men here say that if they can have until the 20th of August, they would raise a whole company, otherwise, I suppose, we shall have to Draft.

Alpheus S. Packard jr son of Prof P. is anxious for the position of Hospital Steward. I do not know who the surgeon is, but we can all commend Mr. Packard as a superior man for the place he wants.

Your Excellency's
obdt. Servt.
J. L. Chamberlain[8]

The Bowdoin faculty's objections to Chamberlain's trading his professor's robe for army tunic apparently did little to impress the governor, and Chamberlain received his commission as lieutenant colonel of the 20th Maine Regiment of Infantry. Recent West Point graduate Adelbert Ames was colonel of the regiment.

Brunswick Aug 8. 1862

Governor Washburn,
My dear Sir

The interval between the mails leaves me only time to thank you & to say I should prefer the office you tender to any other. I shall accept. The College Laws require me to present the matter to the Faculty before the case is finally adjusted, but it can have only one issue, & an hour will settle it. I wait your further orders Shall I go to Augusta?

Very respectfly,
J. L. Chamberlain[9]

Brunswick Aug 11, 1862

My dear Loring,

I have received your favor and shall be extremely happy to do what I can for your friend, who, I learn from all sources, is worthy of the place.

As the Col. will not be here for some time, I suppose I shall have something to say about some of the new appts. I am inclined to think that your letter will secure the place for Mr. Loring. I go to Augusta today & shall attend to the matter.

The faculty here are greatly opposed to my going. They absolutely refuse to give me up, & have passed a vote to that effect, but I feel it is to be my duty to go, & know that I can be of service in the field, where my natural tastes & my early education lead me & for which they in some small degree qualify me.

I dare say those who oppose my going, will say things to break me down if possible, & I hope you will do what you can to countermand such an influence. I thought the "Press" a little hard in the way the Report of my appt. to the Colonelcy was connected, & perhaps it was somewhat injurious to me. I was not responsible in any way for that story. I had only offered my services, in any capacity in which I might be placed. However that is past. Do look after such [ill.] as that, my good friend, & I will thank you.

I told you I could not do much for the Press. Those two letters were written a line at a time in a great hurry. I can hardly do anything more I suppose, so I won't hold you to your promise to send.

I will <u>subscribe,</u> & then do what I can to see that you get correct information of Brunswick & Bowdoin.

Yours truly, J. L. Chamberlain[10]

Chamberlain and the recruits from his area of Maine were about to gather at Camp Mason near Portland, Maine, to come under the command of their colonel, Adelbert Ames. Besides being a graduate of West Point and a Maine man, Ames had "seen the elephant"—had fought in the Battle of Manassas, Virginia, and had been wounded in the thigh. He would receive the Medal of Honor for his actions there as a first lieutenant. The first meeting between Ames and his charges would not be a cordial one. The men were supremely independent; he was a martinet. But they would bend to his stern will and, in the end, become a superb fighting regiment for it.[11]

As part of his early duties, Chamberlain wrote to a military assistant of the governor concerning recommendations for staff appointments.

Brunswick Aug 15th 1862

Dear Col.

As the Governor must be much occupied, I address a note to you in regard to some matters in the 20th Regt.

I have had a great many applications for staff appointments, & have taken some pains to look into their merits, and if I have anything to say about them, I would suggest the following.

<u>Mr. A. L. Loring</u> of Yarmouth for Quarter master. He makes out a strong case.

<u>Mr. Henry S. B. Smith</u> of Brunswick sergeant major. The Governor will recollect Smith's claims.

<u>Thomas D. Chamberlain</u> of Bangor a brother of mine, wants to be Quarter master sergeant. He is abundantly competent for the place having been for some time chief clerk in F. M. Sabine's store, and I should like to have him receive the appointment.

<u>A. S. Packard</u> jr of Brunswick wants the place of Hospital Steward. The surgeon recommends, I believe, but I mention him here.

The above frees my mind and conscience, & as I suppose the appointments will be made when Col. Ames comes I wish to place in your hands whatever I have to suggest in the matter.

I report in Portland Monday.

I am obliged for your courtesy while I was in Augusta.

Very Truly Yours

J. L. Chamberlain

Col. Eugene Hale

Aid de Camp[12]

Early in the Civil War, politics had as much to do with becoming an officer or gaining a post in the army as military training. It was apparently so even after a year of war had taken all the enthusiastic enlistees and either killed or maimed them or sent them home full of tales of army life and combat. More inducements to enlist were offered for the second round of requests for recruits. Though Chamberlain petitioned for certain individuals to serve in positions early in his military career, it was a habit that apparently came from a desire to assist others, since it continued throughout the conflict.

And so, off they went—quartermasters who had done no quartermastering, store clerks, brothers, college professors' sons, and the professor himself, taking on the responsibilities of a lieutenant colonel in a combat-bound regiment of infantry, officially numbered the 20th Regiment Maine Volunteers—little knowing what those responsibilities were, or what they would entail. Later Chamberlain would understand the burden of writing a testimonial for a desiring friend or former student. But in 1862, as he wrote recommendations for his acquaintances and relatives, he had too little experience in the army to realize that for some, he was also writing out their death warrants.

Interestingly enough, though Chamberlain thought he was going to report to Camp Mason near Portland on Monday, the next letter he wrote was from Portland and dated the same day as the previous one from Brunswick, Friday, August 15, 1862. Apparently he made the twenty-mile journey down the coast that day.

[No addressee]

It gives me pleasure to say a word for Mr. A. N. Linscott who wishes an appointment in the military service. I think he has especial qualifications in that line, & am quite sure he would do himself honor.

Chamberlain's wartime equipment: his gauntlet, blanket, sword, saddle, and boots.
PEJEPSCOT HISTORICAL SOCIETY

I should deem it a great accession to have him in the 20th
Regt., but he will do his duty anywhere.

J. L. Chamberlain[13]
Headquarters 20th Regt. Me.Vol.
Portland Aug 15 1862

What Chamberlain imagined military life would be before he entered the
service is not revealed in his earlier letters. One thing he may not have
anticipated was the day-to-day tedium of paperwork and bookkeeping.

Camp Mason Aug. 25th 1862
General Hodsdon[14]
I have the honor here with to transmit the Receipts for Regtl.
Blanks Books &c. received on Saturday.

I am, General,
Very truly yours
J. L. Chamberlain
Lt. Col. 20th Regt. Me.Vols.[15]

In early September 1862, Chamberlain and the men of the 20th Maine
left Portland by train headed for Boston. There they boarded the steamer
Merrimac in Boston Harbor. A four-day cruise down the coast, up the
Chesapeake Bay, and up the broad, winding Potomac brought them to
wartime Alexandria, Virginia. Though they were officially in the Confederacy, Alexandria, with its proximity to Washington, D.C., had been a
Federally occupied city since 1861. It was from Alexandria that McClellan had launched the amphibious force that landed on the Virginia
peninsula in the spring of 1862, then returned, defeated, during the late
summer. It was around this time that the men of the 20th Maine heard of
the Union's most recent defeat at the end of August in a battle on the
same field that saw contending armies in July 1861: a battlefield near
Manassas, Virginia, called Bull Run.

After camping near Alexandria, the men marched across the Potomac
and into Washington. There they were issued Enfield rifle-muskets and
ammunition and encamped in the city.[16] To at least a few of the Mainers,
accustomed to falling asleep to the mournful coos of loons across a
coastal lake, busy, noisy wartime Washington must have been a shock.[17]

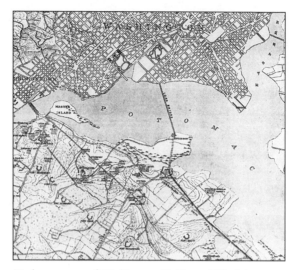

*Early war map of Washington, D.C., and Virginia,
showing Chamberlain's route to Fort Craig.* THE ATLAS
TO ACCOMPANY THE OFFICIAL RECORDS OF THE UNION
AND CONFEDERATE ARMIES, PLATE VI

Soon the green regiment crossed the Long Bridge from Washington back into Virginia. The men made a seven-mile march without a halt in order to reach Fort Craig, where the rest of their brigade awaited. Their appearance was not very military; a frustrated Colonel Ames shouted that if they could not do any better than they did on this march, "you better all desert and go home."[18]

At Fort Craig they joined the 3rd Brigade of the 1st Division, 5th Corps of the Federal Army of the Potomac. The brigade under Gen. Daniel Butterfield had been romantically christened the "Light Brigade." By the time the 20th joined the brigade, Col. T.W. B. Stockton was its commander.

By September 12, 1862, the 1st Division with the 20th Maine left Arlington Heights to recross the Potomac. The next day they marched through Maryland toward Frederick.

September 14 was a particularly hard day for the new troops of the 20th Maine, not quite accustomed to hard marching. They covered fifty-four miles in three days (including a forced march of twenty-four miles in one day) and finally bivouacked at the Monocacy River two miles from Frederick. Chamberlain, always compassionate to his men, carried one soldier's blankets on his horse to help ease the man's load.[19]

On September 15 the men marched through Frederick toward the Catoctin Mountains to the west and encamped near Middletown, Maryland. Early the next morning the 20th left with the rest of the 1st Division, under division commander Maj. Gen. George W. Morell, and marched the National Road through picturesque Turner's Gap across the South Mountains to Boonsboro. Marching through the gap, they witnessed their first casualties of war: the dead of the Confederate Army of Northern Virginia who had opposed the Federals' advance through the gap a day and a half before, many bloated and rank from lying in the September heat. Chamberlain would recall the scene in a speech nearly twenty years later.[20]

They passed through Boonsboro and Keedysville and joined the rest of the Army of the Potomac once again under its former commander, George B. McClellan, at midday September 16. While they marched, they heard the ominous low thud of artillery in the distance. They encamped just beyond Keedysville on the south side of the road.[21]

Confederate general Robert E. Lee had been leading his Army of Northern Virginia across the Potomac and into Maryland on an invasion of the Northern states. McClellan had been watching, concentrating, and maneuvering his Army of the Potomac in order to engage Lee at his own advantage. Now, Lee was cornered inside a bend in the Potomac River near the Maryland village of Sharpsburg behind Antietam Creek. The two armies, fighting with desperation all the next day, would endure the bloodiest single day in American military history. The battle would be remembered by Southerners as the battle of Sharpsburg; to those left to mourn in the North, it was called Antietam.

On September 17 after breakfast, Morell's division with Chamberlain and the men of the 20th Maine moved to guard what was known as the Middle Bridge across Antietam Creek. Stationed behind some hills, they were just north of the road from Boonsboro to Sharpsburg. Chamberlain and some other officers climbed to the high ground in front of their position where the artillery was posted and watched some of the fighting.

Stockton's brigade, with the 20th Maine, was moved to the right a mile or so to support Maj. Gen. William B. Franklin's 6th Corps later that afternoon, but returned at sunset to its original position above the Middle Bridge.

Boteler's Ford near Shepherdstown. BATTLES AND LEADERS OF
THE CIVIL WAR

The next day, September 18, Morell's division, with the 20th Maine
attached, moved south. The men crossed the lower bridge on the Antietam,
the one now known as Burnside's Bridge after the Union commander
who, because of stout Confederate resistance, had had so much trouble getting his men across it.

On September 19 Chamberlain and the men of the regiment
marched across the battlefield and into Sharpsburg, once again surrounded by the awful effluvium of combat: stiff-legged horses rotting in
the sun; the putrefying dead; and wounded men everywhere, giving the
field and the temporary hospitals a peculiar crawling effect, as arms waved
for water or assistance, torsos writhed, and legs twitched in spasms of
pain. Leaving the road outside town heading south, they passed the S. P.
Grove house and bivouacked near the Potomac.[22]

Early on September 20, two divisions from the 5th Corps were
ordered on a reconnaissance in force across the Potomac at Shepherdstown (also known as Boteler's) Ford. The 20th Maine was included in
this reconnaissance and crossed the river. But Confederates under A. P.
Hill returned to the vicinity from their retreating army to act as a large
rear guard. Realizing they were outnumbered, the Union troops retreated
quickly back across the river. By two that afternoon, the Union troops
were back on the Maryland side of the Potomac River and ensconced in
the dry canal bed of the Chesapeake and Ohio Canal. This was the first
time the men of the 20th Maine had actually come under fire, but they
performed the river crossing and retreat admirably. A few were wounded

during the action, and Chamberlain's mount (an animal borrowed to spare Prince, his own prize horse) became just one of several horses to be hit while he was astride during the war.[23]

The next six weeks the men were idle except for the incessant drilling ordered by Colonel Ames. The 20th was encamped in at least one place for a while under unsanitary conditions, then moved camp to Antietam Iron Works near a place called Antietam Ford, where Antietam Creek flows into the Potomac. After several weeks in the field, they still had no tents.[24]

On October 1, 1862, President Abraham Lincoln visited McClellan at his headquarters. Chamberlain observed him riding along reviewing the army. Lincoln commented to McClellan about Chamberlain's beautiful white horse, Prince, as they stopped in front of him.

Apparently there was some problem with the mail, or perhaps Fanny Chamberlain didn't write her husband as often as he would have liked, so Chamberlain began numbering his letters to make sure all were received.[25]

(letter 6th)
Head Quarters 20th Me.
Camp near Antietam Ford
October 10th 1862

My dear Fanny,

It is very evident that you do not get all my letters & perhaps I don't get yours. Now it occurs to me that it would be a good idea to <u>number</u> the letters. I will begin with this, if I can recall all that I have written—this must be at least the 5th letter of mine to you. O! Yes it is the 6th or 7th. I have rec'd 2 from you. I know my letters are very meagre & bald considering the opportunity you imagine I have both of observing & relating. I could <u>talk</u> hours together, but writing does not answer at all. I have so many things I wish to say & know that I shall forget many of them, & have no space left to speak of others that it disconcerts me. Then the surroundings & opportunities are not every thing that could be desired. Does your innocent little head imagine that I could get a <u>photograph</u> (!) taken here? My stars! I fear you have not a <u>high</u> idea of my position. If we can get any thing to eat; or any thing to sleep on except the open ground; or under, save the sky; if we can see a house that is not riddled with shot & shell, or left tenantless through terror, or if we could get a glimpse of a woman who does not exceed the requirements for <u>sweepers</u> in College, we think we are in Paradise. Why you have n't [*sic*] the least idea of the desolation that has swept through this part of the country. You are a very dear little wife to suggest that Mrs. Col. Merrill & Mrs. Col. Sewall are coming this way. Well the difference is this Their Regiments are <u>stationed</u> in permanent fortifications, or camps, & are quite in the rear as I understand, while we are in the very front & as shifting as the nighthawk's flight. I should wonder to see a woman in our camp. Really I think the exposure & hardship would kill her in less than a week. Then we have not half the comforts that most other Regts have because we have not been able to get teams & transportation. I do not imagine <u>any</u> <u>body</u> would be <u>more</u> glad to see <u>any</u> <u>body,</u> that somebody to see somebody who is the constant center of his every dream & the soul of his every thought! But for the present, only dreams & thoughts on that delightful side, & deeds & works on the other. By & by you will be able to come & find me in some civilized shape I hope. My rubber blanket is not quite big enough to accommodate ever so sweet & welcome a guest on the rough hill sides, or in the drenching valleys that constitute my changing homes. I have my care & vexations too; but let me say no danger & no hardship ever makes me wish to get back to that college life again. I cant breathe when I think of those last two years. Why I would spend my whole life in campaigning it, rather that endure that again. One thing though I <u>wont</u> endure it again. My experience here & the habit of command will make me less complaisant—will break upon the notion that certain persons are the natural authorities over me. Well I have been thinking of Wyllys & his birth day & Daisy's too so soon. I wish I could send them something but it would only be a bit of candy which I happen to have, or a piece of a rebel gun or exploded shell, such as cover the ground all around here. Give the Darlings my love & tell them I always think of them.

Fanny my impression is from all [The letter ends here with a page apparently missing. The following note in parentheses is written upside down along the tops of pages 2 and 3.]

(Do prevent Tenney, if you can, from trying to say what I "<u>write</u>" No such thing as he says. We were ordered in to the fight & <u>went.</u> Then the Regt "<u>fired</u>" abundantly at the crossing.)[26]

Chamberlain could not help but tease his wife about her ideas of what war was like. She apparently had not realized the basic nature of the soldier's life or the desolation upon the countryside produced by war.

"Sweepers" in college were the women who cleaned up the dormitories. They were hired primarily because of their lack of comeliness so as not to tempt the male students. Bureaucratic slowness has held up the regiment's amenities; all Chamberlain has to sleep on is his rubber blanket. His current accommodations would be inadequate for a visit by Fanny.

His affection for her is obvious; more surprising is his sudden realization that the life of a college professor has become abhorrent to him. In just over two months, without the outdoor camp training sessions West Pointers endured each summer, Chamberlain has taken to the vigorous life of a soldier both physically and mentally.

Unfortunately, a whole page of the letter is missing. From the tone of the sentence that begins on the previous page, Chamberlain is revealing his impression of something important, perhaps military, especially from the parenthetical statement written upside down across the tops of pages 2 and 3. "Tenney" has apparently misquoted Chamberlain concerning the fight at Boteler's Ford on September 20; he explains what happened in the limited space he has.

On October 12, Chamberlain led a reconnaissance to the South Mountains in an attempt to catch the Confederate cavalry commander J. E. B. Stuart, who was on another raid around the Army of the Potomac. Stuart slipped back across the Potomac before the Union troops could catch up, taking with him more than a thousand Pennsylvania horses and the satisfaction of having destroyed some $250,000 worth of public and railroad property north of the Mason-Dixon line.[27]

As the temperature dropped, Chamberlain and Colonel Ames constructed a fireplace in their tent. Its inefficiency was obvious, but it was typical of the type of makeshift heating systems that could be seen during the cool months wherever either army camped.

No 7.
Hd. Qrs. 20th Me. Regt. Camp
near Antietam Ford Oct. 26th 1862

My dear Fanny;
It is some time since I have written you & a great while since I have heard any thing from you. I dare say you have written me

often, but there is great irregularity about the mails. It is rather dis-
couraging to me to look over a bushel or two of letters & find one
for every body but me. You notice we are here yet. Now & then we
have a little incident to break the monotony. We are now under
orders to be ready to march, we dont know where or when. It may
be we shall stay here several days longer. It is cold weather here.
The Col. and I are crammed into this little tent & at night after
dark we became enterprising. We walked out, ripped up a seam in
our tent, built a fire place of stones & mud, topped out the chim-
ney with a flour barrel & stuffed newspapers into the unmanage-
able gaps, thinking to have comfortable air inside. Since that time
we have not been able to see out of our eyes for smoke, & a dull
north easter coming on, we have to stay inside & be smoked, or
outside & be soaked. Thus far I have preferred the smoke. You
notice by the blots & mistakes that I am occasionally smitten with
total blindness. Multitudes of callers are chatting as long as they can
stand the smoke & I am keeping up two or three characters while
writing, none of which will at all excite your jealousy I am very
sure. We are complete old bachelors here as far as our life is concerned. You cant imagine how curiously void of all reference to the
finer half of humanity our life & business is. You would think us to
be under the influence of <u>ether,</u> in regard to that most ethereal part
of creation. However that does not prevent my thinking of you &
the darlings whenever my thoughts are not absorbed in military
affairs, & dreaming of you every night. It is positively refreshing to
awake, after having spent a <u>whole day</u> with you & Daise[28] & Wyllys.
I am happier all the day. A day or two ago, I was contriving to make
an extemporaneous bridge to throw some men over to defend a
threatened place, & the next night I dreamed of leading them
across some crazy planks over the rushing Antietam, & then taking
Daise on my back & swimming it. While Wyllys looked out for
himself & climbed some huge rocks. I dont dare however dwell too
long on those dear names; it makes me rather disposed to pay you a
short visit, which I dont expect to be able to do very soon. One of
our Captains has the pleasure of having his wife at Boonsboro six
or eight miles from here, but with my duties <u>I</u> could not get away
ten miles once in a month. If by any chance we get into winter
quarters, I shall let you come some <u>where near.</u> You are coming to

Washington at any rate this winter—you & Daise. I want you to do every thing you wish, & go every where you like. I dare say my $100 a month for you, has not reached you yet.

As soon as you get it, I want you to use it. Let me know, if any thing is not going well with you. My health is still good, & I am able to do all my duties. Every third day I am detailed as Field officer of the Day for the Brigade & I have charge of all the outposts & advanced guards for miles around. That gives me a fine chance to ride over the country. I wish you could be beside me on some gentle palfrey plunging into some rich shaded valley, craggy defile, or along some lovely stream. Or perhaps, as a day or two ago, mount to the summit of one of these blue hills, whence you can see forty miles into Virginia—see the long lines of rebel fires fifteen or twenty miles away & villages & streams & bright patches of cultivated fields—& on our own side the great battle field of Antietam the hills trodden bare & the fields all veined with the tracks of artillery trains, or movements of Army corps. I have enjoyed these rides much. Often I am 12 or 15 hours a day in the saddle. We are having rather a peaceful time now—though I did jump up a minute ago, to see what our batteries on the hill were banging at across the Potomac. We have got over being startled by sudden orders to be "ready to spring to arms at a moment's notice." I study, I tell you every military work I can find. And it is no small labor to master the evolutions of a Battalion & Brigade. I am bound to understand <u>every thing.</u> And I want you to send my "<u>Jomini, Art of War</u>" in a package Lt. Nichols is to have sent soon. The Col. & I are going to read it. He to instruct me, as he is kindly doing in every thing now. If you wish to send me drawers & undershirts, you can send in the same way. I do not find myself in need of much. My one suit of clothing is getting a little worn & a little <u>thin.</u> I shall have to replenish in Washington, or wherever else we are. I have not the least idea where we are going. You will see in the papers what are the movements of Porter's Corps, Morell's Division. Give my love to all the friends who think so kindly of me, & treat you so kindly. I feel that it <u>is</u> a sacrifice for me to be here in one sense of the word; but I do not wish myself back by any means. I feel that I am where duty called me. The "<u>glory</u>" Prof. Smythe so <u>honestly</u> pictured for me I do not much dread. If I do return "shattered" & "good-for-nothing", I think there <u>are</u> those who will hold me in some degree of favor better than that which he predicted. Most likely I shall be hit somewhere at sometime, but all "my times are in His hands", & I can not die without His appointing. I try to keep ever in view all the possibilities that surround me & to be ready for all that I am called to. I know that prayers are going up for me from dear hearts & loving lips. I long to see you—to rush in & have a good frolic with the children, & a sweet sit-down with you in the study—take tea with you & Aunty[29]—then dash off again into my work. I tell you Fanny the estimate of men & things is very different here from the popular one at home. Our Maine Regts. & our prominent officers, have quite a different name from the one they are given in the papers. That is, there is a <u>difference</u> in them. Some of our Regts. are not doing much, & some of our officers are not highly held by real judges—compared, I mean, with others of whom you do not hear so much. <u>We</u> employ no reporters—have no partizans at home— the papers do not load us with praise we do not deserve, but in the <u>Army</u> & by Regular officers we are already said to be a marked Regt. We have been applied for by <u>three</u> Generals out of our Brigade, & I believe that no other new Regt. will <u>ever</u> have the discipline we have now. We all <u>work.</u> The rain is <u>pouring,</u> & we are waiting orders to march. Write me a <u>few</u> more letters than you do. I should get one somewhat oftener. Your ever loving Lawrence

You must by all means get <u>Harper's</u> <u>Weekly</u> all the numbers since the battle. You will see <u>some</u> true pictures & a good map of the field. Stanwood has them. Col. Ames sends regards.[30]

Out of the $194 per month he was paid as a lieutenant colonel, Chamberlain sent $100 home to Fanny.[31]

But besides his attention to fiduciary responsibilities to his family, more of Chamberlain's philosophy can be gleaned from his comments concerning the prediction Professor Smythe gave, that he would return to Brunswick wounded, perhaps an invalid, and that would be the only glory gotten from the war. Chamberlain's faith in God and his trust in the intervening prayers from his wife and children would allow him to do his duty no matter how dangerous.

Only six weeks after their own colonel told them they had all better desert, the 20th Maine's constant drilling had turned them into an

Harpers Ferry as it looks today. AUTHOR PHOTO

admired regiment. Their success also must be attributed to their officers. Adelbert Ames, West Point class of 1861, had read at the Military Academy all the manuals of drill and was familiar with the modern style of war. Chamberlain, late professor of theology and logic, Bowdoin College, had read none of that. But as he assured his governor in July, "I <u>know how to learn.</u>" He asked Fanny to send him his copy of *The Art of War* by Antoine Henri Jomini, who had served as chief of staff to Marshall Ney and with Napoleon in his Russian Campaign. Jomini's book was written in 1838, translated from the French, and recommended by the U.S. Military Academy at West Point for both military and lay persons alike in 1862. Chapters covered everything from "The Relation of Diplomacy to War" to "Formation and Employment of Troops for Battle." Of particular interest to Chamberlain, as a lieutenant colonel, would have been the chapter on "Grand Tactics and Battles."

After less than three months in the military, Chamberlain approached the conquest of the art of war with the ardor and prosaic methodology of a scholar and the aggressiveness of a commander of light infantry. The combination worked. No doubt he read as much as he could of Jomini, perhaps all of it, and discussed passages with Ames: "The best thing for an army standing on the defensive is to know *how* to take the offensive at a proper time, and *to take it.*" Perhaps he read with special interest, as a potential combat commander, Jomini's observation that "Every army which maintains a strictly defensive attitude must, if attacked, be at last driven from its position; whilst by profiting by all the advantages of the defensive system, and holding itself ready to take the offensive when

The view from Snicker's Gap, Virginia, is the same today as it was when Chamberlain stood there. AUTHOR PHOTO

occasion offers, it may hope for the greatest success." And it would seem inevitable that he would have studied the passage concerning counterattacks: "When the assailant, after suffering severely, finds himself strongly assailed at the moment when the victory seemed to be in his hands, the advantage will, in all probability, be his no longer, for the moral effect of such a counterattack upon the part of an adversary supposed to be beaten is certainly enough to stagger the boldest troops."[32]

Chamberlain would soon have ample opportunity to practice Jomini's theories.

On October 30 the 5th Corps broke camp and headed south from the ironworks at Antietam Ford in a night march. They camped around midnight.[33] On the books a regiment was supposed to number 1,000 men, but because of attrition, by this time the 20th Maine carried on its rolls about 550 men. Though the unit had engaged in only an hour or so of combat at Boteler's Ford, it was already reduced by almost half. This, however, was typical during the American Civil War; when young men from scattered rural areas were suddenly jammed together with hundreds of others, disease spread quickly through the ranks of men who had never built up immunities to certain illnesses.

The 20th Maine stopped at Harpers Ferry on October 31 after crossing the Potomac. They continued their march below Loudoun Heights south into the Loudoun Valley with the Blue Ridge Mountain just to the west. The next day they marched fifteen miles.[34] That night, November 1, the men from Maine encamped after dark. Shortly, wind and rain blew in off the mountains, with Chamberlain wrapped only in a shawl and rubber talma and sleeping under a tree. His remarks, coming from the former bespectacled professor, are quite revealing as to how he's taken to military life. As well, he draws a fine portrait of himself as a soldier in the field.

3d <u>Brigade</u>
<u>Butterfield's</u>
<u>Division</u>
<u>(now)</u>
(No 8)
Head Qrs. 20th Me Vols. Nov. 3d 1862
Camp or rather Bivouac near
Snicker's Gap. Blue Ridge Va

My dear Fanny

What names they have here in the land of Rebeldom! <u>Snickers</u> Gap! What an undignified name for a battle field. Yet here we are, expecting a battle with the Rebels who are just over the mountain at the other end of the Gap. We are all in fine condition for a fight. To be sure our Regt. is now reduced to about 550. But what there are left are of the right sort. We marched suddenly from Antietam at night—the loveliest night you ever saw & this one of the richest countries. Two days more of marching brought us here. You can find the place on the map I used to look so longingly at. If not buy a map, send for one by Mr. Griffin[35] so that you can keep the <u>run</u> of me, if I do run. We are now under Hooker who had command of the <u>1st Army.</u> Hooker's Porter's & Franklin's corps are joined to make the finest army of the war, & the appearances are that we shall not be slighted in the coming battle. shall certainly beat the Rebels this time, though I expect a hard fight. They are admirably handled & fight with desperation. We were in sight of the artillery skirmish yesterday & are now ready to pitch in when called for. You have not much idea of how I look & fare. You may imagine that I am in a suffering condition, but I am not one of that sort. Mr. Brown says I am the most careless & improvident fellow he ever saw—take no care of myself at all—sleep on the ground when I have the whole Regt. at my command to make house for me. But I hate to see a man always on the spring to get the best of everything for himself. I prefer to take things as they come, & I am as well & comfortable as any body, & no one is worse for it. Picture to yourself a stout looking fellow—face covered with beard—with a pair of cavalry pants on—sky blue—big enough for Goliath, & coarse as a sheep's back—said fellow having worn & torn & ridden his original suit quite out of the question—enveloped in a large cavalry overcoat (when it is cold) of the same color & texture as the pants; & when wearing the identical flannel blouse worn at Portland—cap with an immense rent in it caused by a Picket raid when we were after Stuart's cavalry. A shawl & rubber talma strapped on behind the saddle & the overcoat (perhaps), or the dressing case, before—2 pistols in holsters. Sword about three feet long at side—piece of blue beef & some hard bread in the saddlebags. This figure seated on a magnificent horse gives that peculiar point & quality of incongruity which constitutes the ludicrous. The Col. says the Regt. is recognized every where by that same figure. Rebel prisoners praise the horse & the sword, but evidently take no hang to the man. When we march the baggage trains are behind, & usually do not come up at night within some miles. Yesterday for example, the day was very hot & we marched fifteen miles camping as little as possible, at night, after dark, we halt. A bitter cold north wester from the Blue Mountains tears down upon us. We bivouac as we can—some taking more pains & some less. I take my saddle for a pillow—rubber talma for a bed—shawl for a covering & a big chestnut tree for a canopy & let it blow. A dashing rain & furious gale in the night make me put on a skull-cap (given me by the major) & pull the talma over me—head & all—curl up so as to bring myself into a bunch—& enjoy it hugely. I would confess to anybody but you, that I was cold—feet especially. However I enjoy it I say, & get up, (I dont say wake up) bright as a squirrel & hearty as a bear. Our living, of course, under these circumstances is precarious. Now pretty coarse, & now some luxury such as you seldom get. Say, a supper of fig paste, jellies of all sorts, cans of preserves & fruits &c—bought of some sutler at double price, then a breakfast of salt pork, or hard bread; with maybe, coffee with out milk & alas! without sugar. When we are in one camp for some time however, we fare well & regularly. I am sitting on a pile of husks, writing on my knees, looking down on this great body of men, directing a thousand little matters & trying to say something worth writing to you. You see I dont succeed at all. Some time when I am in the mood, I will give you a better description of our affairs. I do not say much about the army, or Generals, or victories, because I dont know under what scrutiny the letter will pass before it gets to you. I shall find time to write you again perhaps before the battle comes off. Do not be worried about me. I am in the right place, & no harm can come to me unless it is wisely & kindly ordered so. I try to be equal to my duty & ready for anything that may come. I rec'd. your letter enclosing one from Cpt. Badger—another just before as you intimated. Very welcome you may be sure. I wrote Julia Lombard a day or two ago in answer to her two letters to me. Tell Aunty it is rather too late to enclose hers! I directed to <u>30 Oxford St.</u> Is that right? I am surprised at the matter you mention. Hope Julia, sweet girl that she is, will not go & throw herself away on some chance acquaintance for the sake of securing that apparently [*sic*] "only hope" which they speak of so much.

Be sure & treat Capt. Badger with attention. Get everything for the children to wear. Wyllys wants a good big overcoat to go with his boots, & a <u>cap</u> to keep his ears warm. If you do not have as much money as you want let me know at once. Give my love to the kind friends you speak of. I shall write to one or two of them soon, <u>perhaps,</u> & as for yourself <u>be happy</u>—I should be perfectly so if I could see the dear ones under my little roof. You need not have the cellar walls banked unless you like, though I think it would be well to have Mr. Booker put boards & sawdust around. Do as you please. It will not make much difference—about anything. With much reason to love you & being as I contend a reasonable man, you may draw the inference. L![36]

There were so many things Chamberlain wanted to communicate to Fanny in his letters: the conditions in camp, rumors of movements of the enemy, the ill will of the local populace in war-torn Virginia.

His current surroundings and the desolation he saw around Sharpsburg caused by the war may have prompted his advice to Fanny in his next letter concerning the garden, the house, and the coming winter. And his thoughts regarding his relationship with his children are sobering, with their too, too solid logic.

(No. 9)
Head Qrs. 20th Regt. Me Vols. Nov 4th 1862
Camp or rather Bivouac near <u>Snicker's
Gap</u> Blue Ridge Virginia

My dear Fanny,

I had just resolved to burn up a letter I wrote you yesterday & write another in its place when the mail carrier came along & I put the poor thing <u>in</u> rather than miss sending any thing by that mail. You may count that letter as nothing. I will write now until something happens to interrupt me, & then take it up some other time. We have the satisfaction at present of not camping on ground that has been occupied before, but in a fresh sweet valley between beautiful mountains. Still it is difficult to get anything here, because the Rebels who live here will neither sell nor give. One amiable lady of whom we meekly requested some milk, said she would like to kill the whole of us. It is quite possible however that she indirectly contributed to our good <u>living,</u> for I am afraid our naughty boys helped themselves to a few pigs & turkeys & other delicate articles of diet, which must be <u>had</u> even if they could not be bought or accepted as presents. We hear to day that the Rebels have commenced a retreat towards Richmond. If so our opportunity of glory will have to be put off. But there is no counting on those Rebels—they may come pouring through the Gap at any time. We are making ourselves as comfortable as possible. I have contrived a fire place in a corner of the tent. I am afraid you would think it <u>smoked,</u> & be so impolite as to refuse to stay near it. The Major is lying on a sack of straw flat on his back, holding a candle in one hand & Handy Andy in the other his feet on my stone fireplace. Mr. Brown on my left smoking a cigar, I avail myself of the light & fire, take my inkstand in one hand, pen in the other, paper on my knee. You want to know where the Major was during the battles. He was not well the morning of the Great Battle & went back to Washington. He is with us now & pretty well. I had a pleasant call yesterday from Mr. Palmer, chaplain of the 19th. I am sorry he is not with us. As to the Garden I usually have the asparagus covered in the fall two or three inches deep with dressing which is to be raked off in the spring & the surface <u>dug in</u> with a fork carefully. I believe I did not do what I intended with the strawberry bed. I was going to leave <u>one</u> plant in a hill & cover well from cold. If you like you can have some of them fixed. The grape vine should be pruned & covered with straw, or leaves, or something, but if the plaguey thing is not going to <u>bear</u> I dont care for it at all.

Dont be afraid to have it <u>pruned.</u> The currant bushes too. All the dead wood cut out, & the grass dug away from the roots, earth closed up around them & keep warm. You need not try to do anything with the Garden except the asparagus bed unless you choose. Have the stoves arranged to keep you comfortable. If you have taken up the carpet from my college room, why not put it down over the other in the Dining room, & have <u>double</u> <u>windows</u> put on, & keep warm there, & in the sitting room. I think it would be a good idea. I do not expect you to spend the winter in Brunsk. but Aunty & the children will, I suppose. Fanny, I think you had better give Aunty a set of furs. I am sure it will be very well to do so. As for your plans for the winter, I would certainly go to see Jenny Abbott a few days, & stay awhile in New York, & then come to Washington (or Baltimore). I suppose our present campaign will be closed by Christmas at least, but I dont know where we shall go into winter quarters. Maybe near Washington, we hope Richmond, but possibly near here. We shall keep on fighting, I imagine, through the present administration. I see no signs of peace. Good fighting on both sides, but while we will not be beaten, still something seems to strike all the vigor out of our arms just at the point of victory. We have confidence in our officers, & are well prepared for the campaign, & hope for more decided results.

Your letters are the only ones I receive. They do not come quite so often as I could wish, but I read them over often enough to make up. I like to hear all the little particulars you mention. Bless the dear children. I don't dare to think of them too much. It makes me rather sad, & then I do not forget that I am here in the face of death every day. You must not let them dwell too much on me, & keep me too vividly in their affections. If I return they will soon relearn to love me, & if not, so much is spared them. Provide all that they need. <u>Dont</u> have them so lacking as they were last winter. I want you to be cheerful & occupy your mind with pleasant things, so as not to have any time to grow melancholy. You must not think of me much. I am in earnest. Invite the Juniors over &

spend the evening with some of the young ladies, as we used to, &
keep up your character for hospitality, & your spirits at the same
time. I shall write you as often as I can get an opportunity, & you
need not worry if you hear of a battle, until you know that I was in
it; If I am injured, you will hear at once. I expect to get some sort
of a scratch when we "go in", but the chances are it will not be
serious if anything. Give my regards to all my friends, & tell them I
am beginning to understand my business, & shall probably be
enabled to look them in the face again if I get home.

Yours as ever
Lawrence[37]

If I return they will soon relearn to love me, & if not, so much is spared them.
The former professor of logic was almost too logical in his desire to spare
his children and wife the pain of his potential loss. The possibility of
sudden death in an entity created solely to produce it seemed to have
sunk in: *I am beginning to understand my business.*

On November 6 Chamberlain, the 20th Maine, and the rest of the
5th Corps headed south from Snicker's Gap with a new commander—
Maj. Gen. Joseph Hooker, with whom Lincoln had replaced Fitz John
Porter. McClellan too was out of a job; Lincoln gave the command of
the Army of the Potomac to Maj. Gen. Ambrose Burnside.[38]

Camp of the 20th Regt. Maine
Vols.
near Warrington[39] Va
Nov 16, 1862
To His Excellency
I. Washburn Jr. Governor of Maine

Dear Sir,

Recent changes in this army corps, leave all the brigades of this
Division without Brigadier General's to command them. Recognizing the eminent qualifications of Col. Ames, Maj. Genl. Hooker
has written a letter earnestly expressing his "anxiety, that Col. Ames
be promoted to the rank of Brigadier General and be assigned to
duty in his command." The past services of Col. Ames in this war
are as great and as honorable as those of any other officer in the
army. And among military men no one sustains a higher reputation.

We need not say more to you who know him so well, but may add that General's [*sic*] Howard & Berry are warmly engaged in his behalf. We trust you will recommend him to the President and give your aid in securing his promotion. We are Dear Gov. Respectfully your Obt. Servts.

J. L. Chamberlain
Charles D. Gilmore[40]

Ames would get his promotion, but not until the springtime. Whether this endorsement by Lieutenant Colonel Chamberlain and Major Gilmore helped cannot be determined.

Burnside began to concentrate his army near Falmouth, Virginia, on the Rappahannock River opposite the old colonial town of Fredericksburg. The 20th Maine and the 5th Corps marched in from Warrenton, Virginia, and by Thanksgiving the 20th was encamped on a pine-covered hill near Stoneman's Switch on Aquia Creek Railroad about three miles from Fredericksburg.

Now winter closed in. During the night of December 6, it snowed four inches and two men of the 20th Maine were reported frozen to death by morning. On December 10 the regiment came in from picket duty and was ordered to cook three days' rations and prepare to move the next morning.[41]

On December 11 the men marched from Stoneman's Switch to near Army Headquarters, which Burnside established at the house of a local family named Phillips. Though Chamberlain and the men of the 20th did not know it, they were being moved into position to cross the Rappahannock River and become engaged in a battle that would be named after the town through which it would be fought: Fredericksburg. On the morning of December 11, Chamberlain and his adjutant, John M. Brown, rode to the Union batteries on Stafford Heights, then down to a house owned by a local family named Lacy. Chamberlain and Brown got a look at the ground across which they would later be attacking. They slept that night in the woods behind the Phillips's house and remained there the next day and night.[42]

Chamberlain had begun keeping a notebook since his entry into the service. Sadly, the notebook is now lost, but the entries concerning Fredericksburg were published in a Maine newspaper and clipped to become part of Chamberlain's personal scrapbook.

Camp opposite Fredericksburg
Dec. 17th, 1862.

I know how much you desire to hear what I have experienced
during this eventful week. Let me begin by a few extracts from my
note book.

"Dec. 11th, 10 A.M. In the saddle, waiting the word to cross the
Rappahannock in front of Fredericksburg. Hooker's Grand Division,
closed in masses, covering the ground around me as far as the eye
can see. Our batteries open upon the town—forty-five or fifty shots
a minute. We cannot see the river, but are told our engineers are trying to throw across the pontoon bridges, and the rebel sharpshooters
under cover of the town are picking them off as fast as they appear.
Our cannonading is to shell the rebels out of the city. Their formidable batteries in the rear of the town are plainly to be seen, but do not
reply, or but rarely. I asked permission to ride to the front a short
time ago, and with Mr. Brown for companion (one would not wish
for a better one) with some of the rashness of youth perhaps, we
made quite a minute inspection of affairs. Advancing beyond our
line of batteries we were fully within the circle of sharpshooting
operations. But the result repaid the risk. From the famous Lacey
[*sic*] House, directly opposite Fredericksburg and I should think
almost within pistol range, the scene (let the word include sounds as
well as sights) was grand beyond anything I have ever witnessed, or
expected to witness. The flame and smoke, the thunder and scream
of artillery, the shells bursting in the city; the bridge of boats half
done; the rebel sharpshooters running from the shells, and rallying to
the front again; here and there a huge pontoon, whose weight had
broken its carriage, lying like a stranded whale; and on the other
hand a train of ambulances full of wounded, slowly winding its way
to the rear; before us the beautiful city, on fire in a dozen places,
columns of smoke streaming into the sky, and lurid bursts, where
some enormous shell had lifted a brick building in the air, ground to
dust; behind us glittering in the sunlight our countless host—it was a
scene not given to every one to see. Antietam was not anywhere
equal to it, because more extended; this is gathered into one focus.

"Dec. 12th—Not ready yet; moved nearer, however, and waited
yet another day."

Around midday on December 13, the 1st Division moved toward the heights overlooking the Rappahannock River and Fredericksburg. At about three o'clock the 1st Division crossed the pontoon bridges at the steamboat landing on the lower end of the town. The 3rd Brigade was first held in reserve for an hour as the 1st and 2nd Brigades moved toward the river. Shortly, the 3rd Brigade fell in and crossed the bridge to the steamboat landing under artillery fire. In columns of fours, the men of the 3rd Brigade aligned themselves down Prince Edward Street near the station of the Richmond, Fredericksburg, and Potomac Railroad. Their right flank reached Charlotte Street and their left about one hundred yards south of the depot. Behind a small rise, they lay down to endure the Confederate artillery fire coming from Marye's Heights. Veterans of Civil War combat could tell what kind of battle had been fought by the detritus left behind: Infantry left dead and wounded men; artillery, pieces of men. When the 20th Maine reached the site, strewn about and underfoot was the sickening evidence of an artillery battle.[43]

> Dec. 13th—The day opens with sharp musketry, followed by a spirited artillery fire—Griffin's Division is drawn up near the head of one of the pontoon bridges, in full view of the engagement, waiting the critical moment to 'go in.' Line after line advances to the very crest of the hill before the rebel batteries and rifle pits, checked each time by the nature of the ground and the strength of the entrenchments, no less than by the awful fire that seems to scorch them from the hillside. I see tears in the eyes of many a brave man looking on that sorrowful sight, yet all of us are eager to dash to the rescue.
>
> No more of note books now—other work now. Griffin is in motion. The hour is come! It was, perhaps, two or three o'clock. The rebels could see us perfectly well, and had the range of the bridge and roads through which we had to pass. Shot and shell were plunging and bursting around us all the way. We kept under cover of the city as well as we could, though every street was raked by cannon shot. Emerging at last in rear of the town, and in front of the fire, we halted, under the partial cover of a slightly rising ground, but precisely in range of the hottest fire, to form our line. The dead and wounded lay thick even here, and fragments of limbs were trampled under foot. Some of our own men fell here. Suddenly two new

batteries opened; it seemed as if the ground were bursting under foot, and the very sky were crashing down upon us; the bullets hissed like a seething sea. In the midst of the hellish din we heard the bugle call the "3rd Brigade." I was standing with the Colonel, in front of the colors. He glanced up at the batteries—"God help us now!" said he, "take care of the right wing! Forward, the Twentieth!" and forward it did go, in line of battle, smooth as a sunset parade, in face of that terrific cross-fire of cannon and rifle, and underneath the tempest of shell, its gallant commander in the van.

At dusk they advanced, first through the water-filled millrace, leaving the men soaking wet to midthigh. The right wing had to tear down a high board fence, Chamberlain himself beginning the destruction.[44] The regiments were halted, their lines having grown ragged because of obstacles on both the right and left. There was an unfinished railroad before the 83rd Pennsylvania, and the cut in the earth caused the unit to become disorganized. About eight hundred yards from the Confederate main line at the base of Marye's Heights, in an old brick kiln yard, Stockton's brigade prepared to continue the advance.

As the regiment double-quicked toward the wall that lined a sunken road at the base of Marye's Heights, Chamberlain recalled later going over obstacles including four lines of men who were lying on the ground. Some of the prone men grasped at the legs of the men who were advancing, the sacrificed trying to hold back those about to be. The 20th Maine was ordered in advance of the rest of the brigade to relieve a regiment lying before the wall. As the tactics textbook prescribed, the men of the 20th loaded and fired by the number, exchanging volleys with the Rebels behind the wall until the sun set.[45]

For some reason the two regiments on the right of our brigade did not advance with us, and our right wing consequently took the flank fire, as well as the torrent it breasted in front. On we charged, over fences and through hedges, over bodies of dead men and living ones, past four lines that were lying on the ground, to get out of the way of the fire, on to that deadly edge, where we had seen so much desperate valor mown down in heaps. We moved in front of the line already engaged, and thus covered, it was enabled to retire. Then, on the crest of the hill we exchanged swift and deadly volleys with the rebel infantry before us.

Around midnight, Chamberlain and Adjutant Brown moved to the right rear to check on wounded and to search for something to throw over themselves to endure the cold December night, as the officers' blankets had been left on their saddles. Chamberlain apparently found no blanket, for when he returned to his position behind and between three dead men, he carefully covered his head with the skirt of a dead soldier's greatcoat. In the middle of the night, someone—a hospital steward seeking the wounded, or perhaps someone looking for booty from the dead—pulled the skirt from Chamberlain's face and was startled to see living eyes flash back at him. A pocket New Testament fell out of the dead man's cloak, and Chamberlain picked it up, vowing, if he lived, to return it to the family.[46]

Nearby to the right was a brick house with a loose windowshade. Flapping in the night wind against the sash and wall, to Chamberlain it sounded a death chant for the eternities: "Never—forever; forever—never!"[47] Perhaps this was the same brick house described by John W. Ames, brevet brigadier general on the same field:

Here stood a low brick house, with an open door in its gable end, from which shone a light, and into which we peered when passing. Inside sat a woman, gaunt and hard-featured, with crazy hair and a Meg Merrilies face, still sitting by a smoking candle, though it was nearly two hours past midnight. But what woman could sleep, though never so masculine and tough of fiber, alone in a house between two hostile armies,—two corpses lying across her door-steps, and within, almost at her feet, four more! So, with wild-eyes and face lighted by her smoky candle, she stared across the dead barrier into the darkness outside with the look of one who heard and saw not, and to whom all sounds were a terror.[48]

Chamberlain's notebook continued:

Darkness had now come on, and the firing slackened, but did not cease. We felt that we must hold the position, though it was a desperate thing to think of. For the rebels knowing the ground, might flank us in the darkness, and to be found under their very guns at daylight would be offering ourselves to destruction. To retire however was to expose the whole army to defeat. So we lay on the trampled and bloody field. Wet and cold it was too, and we had no blankets—the officers, I mean. Little sleep was had then and there, I assure you. Our eyes and ears were open. We could hear the voices of the rebels in their lines, so near were they, and could see many of their movements. I did sleep though, strange as you may think it, in the very midst of a heap of dead close beside one dead man, touching him possibly—the living and dead were alike to me. I slept, though my ears were filled with the cries and groans of the wounded, and the ghastly faces of the dead almost made a wall around me. It was very cold in the night, and we suffered. Mr. Brown and I wandered over the field hoping to find a blanket or an overcoat on some dead man, but others had been before us. Once, on such an errand perhaps, or it may be to find some friends, a man came and lifted our coat-capes from our faces, peering into our eyes, thinking we were dead.

Dawn, December 14 found the 20th lying in the depression behind the last small swell before the stone wall. To their left, the 83rd Pennsylvania had good cover behind a crest of a small ridge just forward of them. The 20th remained there all day and could move a bit when darkness fell. Griffin's 3rd Brigade was eventually relieved by other Union soldiers and retreated back into the town.[49]

The morning broke—Sabbath morning—silent, serene. There we lay, a little handful, in a slight hollow on the hillside, and only thus protected from the batteries and rifles that swept the crests before us and behind us too. No man could stand, without being shot down; troops ordered to our relief could not come up without being annihilated; the aids that sought to bring us orders, riding at full speed had their horses shot from under them the instant they reached the crest behind us. The enemy tried to dislodge us by shell, but they did not succeed in bursting them exactly over us, and the shot that swept the two crests, just skimmed over our heads, if we kept down. Next they sent three or four hundred skirmishers to get a position on our flank under cover of a ravine, and we had to build a breastwork in the midst of their fire, and under this shelter we succeeded in driving them off with our rifles. We kept up the firing all day, in momentary expectation of some desperate attack, but resolved not to flinch in that fiery ordeal.

At last, on that second midnight, having been in that hell of fire for thirty-six hours, an order came that we were to be relieved. But our dead lay around us, and we could not leave them thus. 'We will give them a starlight burial,' it was said; but Heaven ordained a more sublime illumination. As we bore them, the forms of our fallen heroes, on fragments of boards torn from fences by shot and shell, to their honored graves, their own loved North lifted her glorious lights, and sent her triumphal procession along the arch that spanned her heavens. An Aurora Borealis, marvelous in beauty. Fiery lances and banners of blood, and flame, columns of pearly light, garlands and wreaths of gold—all pointing and beckoning upward. Befitting scene! Who would die a nobler death, or dream of more glorious burial? Dead for their country's honor, and lighted to burial by the meteor splendors of their Northern home! Then making sure that our wounded had all been gathered, cold, wet, and battle-worn, we entered the town, and bivouacked for a few hours on the pavements. Once then before morning we had to rally to repel a night attack.

After so great labors we expected a short relief, that we might be ready for another and victorious charge. But in the morning we were ordered to prepare immediately for action again, and had scarcely fallen asleep on the next night when our brigade was called to arms, and in the darkness and silence we marched over that fatal field once more. Here among the thick strewn dead, and scarcely to be distinguished from them, we found a few troops lying flat on their faces, and fairly trembling with fearful apprehension. And indeed it was a more thrilling and harrowing business to be creeping around in that dark and dangerous place, where you could not see whether a man was friend or foe, only two hundred yards from the enemy's works, amidst all the ghastly relics of the slaughter, than anything we had experienced before. Our friends informed us in tones not calculated to re-assure our feelings, that the rebels were in plain sight extending their rifle pits close up to us, that a whole brigade had been 'rushed off' from that spot a short time before, and that a new battery had been placed there the night before so as to sweep us from the ground at daybreak, and they bade us good bye, saying that we could not stay there two hours. But our order was simple and stern—"Hold that ground <u>at</u> <u>all</u> <u>hazards!</u>" Our regiment was here alone; the others were out of sight to the right and left. We felt that something was at stake, and creeping cautiously up to the very edge of the rifle pits we collected a few picks and spades that had been brought there, and used them with a will, you may be sure. We protected ourselves as well as possible by throwing up little breastworks, and sinking pits, to hold only a few men each, so that a shell or cannon shot striking in one would kill only the few that were in it. Often we were interrupted by alarms, and were fired on whenever seen; but just as we had nearly completed our work a hurried order came to retire in perfect silence, and re-cross the river with all possible dispatch, as our forces <u>had</u> <u>evacuated</u> <u>the</u> <u>city!</u> We had been sent out to hold the front while they retired. So we quietly withdrew, picking our way among the sharp bayonets, and stumbling over dead bodies that lay in heaps around, and wound our way back over the pontoon bridge which had been strewn with earth to deaden the sound of our march, once more north of the Rappahannock.

This was our part in the battle of Fredericksburg—disastrous, as it proved, though we did not suspect that the battle was given up until the order came to retire, and we brought off our gallant little regiment that had so nobly stood the trial, without having once retreated or flinched, or even hesitated in the face of a tempest of death, its ranks thinned, but still unbroken; its colors still afloat, tho' the golden crest was shot away, and the blue field rent by many a ball. Nor did we murmur, though drenched with rain, and having no shelter, obliged to lie on the ground or lean against a tree (as I did) until the murky daylight showed us where we were.

You notice that we passed some hours in Fredericksburg city. It was a strange sight for this age—so completely battered by shell— <u>from</u> <u>both</u> <u>sides,</u> remember; the inhabitants all gone; the houses, with scarcely an exception, broken open; and everything, left evidently in great haste, perfectly exposed to our whole army. Yet it was far more the effect of the shot than of violent hands, that everything was in such confusion and exposure. I saw no ruthless or malicious destruction. What our men <u>wanted</u> <u>for</u> <u>use</u> <u>and</u> <u>could</u> <u>carry,</u> they took with perfect freedom; but I assure you no wanton mischief was done there under my eye. Of course many valuable things must have been taken away; but you must remember that the rebels were throwing shell into the town all the time we were there, and would undoubtedly have destroyed the place. I do not attempt to palliate the possible charge of pillage. I simply deny it, and think that our men showed a great deal of forbearance, considering that the houses had been used as a cover for rebel sharpshooters, and that they were shelling the town more or less all the time. We made our regimental headquarters in a house, and did not displace nor disturb anything; but rebel shells struck the house more than once during our stay, and, if any damage was done there, they did it.[50]

On December 15 the 3rd Brigade stretched along Caroline Street for three blocks, its right flank ending near George Street. The men were there all afternoon, then moved out to the edge of Fredericksburg. But soon they headed back to the front, with the brigade commanded now by Col. Strong Vincent after Stockton fell ill. They marched up Hanover Street, crossed the bridge "above the millrace" under cover of a hill, and continued to the left to the ground they had held before.[51]

They were barely one hundred yards from the enemy, and in some places so close that once Chamberlain walked up and inadvertently talked to an enemy soldier in the dark. The 20th was isolated, when Chamberlain was told to withdraw because everyone else had already gone off. Suddenly in a position where a quick rush by the enemy could have doomed his men, he had them number off. Odds went on digging noisily while the evens withdrew as their turn came. In this manner the men "leapfrogged" back to safety.[52]

Stockton's brigade was one of the last to withdraw from Fredericksburg, acting as rear guard, then finally crossing the pontoons. The brigade halted on the return to Falmouth, Virginia. Chamberlain was among the wounded, grazed by a ball on the right ear and side of the neck.[53]

After the hours of frozen horror on the plain behind Fredericksburg, Chamberlain returned to the duties of military paperwork.

Hd Qrs 20th Regt. Me.Vols.
Camp in Falmouth VA
Dec 20th 1862

John L Hodsdon Adjt. Gen.

General,

Yours of Dec 4th enclosing the commissions of Lts Litchfield & Besse was duly received.

In reply I have the honor to inform you that the rank date of Lt. Besse's is Oct. 10th, of Lt. Litchfield Nov. 20th.

Very respectfully
Your obdt. servt
J. L. Chamberlain
Lt. Col. com. 20th Me.Vols.[54]

The rest of that sad, cold December 1862 was spent in winter camp in Falmouth. On December 25, Maj. Gen. George Gordon Meade took over the 5th Corps.[55]

⇌ 1863 ⇌

What has gone takes something with it, and when this is of the dear, nothing can fill the place. All the changes touched the border of sorrows.
—Maj. Gen. Joshua L. Chamberlain, *The Passing of the Armies*

DURING THE LAST few days of 1862 and the first of the new year, Chamberlain and the 20th Maine accompanied the 1st Division on a three-day reconnaissance to Richard's Ford on the Rappahannock River, a little over a mile from the confluence of the Rappahannock and the Rapidan. After January 1 they settled back into their old camps for a few more weeks.

On January 20 Burnside began one of the most famous failures in the history of the Army of the Potomac. He planned to march his army rapidly up the Falmouth side of the Rappahannock, execute a quick crossing, and flank Lee's army in winter quarters at Fredericksburg. Shortly after the march began, so did the rain. It fell in unceasing torrents. Wagons and artillery pieces sunk to the hubs in the seemingly bottomless Virginia muck; men too were virtually motionless, exhausted from lifting their heavy, mud-caked brogans time and again from the sucking ooze. The 20th began executing orders to corduroy roads when the army got stuck. They all returned to the camps at Falmouth defeated by the weather. The fiasco came to be known as "Burnside's Mud March."[1]

As every soldier in this mostly volunteer army understood, there were matters to take care of at home.

Camp 20th Maine Vols
January 28th 1863

Lieut John M. Brown
Adjutant 20th Me. Vols.
Sir,

I have the honor to request leave of absence for fifteen days to attend to business in the state of Maine, involving pecuniary and other important interests.

I would add that all the Field officers of this Regiment are present.

Very respectfully
Your Obdt. Servt.
J. L. Chamberlain,
Lt. Col. 20th Me. Vols.[2]

Early in February Chamberlain received his leave. While home he went to Augusta, Maine, to talk with Gov. Abner Coburn. Shortly he was back with Fanny and their children in Brunswick, where he wrote the next letter.[3]

Head Quarters 20th Maine Vols
Feb. 26th 1863.

To His Excellency Abner Coburn
Governor of Maine
Dear Governor,

According to the understanding I had with you when I left Augusta I take the earliest opportunity after my return to inform you of the state of affairs in regard to the officers of this Regt.

We have now four Captains in command of their Companies— four first Lieutenants & two second Lts. acting as Captains— five second Lieutenants and four sergeants <u>acting</u> second Lts—most of the second and acting second Lts. of course are actually acting as first Lts. leaving <u>eleven</u> <u>vacancies</u> in the Line.

The Colonel is not prepared, I believe, to recommend candidates for all these vacancies at present. The cases with which he appears to be satisfied, and in which I entirely concur, are the recommendation of Lieut. Fitch of Co. "E." as Captain of Co. "D." Lieut. Land of "G" as Capt of Co. "H." or "B.", and second Lieut.

Abner Coburn, governor of Maine in 1863.
MAINE STATE ARCHIVES

Billings Co "A" as first Lieut. of "D" & second Lieut. Morrill of Co "B." as first Lieut. same Company.

The sergeants appointed to act as Lieutenants are the following.

1. Sergeant Chamberlain Co "I." appointed by the Col. acting 2d Lieut. of Co "D" Nov 20 1862.

2. Sergeant Lincoln Co "A" acting 2d Lieut. Co. "I" Nov. 20th 1862.

3. Sergeant Major Keene acting 2d Lieut. Co. "A" Dec. 10th 1862.

4. Sergeant Plumer Co H. acting 2 Lieut Co. "C." Dec 10th 1862

These officers have all been constantly on duty in the above capacity since their appointment & having given entire satisfaction, have been, I believe, recommend by the Col. to your Excellency for promotion.

Upon the appointment of Lieut. Land of Co "G." as acting capt of Co "H." sergeant Chamberlain was transferred by order of the Col. to act as first Lieut. of Co. "G." agreeably to the request of Capt. Spear, and he has since been acting in that capacity.

The good conduct of all the above named officers on the battle field as well as upon other occasions has led to their appointment to the positions in which they now act, and the granting of their commissions for these places would be no more justice to their merits, than a benefit to the Regiment.

I hope the recommendations already made will meet your entire approval, and receive early attention for the sake of the well-being of the Regt.

My letter is, I fear, too long; but I wish to give you a clear idea of what we need Other vacancies can be filled whenever you shall judge it necessary or proper.

Hoping that by our continued good conduct your Excellency may have a better opinion of us than you were pleased to express to me, and believing that the good name we hold in the army will before long reach our home in the state we honor,

I am with the highest respect,
Your friend & servant,
J. L. Chamberlain,
Lieut. Col. 20th Maine Vols.[4]

Apparently the reputation of the 20th Maine in the state capital was not as good as it was in the army. Chamberlain complained of this fact several times in his letters.

Chamberlain's brother Tom received his promotion from sergeant to lieutenant.

In early April, Chamberlain wrote to the regiment's acting adjutant—his brother Tom—to request five days' personal leave. He met Fanny in Washington.[5]

Camp 20th Maine Vols.
April 12, 1863.

Lieut. T. D. Chamberlain
Acting Adjt 20th Me Vols.
Sir,

I have the honor to request leave of absence for five (5) days to go to Washington & Baltimore on business.

Very respectfully
Your obdt. servt.
J. L. Chamberlain
Lieut. Col. 20th Me Vols.[6]

20th Regt. Maine Vols.
Camp near Falmouth Va
April 20th 1863.

Major Genl. Butterfield
Chief of Staff
General:

In my conversation with you this morning I seemed not to have conveyed the precise impression I designed.

The object of my visit was not to complain that my Regiment was to be detained, but convinced of the necessity ["of the necessity" is written inadvertently a second time and crossed out] of that, to ask that if possible I might be enable [*sic*] to participate in the active operations about to commence, in some position where I might be of service.

Major Genl. Howard knowing ["knowing" is repeated and inserted above the line   perhaps the first was not legible enough for Chamberlain] the circumstances of the case has unsolicited given me the enclosed letter, with directions to present it in person to the General Commanding, with explanations.

I have taken the liberty to rely on your kind interest, in addressing you, and leave it with your judgement whether it would be expedient to bring the matter to the notice of the General.

It seems unnecessary for all the field officers of the Regiment to remain in charge of the hospital camp, when it is the earnest recommendation of the surgeon in charge that as few officers as possible should be thus detained.

If Genl. Howard's views are not practicable, is it possible for me to be permitted to serve on the staff of some General officers until the Regt. is fit for duty?

You, General, will surely understand and appreciate my feelings in being prevented from taking into the field a Regiment upon which I have bestowed so much care and in whose efficiency I have so much confidence and pride.

It would be some relief in the mean time if I could be permitted to render such personal service as your judgement might suggest.

Yours [signature torn][7]

On April 22 the 20th Maine moved about a mile away from the rest of the army to a place called—ominously—"Quarantine Hill."

New Camp April 24th 1863.

My precious wife,

It has rained pouring ever since we started to move camp, so that the most we could do was to get our things into a tolerably compact heap, & keep them from a thorough wetting. I had some important letters to write this evening, & have been scrambling about to prepare for it—looking at the dry side of a board for a table—ransacking after a piece of a candle & pen, ink, & paper—humming a little air meantime to counteract the gloomy influence of the storm & confusion, when I found that I had been singing in the air of "Sleeping I dream Love", this very foolish & boyish song, "<u>First</u> <u>to</u> <u>my</u> <u>Dear</u> <u>One,</u> <u>First</u> <u>to</u> <u>my</u> <u>Love.</u>" Because I am always thinking first of you.

You were too sad, Darling, when you wrote, but my mind was dwelling on you, even more than usual, all that very time. I do not think you can have any particular occasion to feel apprehensive either for yourself or for me. I trust that before this time you are in a happier mood.

The most that troubles me now is that I may not be able to take part in the next fight. Here we are in an isolated camp, with direful looking placards posted at every entrance "<u>Small</u> <u>Pox</u>," the Surgeons giving opinions that we cannot move for a fortnight at least. If in the mean time there is a battle, & I am left here in a pesthouse, I shall be desperate with mortification. I have tried to make conditional arrangements to get placed on some General's staff but things are so uncertain in regard to the Army & to our Regt. that even this could not be done at present.

Meantime I have had printed notice of an appointment for the proving & allowing of Capt. Badger's Will on the first Tuesday in May, & if I have any thing to do with it as an Executor, it is necessary for me to be present, at that time & place. Nothing would induce me to be absent from my Regt. when they went into a battle, and even if they did not engage, I should make every effort to to [*sic*] obtain permission to render some service personally on the field. Now if I were at all sure there would be a movement within a fortnight, & I could be permitted to take an honorable part in a battle, I would throw up all idea of serving as Executor in this case. But you see every thing is uncertain—the probability is that I could attend to this matter & return before the <u>Regt.</u>, at any rate, moved. At the same time it seems half disgraceful to ask for leave of absence just when it is possible there may be a battle impending.

You see my perplexity. If the settling of this Estate were a matter of ordinary importance I might easily fore go all thought of it. But it seems hardly right for me to neglect a business of so much interest to me personally; for I suppose Capt. B. intended by appointing me to do me a favor in the pecuniary advantage it would be to execute this trust. If I should give it up now, & then find that I must stay here in this hospital camp a longer time than I should require to transact the business it would be a great vexation.

I feel quite puzzled,—<u>cornered</u> expresses it.

Apr. 27. Well here we are at length—<u>left</u>—the Col. gone, & I put in charge of the Regt. We saw our Division & Brigade move off, & we felt lonesome, I assure you. However by not granting me permission to go forward, I suppose the Regt. will be ordered to move very soon. I wish you could be here now. I could endure it. I suppose I shall have to give up the Badger Will case which I am sorry to do.

You do not know how I want to see you, dearest; this disappointment in not being able to go on with the army, nor obtaining leave to go & attend to the Will business, keeping me in a sick camp I do not at all enjoy.

I have not the slightest idea when or where I shall go next.

You had better go on without me where you wish.

I have only time to say pay Mrs. Harris amply—say $10.00 a week. I have reason to believe she would be obliged to have that to save herself

In haste your own L.[8]

On April 27 the rest of the Army of the Potomac, under Maj. Gen. Joseph Hooker since late January, began their spring offensive against Robert E. Lee and his Army of Northern Virginia. When Hooker took over from Burnside, he reorganized the army into seven corps. On April 27 three of his corps headed up the Rappahannock River. The 5th Corps, leaving Chamberlain and the men of the 20th Maine behind, followed the 11th and 12th Corps to Kelly's Ford on the Rappahannock, crossed there, and headed toward a small crossroads called Chancellorsville.[9]

On April 29, Maj. Gen. John Sedgwick's 6th Corps was ordered to cross the Rappahannock at Fredericksburg and occupy the Confederates in that area, following and pressing them if they fell back. The 1st Corps under Maj. Gen. John F. Reynolds was to do the same farther downstream.[10]

The battle known as Chancellorsville had raged through an area of Virginia called "the Wilderness" for two days while the 20th Maine sat in quarantine. Colonel Ames, realizing that though his unit might not be serviceable, he himself could still be of help, presented himself to Maj. Gen. George G. Meade's 5th Corps headquarters, leaving Chamberlain in charge of the regiment.

Chamberlain listened to the firing in the distance and yearned to be in the action. Unknown to Chamberlain, the firing he heard late on the afternoon of May 2 was directed at fellow Bowdoin alumnus Maj. Gen. Oliver Otis Howard, now in command of the Union army's 11th Corps. Confederate generals Robert E. Lee and "Stonewall" Jackson had come up with their most audacious plan yet: While the Union army flanked them, they would flank it. Splitting his army into three parts in the face of the enemy, Lee held Sedgwick off at Fredericksburg, froze Hooker's main force as it curved around Chancellorsville, and sent Jackson on a march swinging to the left around the Union army's right flank, falling on the rear of Howard's lounging troops. Chaos ensued. After darkness fell, Jackson was accidentally shot by his own men. Maj. Gen. J. E. B. Stuart, commander of the Confederate Cavalry Division, was called from outpost duty at Ely's Ford to take command of Jackson's corps and press the attack early the next morning, May 3.

Meanwhile, Chamberlain petitioned in person to get his unit into action. After midnight on May 2–3 he finally received orders to move to Banks' and U.S. Fords on the Rappahannock River and arrived there with his unit on Sunday, May 3. His men were to watch over the telegraph wires and guarantee communications between Hooker's headquarters and the rest of the army.[11]

That morning the Confederate attack continued, advancing from the west while Union troops under Sedgwick fought a battle of their own around Salem Church once they cleared the town of Fredericksburg. Chamberlain rode all night inspecting telegraph wires, which were constantly being broken. The crossing at Banks' Ford, guarded by the 20th

Maine, grew in importance, as it appeared that Sedgwick might have to use it to extract his men from Confederates attacking on two fronts.[12]

Chamberlain joined the 2nd Brigade of Griffin's division on May 4. Although his magnificent horse, Prince, was wounded in the head,[13] most of the hard fighting was over. By May 6 Hooker's army had recrossed the Rappahannock.

After Chancellorsville, the Army of the Potomac retreated to their Falmouth camps through a pouring rain.

Chamberlain found time to write a letter to his daughter Daisy, now six years old. He printed each word so that she could read it herself. The letter seemed to provide him an escape from his present martial position to the tranquil, domestic life, if only for a little while.

May 1863

My dear little Daisy,

I began a letter to you before the battle, but in the hurry of our moving it was lost. It was night too, so that we could not see much. I am sorry I lost the letter, for it was almost done. There has been a big battle, and we had a great many men killed or wounded. We shall try it again soon, and see if we cannot make those Rebels behave better, and stop their wicked works in trying to spoil our Country, and making us all so unhappy.

I have looked for the letter a great deal, but I shall enjoy writing another to you. You see I cannot write very well in this way; I believe you could write better if you should try.

I am very glad to have so many nice letters from you. I sent the last ones to dear Mamma. I shall want another soon. I suppose Mamma is at home by this time, so I shall have the pleasure of a letter from both of you next time.

Do you and Wyllys have a pleasant time now-a-days? I think dear Aunty must make you very happy. She has such kind ways. I should like to see you all. What a charming little home you have, especially if dear Mamma is with you. Does Master Wyllys call her Fanny yet? You must have a garden to work in. It is very hot here, so that we can hardly bear to have our clothes on. But we do not have any Mayflowers here. All the ground is so trampled by the Army that even the grass will not grow much. How I should enjoy a May-walk with you and Wyllys and what beautiful flowers we could bring home to surprise Mamma and Aunty! I often think of all our paths and sunny banks where we are always sure to find the wild-flowers. Do the beautiful birds sing about the trees, and look for places to build nests near the house, as they used to do?

I am suddenly ordered to go to the front and take command of our pickets. Mamma will tell you what they are, so good bye once more.

Papa.[14]

All too suddenly he was pulled back into the realities of war.

By mid-May the quarantine had been lifted and the 20th was back on picket duty. Chamberlain was back to army paperwork: he was required to submit a monthly return of the regiment for January.

Head Quarters 20th Me
May 18, 1863.

John L. Hodsdon,
Adjt Genl. State of Maine,
General,

I have the honor herewith to transmit to you a copy of the return of this regiment for the month of January. I regret that you did not receive the return which was sent last January.

I am sir,
Very respectfully
Your obdt servt
J. L. Chamberlain
Lieut Col. Comdg
20th Me.[15]

On May 20 Adelbert Ames, for service rendered under Meade, received a promotion to brigadier general and the command of a brigade in Howard's 11th Corps. Joshua L. Chamberlain became the colonel in command of the 20th Maine.

A number of other promotions occurred to fill vacancies: Major Gilmore became lieutenant colonel of the regiment; Ellis Spear of Company G was expected to become major; and a handsome, youthful Pennsylvanian named Strong Vincent became commander of the 3rd Brigade, taking Stockton's place. Tom Chamberlain, Lawrence's brother, remained acting adjutant.[16]

Command of the 20th was received proudly by the former professor from Bowdoin. But along with the elation of command came its burdens. One of the first problems Chamberlain had to solve was an apparent injustice to one of his young officers. Even in his postwar writings, no matter the accolades he was to receive for his role in the war, Chamberlain always laid the honors on "the Army"—meaning, of course, the men he commanded. His letters show a compassion, a fatherly concern, for the common soldier.

Though he was *de facto* colonel of the regiment, the official paperwork had not yet arrived, so he still signed this letter "Lieut Colonel."

> Head Qrs 20th Maine Vols.
> Camp near Falmouth Va
> May 21, 1863.

Brig Genl L. Thomas
Adjt. Genl. U. S. A.
General,

I beg leave respectfully to call attention to the case of 2 Lieut. Mattson C. Sanborn of 20th Regt. Maine Vols whose appointment was revoked by order of War Department—Special Order No. 164; date of April 10, 1863—in consequence of his not having joined the regiment.

Lieut. Sanborn was Sergeant in the 1st Maine Battery, stationed near New Orleans and by reason of sickness he was unable to join this regiment until April 1, 1863.

His papers show that he was absent by proper authority, although the evidence at the time did not reach the Adjutant of this regiment.

He is a deserving young man and being satisfied that he is guilty of no negligence in the matter, I respectfully request that he may be restored to his appointment.

> I have the honor to be
> Very respectfully
> Your obdt sevt.
> J. L. Chamberlain,
> Lieut Colonel. Comdg,
> 20th Maine[17]

Believing that the army will remain in the present camps for a while, Chamberlain invites his younger brother John to visit. But before they would get together, both would be engaged in the most important campaign of the war to date, challenging John to a more difficult and eventful journey than either had ever anticipated.

H. Q. 20th Maine Vols.
May 22d. 1863

Dear John,

I thank you much for your kind letters. You may be sure I value them, & think of them a great deal.

I got acquainted with you in college, somewhat in the way I would with any young man, & that in addition to some previous & subsequent acquaintance from the time you used to ask for "nickes on capin", to the tree-climbing on Mount Monsummon, makes me believe I am not mistaken in holding a high opinion of you.

I write now chiefly to give one illustration of my good opinion by asking for the pleasure of your society for a few weeks.

We shall probably be situated for some little time so that you could find it pleasant to visit us. The season is glorious. Our camp is fine & you would thoroughly enjoy it.

I shall be expecting you now soon.

You can get a transfer ticket from Boston to Washington—perhaps from Bangor. Then get a pass at Lt. Col. Conrad's 132 Penn. Avenue up beyond White House.

Thomas is well & doing well. Mother wrote him a beautiful letter a few days ago. He thinks a great deal of you at home.

I am in command here now. We receive the three years men of the 2d Maine tomorrow morning, & that will make us by all odds the best Regt. from Maine.

Where is Miss Sae now-a-days? I shall write her when I get a pen that will make a mark the 2d or 3d time going over the paper.

Love to Father & Mother & all.

J. Lawrence C.[18]

Chamberlain's compassion for the common soldier would prove valuable in handling a situation concerning the arrival of some disgruntled men from the 2nd Maine. Their papers said that they were enlisted for three years, but they had been told upon enlisting that, like others in the unit, they would be held to only two years' service. They had been duped by the recruiter, however, and as they watched the rest of the unit head home to the woods and rocky shores of their beloved Pine Tree State, they felt extreme indignation. Though Chamberlain did not know it yet, their arrival would test his ability to command and his own humanity in a war that was shredding civil comportment by the day.

Head Quarters 20th Maine Volunteers
May 25th 1863.

To His Excellency Gov. Coburn,
Governor,

I have the honor to acknowledge the receipt of your favor of the 20th instant, addressed to Col. Ames, and sent to me as the present commanding officer of this Regt. Col. Ames having been appointed Brigadier Gen., has taken his oath of office & been assigned a Brigade in Gen Howard's Corps, where he is now on duty.

In reply to your favor I am very happy to say that Dr. Monroe by the efforts of his friends in the Regt. & elsewhere has been reinstated & honorably discharged. We were sorry to lose him, but he felt it his duty to go.

It is very important to the welfare of the men that we have a good Surgeon, & it is a matter about which I feel a great deal of anxiety.

We should all welcome Dr. Hersom. I shall act upon your suggestion, & see Col. Roberts of the 17th. I am aware of the difficulty with which transfers between different Corps are made, but it is possible the arrangement you suggest can be carried out. We should all greatly prefer that, to the other course by which Dr. Hersom would be exchanged for Dr. Wescott & neither Regt. perhaps so well satisfied.

There is another matter, Governor, about which I wish to have a word with you. The transfer of the "three years men" of the 2d Maine has been so clumsily done, that the men were allowed to grow quite mutinous—left uncared for in their old camp after the 2d had gone for several days, & having time and provocation to work themselves up to such a pitch of mutiny that Gen Barnes had to send them to me as prisoners, liable to severe penalties for disobedience of his orders. You are aware, Governor, that promises were made to induce these men to enlist, which are not now kept, & I must say that I sympathize with them in their view of the case. Assured as they were that they should be mustered out with the 2d, they cannot but feel that they are falsely dealt with in being retained & sent to duty in other Regts. They need to be managed with great care & skill; but I fear that some of them will get into trouble for disobedience of orders or mutiny. My orders are to take them & put them on duty—which they have already refused to Gen. Barnes & others. I shall carry out my orders whatever may be the consequence; but I sincerely wish these men were fairly dealt with by those who made them their promises. All their <u>papers</u> say they are enlisted for <u>three years</u>—just as the men of this Regt. are, & for us in the field there is no other way but to hold them to it. What you may be able to do for them I do not know.

I think with pleasure of your short visit to us, & am only sorry I could not do more to make your stay agreeable.

The Regiment was enabled to do good & important service during the fight although we were not allowed to mingle with the rest of the Army. I had a midnight order from Gen Butterfield to take possession of the signal wire from the Battle field to Head. Qrs. of the Army. This gave us enough to do, as the wire was tampered with & broken many times a night, & communication was of the utmost importance. I was in my saddle <u>all</u> the nights inspecting every inch of the line. The Regt. is in good health—never so free from sickness—small pox entirely disappeared.

I have said nothing about promotions of Field officers in this Regt. I have not supposed that you needed any testimonials; if you wish them they can easily be furnished. But you have seen & known us, & we are willing to leave the matter to your own best judgment.

I am Governor
Very respectfully
Your obdt servt.
J. L. Chamberlain
Lt. Col. 20th Maine Vols.[19]

Again Chamberlain lobbies for one of his subordinates.

                                  Head Qrs. 20th Maine Vols.
                                       May 26th, 1863.

To John L. Hodsdon,
Adjt. Genl. State of Maine
Genl.
    I have the honor herewith to transmit to you a copy of a letter
addressed to Brig Genl. Thomas in behalf of 2d Lieut. Sanborn. I
think it is very desirable that he be restored to his appointment.
                                  Very respectfully
                                  Your obdt. servt.
                                  J. L. Chamberlain
                                  Lieut. Col. Comdg.
                                  20th Maine.[20]

The men of the 2nd Maine continued to be on the verge of mutiny.
Though Chamberlain required of them their duty as soldiers, both they
and he anticipated some direction from the governor as to a solution for
the problem. The situation continued for at least another month, and
Chamberlain had to handle this one on his own.

                                  Head Quarters 20th Maine
                                       May 27, 1863.

Hon. A. Coburn
Governor of Maine
Dear Governor,
    I find that it is going to involve great trouble to obtain the
transfer of Drs. Hersom or Wescott. They do not like to give up Dr.
Hersom in the 17th, I learn.
    And if we cannot obtain Dr. Hersom, we should prefer Dr.
Martin of Presque Isle formerly Asst. Surgeon of the "6th" Maine
& late surgeon of the "4th" We hear no one so highly spoken of, &
although I do not know him personally, I should feel entirely safe
in trusting the health of the Regt in his hands
    The men of the "2d" are quite unhappy; still feeling that great
injustice has been done them in holding them to service longer I

have taken a liberal course with them, because they are nearly all good & true men, but I shall be obliged to carry a firm hand. They are now ordered on duty, & their orders must be carried out.

They are expecting to hear from you, in reply to a communication of theirs & their expectation of this keeps them in an undecided state of mind as to doing duty.

I sympathize with the men, but while under my orders, they will be strictly held to obedience.

Hoping to hear soon in reference to these matters

I am Governor
Very respectfully
Your Obdt servt.
J. L. Chamberlain
Lieut Col. Comdg.
20th Maine[21]

On May 28 the 1st Division of the 5th Corps broke camp to guard the crossings of the Rappahannock.[22] By May 30 the 20th was guarding U.S. Ford downstream to Horse Pen Run, one of the small tributaries emptying into the Rappahannock River.

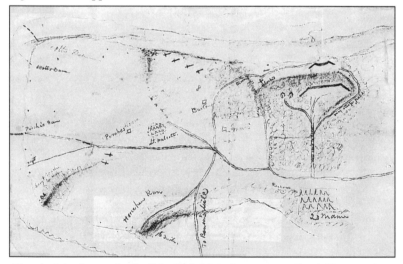

Chamberlain drew a sketch of the 20th Maine's camp near Scott's Dam on the Rappahannock River. LIBRARY OF CONGRESS

A map of the area accompanied the next letter, which was unsigned. The letter ended in mere notes, indicating that the dictation was interrupted, perhaps for the regiment's move upriver to Ellis Ford. From its provenance—"Hd. Qrs. 20th Maine Vols."—Chamberlain no doubt would have signed it had it been finished.

Hd. Qrs. 20th Maine Vols.
June 3rd 1863

Lieut.

In obedience to orders I have the honor to report the following information in regard to the Fords.

I divide my front into four Sections Viz.

Section I From the lower Island to U. S. Ford

Section II U. S. Ford 100 Rods front

Section III From U. S. Ford to Scotts Dam

Section IV From Scotts Dam to Horse pen Run

The river front of section I is fordable as to depth and bottom nearly every where. The water is no where over three feet deep here excepting opposite a perpendicular ledge a short distance above U. S. Ford. The banks along this front are mostly very steep and high. There are two approaches on the other side, only one on this side. This is practicable for Cavalry & Artillery. Opposite the lower Island at what is called Low Ford. I have a permanent Post here. Men could ford here with any front but could not land with a wider front than four men abreast. The road could be easily obstructed by felling trees.

The river in front Section II including the ford proper is fordable in many places. Generally 3 feet of water. The bottom however is rough. The approaches on the Rebel side are numerous & easy on our side, the only roads practicable for Artillery or Cavalry are effectually blocked. A very steep bridle path leads to our lower rifle. This will soon be commanded by a small breast work. The banks all along there are very precipitous. A landing nearly could be effected so far as the bank is concerned for 100 yards at the Ford but at present the trees which have been fellen [*sic*] completely obstruct the passage & a completed rifle pit extends the whole distance not more than 20 yards from the water. Our heavy breastwork on the crest directly above & some 300 yards from the water is nearly completed. The rebel works opposite are strong. Sec. III from U. S. Ford to Scotts Dam 1 1/2 miles has no fordable place except 1/4 of a mile above & immediately below the dam. Infantry & Cavalry could cross in single file 1/4 mile above. Artillery not at all. The banks are very steep every where for a small distance there is a level fringe before the bluff rises every thing by way of approach can be obstructed water deep.[23]

After picketing the Rappahannock River from Horse Pen Run to the Lower Island, Chamberlain and the 20th Maine were moved to Ellis Ford by June 5.

Around June 13 the 20th Maine and the 5th Corps moved from Ellis Ford to Morristown, then to Catlett's Station. On June 15 they halted at Manassas Junction.[24] The men were beginning to realize, after having spent nearly a month guarding the fords along the Rappahannock, then pulling out to endure several days of rapid marching during a late spring heatwave, that something was up. That they were heading northward gave them another clue: Lee must be on the move.

When the 20th Maine reached Gum Springs, Chamberlain succumbed to sunstroke and was taken to a nearby house to recuperate. The 20th marched on to Aldie, Virginia, on June 17 without him.

Aldie is located at an important fork in the Little River Turnpike. The southern branch of the fork leads to Snicker's Gap, the other to Ashby's Gap, two important routes through the Blue Ridge Mountains. Confederate general J. E. B. Stuart's mission was to clog up those gaps with his cavalry so that prying Union cavalry could not see what the rest of the Confederate army was doing behind the gap on the west side of the mountains. Union cavalry under Judson Kilpatrick arrived at Aldie at four that afternoon. The 1st Rhode Island Cavalry under Col. Alfred Duffié was sent around the Confederate right flank and rear toward Middleburg, but the Rebels drove them off during the night.

Union reports claim victory at Aldie, and indeed the Confederates withdrew toward Middleburg. But time was what Stuart was buying—time for Lee's army behind him to move father north—and time was just what he gained.

Fighting went on all day June 18 in and around Middleburg with the Confederates slowly retreating. It was the same for the next two days,

Stuart once again using the oldest military equation in the world, trading ground and men's lives for time.

Chamberlain came up on June 20 but was still so sick he could not leave his tent.[25]

On June 21 five of Union general Alfred Pleasonton's cavalry brigades, backed up by Strong Vincent's 3rd Brigade of infantry, launched a two-pronged advance, one through Upperville and the other swinging to the north, driving Stuart's five brigades into Ashby's Gap. Chamberlain was still too sick to participate.

On June 22 Chamberlain's brother John reached the regiment. He had been trying to reach his brother since leaving Brunswick on June 1. On his way through Boston, he joined up with the Christian Commission, a national group formed to see to the spiritual and physical well-being of the soldiers. He visited Philadelphia and Washington, but by the time he got to Stoneman's Station, near Fredericksburg, Virginia, where he was to meet Tom and Lawrence, the army had moved. He performed the duties of a Christian Commission representative while near Falmouth. Finally, after traversing some fairly dangerous sections of Virginia, he met up with his brothers.[26]

Early in the morning of June 26, the 20th Maine resumed the march north. Chamberlain was still sick but insisted on riding his horse rather than using an ambulance. The 5th Corps crossed the Potomac at Edwards Ferry on pontoons. Things began happening quickly now.

On June 27 the troops crossed Monocacy Creek at a ford and encamped that night just a few miles from Frederick, Maryland. On June 28 Maj. Gen. George G. Meade, commander of the Federal 5th Corps, learned he had been assigned to take over the entire Army of the Potomac, relieving Gen. Hooker. Maj. Gen. George Sykes took command of the 5th Corps.

By the twenty-ninth the 5th Corps broke camp and marched through Frederick, continued for eighteen miles and camped. The men resumed the march at 4 A.M. on June 30, marching twenty-three miles, and camped near Union Mills, Maryland, just missing Confederate cavalry under Gen. J. E. B. Stuart by three hours.

Early in the morning of July 1, they continued the march northward, and by early that afternoon, they crossed into Pennsylvania. Brig. Gen. James Barnes's division (which included Vincent's 3rd Brigade and the 20th Maine) arrived near Hanover, Pennsylvania, at about four that afternoon. They prepared to encamp for the evening but had hardly stacked arms when word arrived that part of the Army of the Potomac had fought with the enemy near a small town in southern Pennsylvania called Gettysburg. Orders came to resume the march, and the men, buoyed by the anticipation of meeting the Rebels on Northern soil, "were transformed to boys," unfurled the colors, and marched on through the evening.[27]

The undulating column was greeted on its summer's night's march by the Pennsylvania Dutch womenfolk (nearly all the men had "skedaddled" with the livestock) with waving handkerchiefs and cheers. Down the dark line of march came two rumors: that Maj. Gen. George B. McClellan had taken over the army, and that ahead, through the odd mists that are common in that part of Pennsylvania on summer evenings, was seen a horseman with a cape and tricorn hat. The men at the head of the column had identified him: It was, without a doubt, Gen. George Washington. The ghost of the Founding Father was leading the men to victory to save the Union he loved so dearly![28] *Other orders of beings also share this halt at the bridge of life and death. . . .*[29]

Their commander called a halt after midnight. The men of the 20th Maine rested for three hours. Suddenly, after muscles had cooled and stiffened, they were called out and marched another two or three miles. To one participant's reckoning, they had marched thirty-two miles since the morning of July 1, the last fourteen in the dark. They halted for an hour's rest until daylight, when the company rolls were called, arms and ammunition inspected, and the men ordered to load their weapons.[30]

Somewhere on the march or during one of the halts, the men may have heard the news that two corps of the Union army had been defeated the day before. The Confederates had driven them from some ridges and hills west and north of the small town of Gettysburg and through the town itself. Their defeated and weary comrades waited for daybreak and a renewed battle on some hills and a ridge just south of town. Reinforcements were essential.

Coming toward Gettysburg from the east, the men of the 20th were marched to the left, across Rock Creek, and then north along the Baltimore Pike, which led from Gettysburg south to Westminster, Maryland. They halted near a hill on which the local cemetery had been placed and another hill named after the Culp family, who lived nearby. The Federal

1st and 11th Corps were to their left and front, and they watched as the 12th Corps marched to Culp's Hill to establish battle lines there.[31]

About noon the 5th Corps was moved farther to the left in support of the 3rd Corps. Resting in a peach orchard in the rear of the lines, the men cooked coffee and wrote letters in the dead, stifling air.

Around three o'clock they heard a single cannon fire to their front, then a general cannonade from the same direction.[32] By four the men were up and moving out the road that led from Gettysburg to Taneytown, Maryland. They turned west and marched over the ridge that led southward from Cemetery Hill (soon to be written about as Cemetery Ridge) to a wheatfield to support Maj. Gen. Daniel Sickles's 3rd Corps line. On their way they cut across fields, going through hedges, traversing low swampy ground, climbing over a hill, and leaping several of the ubiquitous stone walls that crisscross the farm fields south of Gettysburg. The regiment could see the soon-to-be-famous Peach Orchard, as well as the Wheatfield, "where heroic men standing bright as golden grain were ravaged by Death's wild reapers from the woods." Chamberlain, caught a glimpse of the left flank of the 3rd Corps in its fight for a jumble of huge boulders called Devil's Den. The 1st and 2nd Brigades of the division went into the gap between the Peach Orchard and the Wheatfield, while Vincent's brigade, including Chamberlain's 20th Maine, was held in reserve.[33]

Behind the brigade was a rounded little hill called Granite Spur or Little Round Top. The west side of the hill had been cleared of timber for firewood by the Weikert family the previous autumn, but the woods on the east slope remained. Atop the hill, Maj. Gen. G. K. Warren of Meade's staff realized that there were no Union troops, save some signalmen, on this hill that lay at the extreme left flank of his entire army. He saw the fighting in Devil's Den but could not see how far the Confederate assault extended because of the thick woods covering a spur of an even higher hill to his south. To see if there were Confederates in those woods, he relied upon human nature, ordering an artillery battery below him to lob a shell into the woods.

The crash of the shell through the woods and the showering of branches caused the men hidden there to flinch and cover, and Warren saw the sunlight reflected off hundreds of burnished musket barrels and bayonets as they moved with the men. There were troops in the woods, and they did not belong to the Union army, so Warren sent two staff officers—

one to Sickles and one to Sykes—down the slope of the smaller hill to find some friendly troops.

Meanwhile, Confederate brigadier general E. M. Law's brigade, as part of the massive Confederate movement through and around Devil's Den, ended up in the woods on the spur of the big hill. One of Law's regiments, the 15th Alabama, commanded by Col. William C. Oates, drew the onerous duty of marching directly up the south slope of the big hill, later called Sugar Loaf or Big Round Top. They ran into a few Yankee sharpshooters on their way up but managed to push them back as they advanced. Some of the way up was hand-over-hand climbing. They had already marched twenty-five miles since 4 A.M. just to get to the battlefield, then several more miles to get into position to attack. Just before they were to move out, a detail was sent to gather all the canteens of the unit and fill them at a well behind the lines. But before the water bearers had a chance to return, the rest of the men were ordered into action. As they reached the summit of Big Round Top, Oates's men virtually collapsed as a regiment from fatigue, the July heat, and lack of water.

Five minutes were spent while the men recuperated; another five passed while Oates argued in vain with Law's assistant adjutant general—who had ascended the summit to get Oates's men moving—about the advantages of his current position. Those may have been the most important ten minutes in the lifetime of the Confederacy.

Had Oates's troops advanced, they would have taken Little Round Top practically without a fight. Confederate artillery, if placed there, would have enfiladed the entire Union line, flank and rear, up to its center on Cemetery Hill. An infantry assault would have rolled the Union line up with a flank attack—similar to what happened to them just two months before at Chancellorsville. If the Confederates had not wished to attack, they could have extended their lines to the east and cut the Taneytown, then the Baltimore Road (they had already captured the Emmitsburg Road), placing them between the Union army and the Federal capital, Washington, D.C.

Instead, Warren made his discovery and was sending word of it down Little Round Top and looking for help. Brig. Gen. Strong Vincent stopped one of Gen. Sykes's aides and demanded to know what was happening. Then he turned his brigade to the rear, ordered them to Little Round Top, and galloped ahead to find positions for them.[34]

Elisha Coan, a member of the 20th Maine, recalled marching in column by the right flank, crossing a muddy run and moving down the valley between Little Round Top and Devil's Den, later to be named by the soldiers "the valley of death."[35] Chamberlain remembered the same, adding that they "found a rude log bridge" over the run and a "rough farm road" that led to the base of Little Round Top. As the men began to climb the slope, some Confederate batteries found their range and began peppering them. The three Chamberlain brothers were riding together when a solid shot whisked past their faces. Chamberlain sent Tom to the rear of the regiment and John to the front, saying, "Another such shot might make it hard for mother."[36]

When they reached the southern face of the hill, Vincent was already there. The 16th Michigan, which had led the brigade up the hill, was moved behind the forming defensive line to the right of the brigade, leaving the 20th Maine at the extreme left of the brigade—and the army. Vincent told Chamberlain that the position he was placing him in must be held at all hazards.[37]

After Vincent left, Chamberlain began placing his line to take best tactical advantage of the rocky slope that faced into the woods on the higher hill to the south. He stripped his unit of one company, B, under Capt. Walter G. Morrill, and sent them to the left to protect the rest of the regiment's flank. Forming the battle line, the 20th Maine was under constant, heavy artillery fire. It was probably here that Chamberlain got his first wound at Gettysburg, to his right instep.[38]

Chamberlain had barely gotten the men into a slightly semicircular position conforming to the curve of the spur when he heard the artillery lift and the center of the brigade, to his right, become engaged. Like a wave breaking on a slanted shore, the Confederate assault rolled toward him and the men of the 20th Maine.

From the Confederate point of view, Law's brigade had begun its attack from the south. Oates's 15th Alabama was originally in the center of the brigade, but the two regiments to his right were moved, leaving the 15th on the extreme right flank of the brigade. Sixty-year-old Lt. Col. Michael Bulger's 47th Alabama was to their left. As Oates roused his men and descended the north face of Big Round Top, he "found the enemy in heavy force, posted in rear of large rocks upon a slight elevation beyond a depression of some 300 yards in width between the base of the mountain and the open plain beyond."[39]

He could see a large park of Federal wagons in the distance and sent Company A to capture them. The rest of the unit continued to advance until they were about forty yards from an irregular ledge of rocks. Suddenly, from this natural breastwork, came "the most destructive fire I ever saw." He had run into the four regiments of Vincent's brigade: on the right of the brigade, the 16th Michigan; to its left, the 44th New York; then the 83rd Pennsylvania; and on the extreme left, the 20th Maine. Chamberlain, though not in action yet, could distinctly hear "the roll of musketry. It struck the exposed right center of our brigade."[40] Oates had his men perform a left wheel: "I could see the men of the Twentieth Maine in front of my right wing running from tree to tree back westward toward the main body, and I advanced my right, swinging it around, overlapping and turning their left."[41] (In his after-action report— his earliest account of the fighting—Oates wrote, "I discovered that the enemy were giving way in my front. I ordered a charge, and the enemy in my front fled, but that portion of his line confronting the two companies on my left held their ground, and continued a most galling fire upon my left.")[42]

What Oates saw in front of his right wing was Chamberlain's response to Oates's movement. Lt. James H. Nichols ran up to Chamberlain from the center of the 20th's line and reported something strange going on in front of his company. Chamberlain clambored atop a large rock in the center of Nichols's company and saw over the heads of the Confederates engaged with the rest of Vincent's brigade: "I was able to see a considerable body of the enemy moving by the flank in rear of their line engaged, and passing from the direction of the foot of Great Round Top through the valley toward the front of my left."[43] Perhaps what Nichols and Chamberlain saw was Shaaf's Company A moving toward the wagon park. The vision of enemy troops moving to his left sparked him into action. Capt. Ellis Spear from the left came up with the same observation. Chamberlain called his company commanders together and gave them orders.

Chamberlain originally ordered the right company of the 20th to move to the extreme left, but realizing that the movement might be interpreted as a retreat and would involve a difficult maneuver under fire, he countermanded his order.[44]

Instead, he immediately had his right wing "take intervals by the left flank at 3 to 5 paces according to the shelter offered by the rocks & trees, thus covering the whole front then engaged;" he moved his left wing "to the left rear making nearly a right angle at the color."[45] Chamberlain reported that the movement was so well executed that the fire from his front did not slacken. This, of course, is what Oates thought was the 20th Maine "giving way" in his front and "running from tree to tree back westward toward the main body," and the continued firing of Chamberlain's right wing produced for Oates what he observed as "a most galling fire upon my left." Oates thought that Vincent's brigade had spent about ten minutes piling a few rocks in a zigzag line before Oates attacked. Chamberlain figured his regiment had gotten into line "not a moment too soon," and his formation was "scarcely complete" when Oates began his assault.[46]

The 47th Alabama under Bulger advanced with only seven companies, the rest performing as skirmishers, and took tremendous fire from the 44th New York and the 83rd Pennsylvania and an oblique fire from the 20th Maine as the Confederate "wave" broke on the Union "shore." During the march over Big Round Top, the left flank of the 47th Alabama had gotten separated from its right flank, creating a gap. When the 47th confronted the 83rd Pennsylvania, the unsupported left flank received oblique fire across that gap from the 44th New York in addition to frontal fire from the 83rd Pennsylvania. Chamberlain thought that all the companies of the 47th attacked his front. In reality, the units overlapped, with only the right three companies of the 47th striking Chamberlain's right companies at first. The fire from two sides upon the 47th Alabama was devastating. The seven companies of the 47th found temporary shelter among the rocks on the slope of Little Round Top while the 15th Alabama continued its left wheel and, coming into line parallel with the 20th Maine, fought to within ten paces of the Northerners before the Yankee volleys brought the Rebel troops to a halt and they withdrew.

Chamberlain believed that the flanking party had worked its way around to his left. Though it had initially gone that way, it could not have

been Oates's Company A; that company would not return to the regiment until the end of the fight. What Chamberlain saw was probably the
15th Alabama sidling more to its right in an attempt to gain his left
flank.[47] From the woods in the little valley below Little Round Top,
Oates's men came on again, this time along the whole front of the 20th
Maine. Oates thought that his line made it about halfway to the Yankees'
position, the men advancing and wavering like "a man trying to walk
against a strong wind."[48] But here and there small groups of Alabamians
broke through Chamberlain's line; here and there Chamberlain's line
retreated up the slope five, ten, twenty paces to another ledge. At other
places Chamberlain's men penetrated the Rebel lines and mingled vio-
lently with the Confederates. "The edge of the fight rolled backward and
forward like a wave."[49] Some men of the 20th Maine were driven nearly
to the summit of the spur only to press back down the hill, forcing the
Confederates back to the base. "The edge of the conflict swayed to and
fro," recalled Chamberlain, "with wild whirlpools and eddies." He saw a
young man shot across the forehead. He sent him back to the field hospital "to die in peace. Within a half-hour, in a desperate rally I saw that
noble youth amidst the rolling smoke as an apparition from the dead,
with bloody bandage for the only covering of his head, in the thick of
the fight, high-borne and pressing on as they that shall see death no
more. I shall know him when I see him again, on whatever shore!"[50]

"When that mad carnival lulled," Chamberlain recalled when in his
eighties, "from some strange instinct in human nature and without any
reason in the situation that can be seen—when the battle edges drew
asunder, there stood our little line, groups and gaps, notched like saw-
teeth, but sharp as steel, tempered in infernal heats. . . ."[51]

Between assaults there were three or four lulls in the fighting.
Between the lines lay the dead and groaning wounded of both sides. But
while Chamberlain and his men had a little time to catch their breath,
the firing to the right, behind them, continued to rise in intensity as
Confederates attacked the rest of Vincent's brigade. Lt. Charles Hazlett's
battery of artillery was being dragged to the summit of Little Round Top
by hand through the woods behind them. Somewhere in the tumult to
the right, Vincent went down, mortally wounded.

During one of the brief lulls, the men of the 20th gathered small
rocks and piled them between some of the larger boulders. They were
not much, but the low rock walls would protect a man lying down—if

he was small. Also, as the firing receded temporarily, Chamberlain's men pulled in the wounded where they could reach them and, after placing them in a relatively safe place, took their cartridges. They pilfered the dead too, for whatever ammunition and working weapons they could find, some men exchanging their Enfields for what they believed were the more serviceable Springfields. Then, suddenly, through the trees, came again the unearthly, banshee cry the Confederates would wail in battle—the "Rebel yell." This time, their lines seemed to have slid even more to the left, lapping against Chamberlain's bent-back left wing.

"I saw around me more of the enemy than of my own men," Chamberlain recalled fifty years later. "Gaps opening, swallowing, closing again with sharp convulsive energy; squads of stalwart men who had cut their way through us, disappearing as if translated. All around, strange, mingled roar—shouts of defiance, rally, and desperation; and underneath, murmured entreaty and stifled moans; gasping prayers, snatches of Sabbath song, whispers of loved names . . . Things which cannot be told—nor dreamed."[52]

Perhaps from somewhere in his scholar's trained memory, Chamberlain recalled some of the Jomini he and Colonel Ames had studied so diligently in their camp over the winter: "Every army which maintains a strictly defensive attitude must, if attacked, be at last driven from its position; whilst by profiting by all the advantages of the defensive system, and holding itself ready to take the offensive when occasion offers, it may hope for the greatest success."

Peering through the cloud of dust and battle smoke, he saw, like an illusion, that the men of the color guard had been shot away except for two men on either side of Sgt. Andrew Tozier. Ghostlike Tozier, appearing then disappearing in the white smoke, had planted the colors into the ground, hooked an elbow around the staff, secured a musket, and was loading and firing as fast as he could. Into the smoky caldron Chamberlain sent his own brother Tom to gather a few men together and close up the gap, or to order Tozier and his guard to pull back and thus plug the hole the devastated salient had created. The bullets whizzed and thudded so frequently that he assumed Tom would never make it to Tozier alive, and so sent another messenger with the same orders.

Colonel Oates led a charge, passing through the line waving his sword, calling "Forward, men, to the ledge!" Again they rolled up the hill and pushed Chamberlain's men back. Oates counted five rallies by the Union troops attempting to drive his Confederates from that position, coming near enough at least twice for his men to use the bayonet and for him to use his pistol within musket length. He described a horrible sight that would remain embedded in his memory for more than forty years:

> About forty steps up the slope there is a large boulder about mid-way the Spur. The Maine regiment charged my line, coming right up in a hand-to-hand encounter. My regimental colors were just a step or two to the right of that boulder, and I was within ten feet. A Maine man reached to grasp the staff of the colors when Ensign Archibald stepped back and Sergeant Pat O'Conner stove his bay-onet through the head of the Yankee, who fell dead.[53]

Oates saw his brother shot down, riddled. Chamberlain comforted a dying young private whose sergeant's stripes had been wrongfully stripped from him; he restored George Washington Buck's rank on the field, and the young man died a sergeant. Oates saw the blood pooling on the rocks. Chamberlain took another wound when a bullet hit his scabbard and hammered it against his left thigh. Both watched as the boys from Maine fought those from Alabama, and the Yankees finally were fended off at bayonet point.

There was one more lull as the Confederates reorganized and moved even farther to their right. All the wounded and dead in front of the 20th Maine's lines had been stripped of their ammunition and usable weapons. Suddenly, up the slope came the Confederates for another try.

Oates thought the 47th Alabama had disappeared from his left, retreating back to the wooded side of Big Round Top; Chamberlain thought it had reorganized and was assailing him on his right front while more of Oates's men worked their way around to his left wing. The Maine men began to turn to Chamberlain from his thinning line; with-out cartridges they need not seek the enemy anymore. They sought instead a leader, a commander who could tell them now, at their most desperate hour, what to do. A half century later, Chamberlain could afford an understatement: "My thought was running deep."

Jomini had virtually described the situation Chamberlain found himself in: "When the assailant, after suffering severely, finds himself strongly assailed at the moment when the victory seemed to be in his hands, the advantage will, in all probability, be his no longer, for the

moral effect of such a counter-attack upon the part of an adversary supposed to be beaten is certainly enough to stagger the boldest troops."

The two wings of Chamberlain's line, though within shouting distance, were now practically fighting two different battles. Chamberlain's
right wing had been engaged with some of the right-hand companies of
the 47th Alabama[54] and the left wing of the 15th Alabama, and his left
wing engaged entirely with the 15th as it kept attempting to edge
around his left flank. The small spur upon which the 20th was fighting
had a little hogback that ran between the two bent-back wings so that
from Captain Spear's position on the left, only Tozier was visible—when
the battlesmoke allowed—clutching his cherished colors. Spear walked
quickly over to Chamberlain when the fire on the left slackened a bit. "I
was combining the elements of a 'forlorn hope,' and had just communi-
cated this to Captain Spear of the wheeling flank, on which the initiative
was to fall."[55]

Out of the smoky center came Lt. Holman S. Melcher of Company
F. Moved by the suffering wounded out on the exposed slope—his own
color company had lost some 50 percent—he approached Chamberlain
and asked if he might take his company down the slope to bring in a few
of his wounded. It was a noble and courageous request, since it was
indeed a killing ground ahead. Chamberlain assured him that he would
have help going forward: "I am about to order a charge!" Bold Melcher's
request was answered with a bolder decision.

Melcher moved a few steps back to the colors, apparently on one
side of them while Chamberlain stepped to the other.

Did Chamberlain recall Jomini's words then? Did his scholar's training and the desperate circumstances help him remember what to do? He
left no record, but his actions followed exactly the book he had studied
so intently: "The best thing for an army standing on the defensive is to
know *how* to take the offensive at a proper time, and *to take it.*"

The men looked to him for direction. Chamberlain called out one
word: "Bayonet!" Along the line steel rang as the men pulled their bayonets and fastened them to their musket barrels. Further orders were
needless, if not impossible. No doubt Chamberlain called out the next
order—"Forward!"—as did others, company commanders repeating it
down the line, but the men were already up and out from behind the
small rock wall and rushing full speed down the slope.

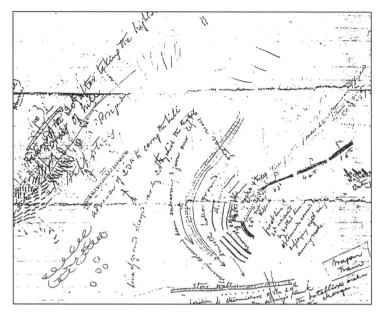

Chamberlain's sketch of the action of the 20th Maine at Little Round Top on July 2, 1863. LIBRARY OF CONGRESS

It was a wild charge with an impetus of its own. And it was irresistible. Part of the reason it was so successful, at least according to Oates, was because he had already ordered a retreat. He had gotten reports of Federal infantry on his right and erroneous reports of two regiments in his rear and dismounted cavalry about to close off his last avenue back to Confederate lines. He saw men struck by two or three minié balls from different directions and decided that they should not try to retreat in order, "but every one should run in the direction from whence we came."[56]

The forward motion of Chamberlain's right wing was held up by the mass of Confederates retreating down the valley between Little and Big Round Tops directly in front of them. As well, the right-hand company was still attempting to maintain contact with the 83rd Pennsylvania so as not to leave its left flank "in the air." Some of Oates's men made a stubborn stand in front of Chamberlain's moving line. Chamberlain himself rushed right up to a Rebel officer, who fired a huge navy revolver in

Chamberlain's face. Incredibly, the ball missed. Chamberlain had his swordpoint to the man's throat in an instant, and the Southern officer turned over both his sword and the nearly fatal revolver.

Spear, on the other wing, never got a formal order to charge. From his right he heard someone shout "Forward!" and saw Tozier and the colors begin to move. He immediately transmitted the order to his men, and down the slope they plunged.

Spear's wing faced less enemy resistance than Chamberlain's. Oates had already given the order to retreat, believing that his men were being shot from front and back.[57] There was no natural sluiceway in front of Spear's wing into which the men poured and were jammed as in front of Chamberlain's right wing. Instead, the Confederates retreated straight back—and into the volleying muskets of Morrill's Company B, crouched behind a rock wall south of the fenced-in Weikert farm lane. Spear recalled seeing some Confederates shot as they tried to climb the fences along the lane. Perhaps it was because of this lack of resistance that Spear's wing and the left of Chamberlain's wing wheeled around a little more to the right and then down the gully between the Round Tops. Perhaps Spear's men saw Morrill's men firing at the Confederates and moved to their right to get out of the way of the friendly fire. Perhaps it was easier for the men to run down the valley between the Round Tops. No doubt all of these factors accounted for the right wheeling motion of Spear's wing and the slower descent of Chamberlain's right wing.[58]

On the way down, Chamberlain passed old Lieutenant Colonel Bulger and apparently exchanged words with him.[59] Oates was horrified to see a man to his right who had his throat cut by a bullet run by him wheezing blood out of the gap under his chin.

Oates's Company A, lost in the woods to the east of his charge, had run into Chamberlain's Company B and went no farther. The men had now returned and were made to stand and deliver fire into Chamberlain's men, who had made it to the front of the 44th New York. Chamberlain was having trouble halting his men, who thought by now they were on their way to Richmond. This fire may have helped Chamberlain bring his men under control.

To Chamberlain, the fighting on this segment of Little Round Top seemed to last from one to two hours (depending on which report one reads).[60] After Chamberlain got his men under control, they returned to their hard-won position on the south spur of Little Round Top.

Battle numbers and losses are always unreliable. Chamberlain thought that there were between 100 and 150 of the enemy killed and wounded—of which approximately 50 were dead—out in front of his line. In the same space—the sixty or seventy yards on the side of the rock-strewn spur between the lines—lay 30 of the Maine men killed in the action. About 105 men and officers, including Chamberlain, were wounded.

The sun was setting and the fighting was dying down when orders came from Col. James Rice, now brigade commander after Vincent's mortal wound. Big Round Top, commanding even Little Round Top and therefore the rest of the Union line, must be taken and secured for the night. The men of the 20th Maine were completely exhausted after nearly two hours of fighting, after the exertion and exhilaration of chasing the enemy from their front. They lay sprawled, many asleep. Chamberlain, realizing his men were played out, merely called what was left of the color guard to him and told the men that he was going up; any who felt they could follow should do so. It was command by example; it was command by compassion.

The two hundred men from Maine wearily rose and advanced up the slope of Big Round Top, following their colors and their colonel, not knowing what to expect. They took some fire without returning it, since they did not want to give away how few they were, and since most had little or no ammunition.

There was confusion and fear on the hilltop in the dark. There was firing in the gloom and men got lost. Finally, after some Confederates were captured and the 20th took some enemy volleys in silence, the night became relatively quiet. More Union troops arrived to support the 20th Maine, and they stayed on the height until the next morning, July 3.[61]

The 20th Maine was relieved on July 3 and sent north of Little Round Top to the right near corps commander Sykes's headquarters. From that point the men heard and felt—"like an earthquake"—the incredible two-hour cannonade preceding Lt. Gen. James Longstreet's grand assault. The 20th Maine's contribution to history at the Battle of Gettysburg, however, was over. The men heard and may have seen "Pickett's Charge," but they were not engaged.

On July 4 Chamberlain and the 20th Maine were sent to scout the area where General Sickles's men had fought and from which they were driven. They pushed past Willoughby Run before returning.[62] The sights, smells, and sounds they witnessed were beyond description. The dead were hideous in their random positions and causes of death, from being torn completely apart by artillery to appearing merely asleep, killed perhaps by concussion. The wounded were heartrending with their pitiful pleadings for water, or a surgeon, or their mothers, or for someone to have mercy and kill them. Worst of all, Chamberlain and the men returned to where the young men of Maine had died and were laid out in rows for burial: "There they lay, side by side, with touch of elbow still; brave, bronzed faces where the last thought was written: manly resolution, heroic self-giving, divine reconciliation; or where on some young face the sweet mother look had come out under death's soft whisper."[63]

All this—the horror, the heartbreak—in typical Victorian fashion Chamberlain kept from his wife and those at home.

> Field near Gettysburg
> July 4th 1863.

Dear Fanny,

We are fighting gloriously. Our loss is terrible, but we are beating the Rebels as they were never beaten before.

The 20th has immortalized itself. We had the post of honor in the severe fight of the 2d, on the extreme left where the enemy made a fierce attempt to turn the flank. My Regt was the extreme left & was attacked by a whole Brigade.

We not only held our ground but charged on the Rebels & drove them out of all sight & sound & killing & wounding over 100 & taking 200 prisoner, including 6 officers one the inspector Gen. of the Brigade. I received the thanks of my superior officers on the field. After our charge I was asked if my men could carry a high hill, which was a strong hold of the enemy, being covered with trees & large rocks.

I had lost at that time almost half the effective men I took in, but I went in with charged bayonets & line of battle & swept every thing before us taking many prisoners.

Col. Vincent is mortally wounded—the greatest loss that could have befallen this Brigade.

Six officers in the 20th wounded—135 men killed & wounded.

I am receiving all sorts of praise, but bear it meekly.

Our army is in fine spirits.

Many Generals on our side were killed. <u>Ames</u> & <u>Brown</u> of the 11th Corps have covered themselves with glory.

You shall hear from soon [*sic*] again, if I am spared.

I shall tell of some little incidents, such as my taking officers prisoners & receiving swords & pistols &c. We captured one whole Rebel Regt.

> Hoping you are all well.
> Yours,
> L.[64]

In the rain and pitch black night of July 5, the 20th Maine began to march away from Gettysburg, from both the glory and the horror. The men reached swollen Marsh Creek and halted for the night along the road to Emmitsburg, Maryland.[65]

The next day they marched from their camp on Marsh Creek southward toward Emmitsburg, about one mile, then spent the remainder of July 6 resting. During this repose, Chamberlain had an opportunity to write two, and possibly as many as four, reports of the action to his various superiors.[66]

General Barnes
Comd 1st Div. 5th Corps
General,

In accordance with your permission I beg leave to submit, unofficially, the following memoranda (which I have hardly had time to condense as I could wish) of the part taken by the 20th Maine Vols. on the left of your Div. in the action of July 2d at Gettysburg.

This Regt. was on the extreme left of our line of battle, & its original front was very nearly that of the rest of the Brigade. At the general assault of the enemy on our lines, my Regt. from the first received its full share. While we were warmly engaged with this line, as I stood on a high rock by my colors I perceived a heavy body of the enemy moving by the right flank in the direction of our left & rear. They were close upon me, & I had but a moment in which to act. The head of their column was already coming to a front, in direction only a little oblique to that of the rest of our Brigade. Keeping this movement of the enemy from the knowledge of my

men, I immediately had my right wing take intervals by the left
flank at 3 to 5 paces according to the shelter afforded by the rocks &
trees, thus covering the whole front then engaged; & moved my left
wing to the left & rear making nearly a right angle at the color.

This movement was so admirably executed by my men, that our
fire was not materially slackened in front, while the left wing was
taking its new position. Not more than two minutes elapsed before
the enemy came up in column of Regiments with an impetuosity
which betrayed their anticipation of an easy triumph. Their astonishment was great as they emerged from their cover, & found
instead of an unprotected rear, a solid front. They advanced however within ten paces of my line, making what they call a
"charge"—that is, advancing & firing rapidly. Our volleys were so
steady & telling that the enemy were checked here, & broken.
Their second line then advanced, with the same ardor & the same
fate, & so too a third & fourth. This struggle of an hour & a half,
was desperate in the extreme: four times did we lose & win that
space of ten yards between the contending lines, which was strewn
with dying & dead. I repeatedly sent to the rear reports of my condition, that my ammunition was exhausted, & that I could hold the
position but a few minutes longer. In the mean time I seized the
opportunity of a momentary repulse of the enemy, to gather the
contents of every cartridge box of the dead & dying, friend & foe,
& with these we met the enemy on their last & most desperate
assault. In the midst of this, our ammunition utterly failed, our fire,
as it was too terribly evident, had slackened, half my left wing lay
on the ground, & although I had brought two companies from the
right to strengthen it, the left wing was reduced to a mere skirmish
line. Officers came to me, shouting that we were "annihilated", &
men were beginning to face to the rear. I saw that the defensive
could be maintained not an instant longer, & with a few gallant
officers rallied a line, ordered "bayonets fixed," & "forward" at a run.
My men went down upon the enemy with a wild shout, the two
wings were brought into one line again. I directed the whole Regiment to take intervals at 5 paces by the left flank, & change direction to the right, all this without checking our speed, thus keeping
my right connected with the 83rd Penna, while the left swept
around to the distance of half a mile. In this charge the bayonet

only was used on our part, & the rebels seemed so petrified with astonishment that their front line scarcely offered to run or to fire—they threw down their arms & begged "not to be killed", & we captured them by whole companies. We took in this charge 368 prisoners, among them a Colonel, Lieut. Col. & a dozen other officers who were known. I had no time to inquire the rank of the prisoners, but sent them at once to the rear.

The prisoners were amazed & chagrinned [*sic*] to see the smallness of our numbers, for there were only one hundred & ninety eight men who made this charge, & the prisoners admitted that they had a full Brigade.

I reported at once to Col. Rice, who immediately came up, & who with the greatest promptitude brought up a Brigade as a support, & a supply of ammunition. We then threw up a small breastwork of rocks, & began to gather up the wounded of both parties. 21 of my men lay dead on the field, & more than 100 wounded. 50 of the enemy dead were counted in our front, their wounded we could not count. What is most surprising is that often as our line was forced back & even pierced by the enemy, not one of my men was taken prisoner, & not one was "missing".

It was now nearly dark, & Col. Rice ordered me to take the high & difficult hill on the left of our general line of battle, (but more nearly in front of my own line) where the enemy appeared to have taken refuge on their repulse. My men were exhausted with toil & thirst, & had fallen asleep, many of them, the moment the fighting was over, but the order was given, & the little handful of men went up the hill with fixed bayonets, the enemy retiring before us, & giving only an occasional volley. Not wishing to disclose my numbers, & in order to avoid if possible bringing on an engagement in which we should certainly have been overpowered. I went on silently with only the bayonet. We carried the hill, taking twenty five prisoners, including some of the staff of Gen. Laws commdg the Brigade. From these I learned that Hoods Division was massed in a ravine two or three hundred yards in front of me, & that he had sent them out to ascertain our numbers, preparatory to taking possession of the hill with his Division. Fortunately I was able to secure all this party, by sending out one of my own more cautious than they, so that Gen. Hood never received the reports of his scouts. My men stood in line that night, & received the volleys of the enemy without replying, & the enemy apparently puzzled, desisted from their attempts. In this movement I lost one officer mortally wounded, & one man taken prisoner in the darkness. The prisoners in all amounted to 393 who were known; 300 stand of arms were taken from the enemy. We went into the fight with 380 officers & men, cooks & pioneers & even musicians fighting in the ranks, my total loss was 136 as more fully appears in the tabular report already sent you.

We were engaged with Laws' Brigade, of Hood's Division, Longstreets Corps,—the 15th & 47th Alabama 4th & 5th Texas: our prisoners were from all these Regts.

My authority for some of my statements are Col. Powell 15th Ala. Lt. Col. Bulger, comdg the 47th Ala. Capt. Johnson of the 5th Texas, & Lt. Christian, Inspector Genl. Laws' Brigade who were among our prisoners.

The Hill carried in the evening is said to be Round Top, or Sugar Loaf, reported by Col Rice as "Wolf Hill."

Justice required me to express my gratitude for the admirable support I received from the 83d Penna. Capt. Woodward comdg.

> I am, General,
> Very respectfully
> Your obdt servt.
> J. L. Chamberlain
> Col. 20th Maine Vols.[67]

The next report was written just outside of Gettysburg, probably in the 20th Maine's camp along Marsh Creek. In it he has revised his figures somewhat, and he gives an early clue as to exactly what orders were given by him and how the great right wheel was effected when he writes, "As a last, deperate resort, I ordered a <u>charge</u>. . . ."

> Head Quarters 20th Maine Vols.
> Field near Gettysburg, Pa.
> July 6th 1863

Lieut,

In compliance with orders from Brigade Hd. Qrs. I have the honor to submit the following Report of the part taken by the 20th Regt. Maine Vols, in the action of July 2d and 3d near Gettysburg, Pa.

On reaching the field at about 4 P.M. July 2d, Col. Vincent commanding the Brigade, placing me on the left of the Brigade and consequently on the extreme left of our entire line of battle, instructed me that the enemy were expected shortly to make a desperate attempt to turn our left flank, and that the position assigned to me must be held at every hazard.

I established my line on the crest of a small spur of a rocky and wooded hill, and sent out at once a company of skirmishers on my left to guard against surprise on that unprotected flank.

These dispositions were scarcely made when the attack commenced, and the right of the Regt. found itself at once hotly engaged. Almost at the same moment, from a high rock which gave me a full view of the enemy, I perceived a heavy force in rear of their principal line, moving rapidly but stealthily toward our left, with the intention, as I judged, of gaining our rear unperceived. Without betraying our peril to any but one or two officers, I had the right wing move by the left flank, taking intervals of a pace or two, according to the shelter afforded by rocks or trees, extending so as to cover the whole front then engaged; and at the same time moved the left wing to the left and rear, making a large angle at the color, which was now brought to the point where our left had first rested.

This hazardous maneuver was so admirably executed by my men that our fire was not materially slackened in front, and the enemy gained no advantage there, while the left wing in the mean time had formed a solid and steady line in a direction to meet the expected assault. We were not a moment too soon; for the enemy having gained their desired point of attack came to a front, and rushed forward with an impetuosity which showed their sanguine expectations. Their astonishment, however was evident, when emerging from their cover, they met instead of an unsuspecting flank, a firm and steady front. A strong fire opened at once from both sides, and with great effect—the enemy still advancing until they came within <u>ten</u> <u>paces</u> of our line, where our steady and telling volleys brought them to a stand. From that moment began a struggle fierce and bloody beyond any that I have witnessed, and which lasted in all its fury, a full hour. The two lines met, and broke and mingled in the shock. At times I saw around me more of the enemy than of my own men. The edge of conflict swayed to and fro—now one and now the other party holding the contested ground. Three times our line was forced back, but only to rally and repulse the enemy. As often as the enemy's line was broken and routed, a new line was unmasked, which advanced with fresh vigor. Our "sixty rounds" were rapidly reduced. I sent several messengers to the rear for ammunition, and also for reinforcements. In the mean time we seized the opportunity of a momentary lull, to gather ammunition and more serviceable arms, from the dead and dying on the field. With these we met the enemy's last and fiercest assault. Their own rifles and their own bullets were turned against them. In the midst of this struggle, our ammunition <u>utterly</u> <u>failed.</u> The enemy were close upon us with a fresh line, pouring on us a terrible fire. Half the left wing already lay on the field. Although I had brought two companies from the right to its support, it was now scarely more than a skirmish line. The heroic energy of my officers could avail us no more. Our gallant line writhed & shrunk before the fire it could not repel. It was too evident that we could maintain the <u>defensive</u> no longer. As a last, deperate resort, I ordered a <u>charge.</u> The word "fix bayonets" flew from man to man. The click of the steel seemed to give new zeal to all. The men dashed forward with a shout. The two wings came into one line again, and extending to the left, and at the same time wheeling to the right, the whole Regiment described nearly a half circle, the left passing over the space of half a mile, while the right kept within the support of the 83d Penna. thus leaving no chance of escape to the enemy except to climb the steep side of the mountain or to pass by the whole front of the 83d Penna. The enemy's first line scarcely tried to run—they stood amazed, threw down their loaded arms and surrendered in whole companies. Those in their rear had more time and gave us more trouble. My skirmishing company threw itself upon the enemy's flank behind a stone wall, and their effective fire added to the enemy's confusion. In this charge we captured three hundred & sixty-eight prisoners, many of them officers, and took three hundred stand of arms. The prisoners were from four different regiments, and admitted that they had attacked with a Brigade.

At this time Col. Rice commanding the Brigade (Col. Vincent having been mortally wounded) brought up a strong support from

Genl. Crawford's command, and 3000 rounds of ammunition. The
wounded and the prisoners were now sent to the rear, and our
dead gathered and laid side by side.

Shortly after Col. Rice desired me to advance and take the high
steep hill, called "Wolf Hill" or "Round Top" half a mile or more
to our left and front, where the enemy had assembled on their
repulse—a position which commanded ours in case the assault
should be renewed.

It was then dusk. The men were worn out, and heated and
thirsty almost beyond endurance. Many had sunk down and fallen
asleep the instant the halt was ordered. But at the command they
cheerfully formed their line once more, and the little handful of
men went up the hill, scarcely expecting ever to return. In order
not to disclose our numbers—as I had now but two hundred
guns—and to avoid bringing on an engagement in which I was
sure to be overpowered, I forbid my men to fire, and trusted to the
bayonet alone. Throwing out two small detachments on each flank,
we pushed straight up the hill. The darkness favored us, concealing
our force and preventing the enemy from getting range so that
their volleys went over our heads, while they deemed it prudent to
retire before us. Just at the crest we found more serious difficulty
and were obliged to fall back for a short time. We advanced again
with new energy, which the knowledge of our isolated and perilous position rendered perhaps desperate, and carried the desired
point. We took twenty five prisoners in this movement, among
them some of the staff of Genl. Laws. From these officers I learned
that Hoods whole Division was massed but a short distance in
front, that he had just prepared to advance and take possession of
the heights, and was only waiting to ascertain the number and position of our force. I posted my command among the rocks along the
crest in line of battle, and sent two companies in charge of judi-
cious officers to reconnoitre the ground in front. They reported a
large body of the enemy in a ravine not more than two or three
hundred yards distant. I therefore kept these two companies out,
with orders to watch the enemy, while our main line, kept on the
alert by occasional volleys from below, held its position among the
rocks throughout the night. In the meantime the 83d Penna. and

the 5th & 12th Penna. Reserves came up and formed as a support. The next day at noon we were relieved by the 1st Brigade.

We were engaged with Laws' Brigade, Hood's Div. The prisoners represented themselves as from the 15th and 47th Alabama and the 4th and 5th Texas Regts. The whole number of prisoners taken by us is three hundred & ninety three—of arms captured three hundred stand. At least one hundred and fifty of the enemy's killed and wounded were found in front of our first line of battle.

We went into the fight with three hundred & fifty eight guns. Every pioneer and musician who could carry a musket was armed and engaged. Our loss is one hundred & thirty six—thirty killed, one hundred & five wounded—many mortally—and one taken prisoner in the night advance. Often as our line was broken and pierced by the enemy, there is not a man to be reported "missing."

I have to regret the loss of a most gallant young officer. Lt. W. L. Kendall, who fell in the charge also Capt. C. W. Billings mortally wounded early in the action, and Lieut. A. N. Linscott mortally wounded on the crest of "Wolf Hill." Our advantage was dearly bought with the loss of such admirable officers as these.

As for the conduct of my officers and men, I will let the result speak for them. If I were to mention any, I might do injustice by omitting some equally deserving. Our roll of Honor is the three hundred eighty officers and men who fought at Gettysburg.

My thanks are owe[d] the 83d Penna, Capt Woodward comdg. for their steady and gallant support, and I would particularly acknowledge the services of Adjt. Gifford of that Regt. who exposed himself to the severest fire to render me aid.

> Very respectfully
> Your obdt. servt.
> J. L. Chamberlain
> Col. 20th Maine Vols.
> Lt. Geo. B. Herendeen
> Act. asst. adjt. Genl.
> 3d Brigade 1st Div. 5th Corps.[68]

The following report was written next, since Chamberlain had moved closer to Emmitsburg when he wrote it. It became the report published

in *War of the Rebellion: Official Records of the Union and Confederate Armies*
in 1889.[69]

No. 196
Report of Col. Joshua L. Chamberlain,
Twentieth Maine Infantry.
Field near Emmitsburg, July 6, 1863.

Sir: In compliance with the request of the colonel commanding
the brigade, I have the honor to submit a somewhat detailed
report of the operations of the Twentieth Regiment Maine Volunteers in the battle of Gettysburg, on the 2d and 3d instant.

Having acted as the advance guard, made necessary by the proximity of the enemy's cavalry, on the march of the day before, my
command on reaching Hanover, Pa., just before sunset on that day,
were much worn, and lost no time in getting ready for an expected
bivouac. Rations were scarcely issued, and the men about preparing supper, when rumors that the enemy had been encountered
that day near Gettysburg absorbed every other interest, and very
soon orders came to march forthwith to Gettysburg.

My men moved out with a promptitude and spirit extraordi-
nary, the cheers and welcome they received on the road adding to
their enthusiasm. After an hour or two of sleep by the roadside just
before daybreak, we reached the heights southeasterly of Gettysburg at about 7 a.m., July 2.[70]

Somewhere near 4 p.m. a sharp cannonade, at some distance to
our left and front, was the signal for a sudden and rapid movement
of our whole division in the direction of this firing, which grew
warmer as we approached. Passing an open field in the hollow
ground in which some of our batteries were going into position,
our brigade reached the skirt of a piece of woods, in the farther
edge of which there was a heavy musketry fire, and when about to
go forward into line we received from Colonel Vincent, commanding the brigade, orders to move to the left at the double quick,
when we took a farm road crossing Plum Run in order to gain a
rugged mountain spur called Granite Spur, or Little Round Top.

The enemy's artillery got range of our column as we were
climbing the spur, and the crashing of the shells among the rocks
and the tree tops made us move lively along the crest. One or two

shells burst in our ranks. Passing to the southern slope of Little Round Top, Colonel Vincent indicated to me the ground my regiment was to occupy, informing me that this was the extreme left of our general line, and that a desperate attack was expected in order to turn that position, concluding by telling me I was to "hold that ground at all hazards." This was the last word I heard from him.

In order to commence by making my right firm, I formed my regiment on the right into line, giving such direction to the line as should best secure the advantage of the rough, rocky, and stragglingly wooded ground.

The line faced generally toward a more conspicuous eminence southwest of ours, which is known as Sugar Loaf, or Round Top. Between this and my position intervened a smooth and thinly wooded hollow. My line formed, I immediately detached Company B, Captain Morrill commanding, to extend from my left flank across this hollow as a line of skirmishers, with directions to act as occasion might dictate, to prevent a surprise on my exposed flank and rear.

The artillery fire on our position had meanwhile been constant and heavy, but my formation was scarcely complete when the artillery was replaced by a vigorous infantry assault upon the center of our brigade to my right, but it very soon involved the right of my regiment and gradually extended along my entire front. The action was quite sharp and at close quarters.

In the midst of this, an officer from my center informed me that some important movement of the enemy was going on in his front, beyond that of the line with which we were engaged. Mounting a large rock, I was able to see a considerable body of the enemy moving by the flank in rear of their line engaged, and passing from the direction of the foot of Great Round Top through the valley toward the front of my left. The close engagement not allowing any change of front, I immediately stretched my regiment to the left, by taking intervals by the left flank, and at the same time "refusing" my left wing, so that it was nearly at right angles with my right, thus occupying about twice the extent of our ordinary front, some of the companies being brought into single rank when the nature of the ground gave sufficient strength or shelter. My officers and men understood my wishes so well that this movement was executed under fire, the right wing keeping up fire, without giving the enemy any occasion to seize or even to suspect their advantage. But we were not a moment too soon; the enemy's flanking column having gained their desired direction, burst upon my left, where they evidently had expected an unguarded flank, with great demonstration.

We opened a brisk fire at close range, which was so sudden and effective that they soon fell back among the rocks and low trees in the valley, only to burst forth again with a shout, and rapidly advanced, firing as they came. They pushed up to within a dozen yards of us before the terrible effectiveness of our fire compelled them to break and take shelter.

They renewed the assault on our whole front, and for an hour the fighting was severe. Squads of the enemy broke through our line in several places, and the fight was literally hand to hand. The edge of the fight rolled backward and forward like a wave. The dead and wounded were now in our front and then in our rear. Forced from our position, we desperately recovered it, and pushed the enemy down to the foot of the slope. The intervals of the struggle were seized to remove our wounded (and those of the enemy also), to gather ammunition from the cartridge-boxes of disabled friend or foe on the field, and even to secure better muskets than the Enfields, which we found did not stand service well. Rude shelters were thrown up of the loose rocks that covered the ground.

Captain Woodward, commanding the Eighty-third Pennsylvania Volunteers, on my right, gallantly maintaining his fight, judiciously and with hearty co-operation made his movements conform with my necessities, so that my right was at no time exposed to a flank attack.

The enemy seemed to have gathered all their energies for their final assault. We had gotten our thin line into as good a shape as possible, when a strong force emerged from the scrub wood in the valley, as well as I could judge, in two lines in <u>echelon</u> by the right, and, opening a heavy fire, the first line came on as if they meant to sweep everything before them. We opened on them as well as we could with our scanty ammunition snatched from the field.

It did not seem possible to withstand another shock like this now coming on. Our loss had been severe. One-half of my left wing had fallen, and a third of my regiment lay just behind us, dead or badly wounded. At this moment my anxiety was increased by a great roar of musketry in my rear, on the farther or northerly slope of Little Round Top, apparently on the flank of the regular brigade, which was in support of Hazlett's battery of the crest behind us. The bullets from this attack struck into my left rear, and I feared that the enemy might have nearly surrounded the Little Round Top, and only a desperate chance was left for us. My ammunition was soon exhausted. My men were firing their last shot and getting ready to "club" their muskets.

It was imperative to strike before we were struck by this overwhelming force in a hand-to-hand fight, which we could not probably have withstood or survived. At that crisis, I <u>ordered the bayonet.</u>[71] The word was enough. It ran like fire along the line, from man to man, and rose into a shout, with which they sprang forward upon the enemy, now not 30 yards away. The effect was surprising; many of the enemy's first line threw down their arms and surrendered. An officer fired his pistol at my head with one hand, while he handed me his sword with the other. Holding fast by our right, and swinging forward our left, we made an extended "right wheel," before which the enemy's second line broke and fell back, fighting from tree to tree, many being captured, until we had swept the valley and cleared the front of nearly our entire brigade.

Meantime Captain Morrill with his skirmishers (sent out from my left flank), with some dozen or fifteen of the U. S. Sharpshooters who had put themselves under his direction, fell upon the enemy as they were breaking, and by his demonstrations, as well as his well-directed fire, added much to the effect of the charge.

Having thus cleared the valley and driven the enemy up the western slope of the Great Round Top, not wishing to press so far out as to hazard the ground I was to hold by leaving it exposed to a sudden rush of the enemy, I succeeded (although with some effort to stop my men, who declared they were "on the road to Richmond") in getting the regiment into good order and resuming their original position.

Four hundred prisoners, including two field and several line officers, were sent to the rear. These were mainly from the Fifteenth and Forty-seventh Alabama Regiments, with some of the

Fourth and Fifth Texas. One hundred and fifty of the enemy were found killed and wounded in our front.

At dusk, Colonel Rice informed me of the fall of Colonel Vincent, which had devolved the command of the brigade on him, and that Colonel Fisher had come up with a brigade to our support. These troops were massed in our rear. It was the understanding, as Colonel Rice informed me, that Colonel Fisher's brigade was to advance and seize the western slope of Great Round Top, where the enemy had shortly before been driven. But, after considerable delay, this intention for some reason was not carried into execution.

We were apprehensive that if the enemy were allowed to strengthen himself in that position, he would have a great advantage in renewing the attack on us at daylight or before. Colonel Rice then directed me to make the movement to seize the crest.

It was now 9 p.m. Without waiting to get ammunition, but trusting in part to the very circumstance of not exposing our movement or our small front by firing, and with bayonets fixed, the little handful of 200 men pressed up the mountain side in very extended order, as the steep and jagged surface of the ground compelled. We heard squads of the enemy falling back before us, and, when near the crest, we met a scattering and uncertain fire, which caused us the great loss of the gallant Lieutenant Linscott, who fell, mortally wounded. In the silent advance in the darkness we laid hold of 25 prisoners, among them a staff officer of General [E. M.][72]Law, commanding the brigade immediately opposed to us during the fight. Reaching the crest, and reconoitering the ground, I placed the men in a strong position among the rocks, and informed Colonel Rice, requesting also ammunition and some support to our right, which was very near the enemy, their movements and words even being now distinctly heard by us.

Some confusion soon after resulted from the attempt of some regiment of Colonel Fisher's brigade to come to our support. They had found a wood road up the mountain, which brought them on my right flank, and also in proximity to the enemy, massed a little below. Hearing their approach, and thinking a movement from that quarter could only be from the enemy, I made disposition to receive them as such. In the confusion which attended the attempt to form them in support of my right, the enemy opened a brisk fire, which disconcerted my efforts to form them and disheartened the supports themselves, so that I saw no more of them that night.

Feeling somewhat insecure in this isolated position, I sent in for the Eighty-third Pennsylvania, which came speedily, followed by the Forty-fourth New York, and, having seen these well posted, I sent a strong picket to the front, with instructions to report to me every half hour during the night, and allowed the rest of my men to sleep on their arms.

At some time about midnight, two regiments of Colonel Fisher's brigade came up the mountain beyond my left, and took position near the summit; but as the enemy did not threaten from that direction, I made no effort to connect with them.

We went into the fight with 386, all told—358 guns. Every pioneer and musician who could carry a musket went into the ranks. Even the sick and foot-sore, who could not keep up in the march, came up as soon as they could find their regiments, and took their places in line of battle, while it was battle, indeed. Some prisoners I had under guard, under sentence of court-martial, I was obliged to put into the fight, and they bore their part well, for which I shall recommend a commutation of their sentence.

The loss, so far as I can ascertain it, is 136—30 of whom were killed, and among the wounded are many mortally.

Captain Billings, Lieutenant Kendall, and Lieutenant Linscott are officers whose loss we deeply mourn—efficient soldiers, and pure and high-minded men.

In such an engagement there were many incidents of heroism and noble character which should have place even in an official report; but, under present circumstances, I am unable to do justice to them. I will say of that regiment that the resolution, courage, and heroic fortitude which enabled us to withstand so formidable an attack have happily led to so conspicuous a result that they may safely trust to history to record their merits.

About noon on the 3d of July, we were withdrawn, and formed on the right of the brigade, in the front edge of a piece of woods near the left center of our main line of battle, where we were held in readiness to support our troops, then receiving the severe attack of the afternoon of that day.

On the 4th, we made a reconnaissance to the front, to ascertain the movements of the enemy, but finding that they had retired, at least beyond Willoughby's Run, we returned to Little Round Top, where we buried our dead in the place where we had laid them during the fight, marking each grave by a head-board made of ammunition boxes, with each dead soldier's name cut upon it. We also buried 50 of the enemy's dead in front of our position of July 2. We then looked after our wounded, whom I had taken the responsibility of putting into the houses of citizens in the vicinity of Little Round Top, and, on the morning of the 5th, took up the march on the Emmitsburg road.

> I have the honor to be, your obedient servant,
> Joshua L. Chamberlain,
> Colonel, Commanding Twentieth Maine Volunteers.
> Lieut. George B. Herendeen
> A. A. A. G., Third Brig., 1st Div., Fifth Army Corps.[73]

On July 7 the 20th Maine, marching with the 5th Corps, covered eighteen miles. At six that evening the troops encamped about five or six miles above Frederick, Maryland. On July 8 the men marched in pouring rain across the Catoctin Mountains. They camped near Middletown, Maryland, that afternoon. They marched early on July 10 and struck a contingent of the enemy rear guard at Jones' Cross-Roads where the Sharpsburg Pike crosses the road to Williamsport; there the retreating Confederate army was establishing its defensive lines. The regiment was soon "warmly engaged" as skirmishers, lost two men killed and six wounded or missing, but held the Pike. By July 11 they moved only two miles to the west along the Pike "through field and wood," and there they bivouacked.[74]

> Hd. Qrs. 20 Maine Vols.
> Field near Hagerstown July 11th 1863

Gen. John L. Hodsdon
Adjt. Gen of Maine
Genl.

I have the honor to acknowledge the receipt of a commission for myself as Colonel of the 20th Regt. & for Maj. Gilmore as Lieut. Colonel of the same. The commissions will bear date <u>May</u>

20th 1863. from which time there has been a vacancy in the office of Colonel, & to which time we are mustered back, by the regular mustering officer of the 5th Corps Capt. Barnard. Our Corps has been so cut off from the main army for two months past that we have been sometimes three weeks without a mail, & our baggage & papers have not been up with us for nearly a month.

I shall lose no time in informing you of the gallant part the 20th has had in all that has been done here the moment I can get time & paper. We are now making rapid marches, & expecting another big fight somewhere in this vicinity.

I am aware that many reports &c are due your office, which shall be sent as soon as we can get at our papers.

I can only add at this brief halt & mite bit of paper accidentally found, that this Regt. has been engaged in three battles within as many weeks, one in Virginia one in Penna. & one in Maryland, in all of which we have received especial commendation, as I will soon more particularly inform you.

At Middleburg Va. near Ashby's gap we lost 1 killed & 7 wounded—at Gettysburg 30 killed 100 wounded & six missing probably prisoners taken on the skirmish line—at Jones' cross roads, on the Sharpsburg & Hagerstown pike, where I had command of our advance, we had a fight in which we lost 8 killed, wounded & missing—this was July 10th—day before yesterday.

For our conduct at Gettysburg, I have rec'd the particulars & personal thanks of Brigade & Division & Corps commanders. We held the extreme left of our line when the most furious attack was made.

very respy your obdt. servt

J. L. Chamberlain, Col. 20th Me[75]

Lee's battered but still belligerent Army of Northern Virginia had its back up against the swollen and unfordable Potomac River in extensive fortifications between Hagerstown and a northern loop in the river south of Downsville. Lee planned to cross at Williamsport and Falling Waters as soon as he could. The battles and skirmishes between the two armies during the week and a half since they left Gettysburg were mostly rearguard actions.

The following was attached to the casualty lists for Gettysburg and the fight with Lee's retreating forces at Jones' Cross-Roads on July 10:

Field near Hagerstown
July 13, 1863

Gen. Hodsdon

I have had the foregoing list of casualties carefully made out, & have verified it by strict examination. I feel sure that it may be relied upon as correct.

Some who were very slightly struck, are not reported here. Hardly any one in the Regt. escaped without some mark—in his clothing, at least. All who are at all <u>hurt</u> are reported here.

Your obdt. servt
J. L. Chamberlain
Col. Comd. 20th Maine Vols.[76]

On July 14 Lee finally crossed the Potomac, and Meade followed on the Maryland side of the Potomac. The 20th Maine marched twenty miles to Williamsport, then returned, marching through Keedysville, across the South Mountains, and encamping near Burkittsville, Maryland. On the sixteenth they moved to near Berlin, Maryland, and bivouacked until July 17, when the 5th Corps crossed the Potomac into Virginia, then marched down the Loudoun Valley between the Catoctins and the Blue Ridge Mountains to Lovettsville, Virginia.[77]

Between July 16 and 17 Chamberlain temporarily took command of the 3rd Brigade when Rice was arrested for allowing his men to sleep on sheaves of wheat.[78]

In spite of all the marching and combat, Chamberlain still had monthly reports to submit—even if they were a bit late.

Head Quarters 20th Me
Camp near Berlin Md
July 17th 1863

John L. Hodsdon. Adjt Genl
General

I have the honor herewith to transmit to you the monthly return of this reg't for the month of May.

very respectfully
Your obt servt
J. L. Chamberlain
Col 20th Maine Vols[79]

If there is time for a monthly report, there is time for a letter to Fanny.

Camp near Berlin Md.
July 17th 1863

My dear Fanny

I was very much surprised to have a letter from you dated at New York. I have been writing you at Brunswick. I wrote you on my knee in the battle of Gettysburg, after our terrible fight in which the 20th held the post of honor on the extreme left of the whole army where the fiercest attack was made. I will tell you sometime of the magnificent conduct of the Regt.—I was attacked by a whole Rebel Brigade & after two hours fighting during which we exhausted our ammunition & snatched the full cartridge boxes from the dead & dying friend & foe, & when that was gone & we were pressed two to one, & had lost one hundred & forty from the field, we <u>charged</u> & utterly routed the whole Brigade— killed & wounded 150 & took 308 prisoners & 300 stand of arms.

Afterwards I was ordered to carry a height with my remaining 200 & <u>did it</u>—at the point of the bayonet—an achievement which Gen Sykes said was one of the most important of the day. & for which I recd the personal thanks of all my commanders.

When we were relieved & I rode off from the field at the head of my little scarred & battle-stained band the Brigade Commander took me by the hand, & said "Col. C. your gallantry was magnificent, & your coolness & skill saved us."

I left 32 noble fellows dead—gathered them all & laid them side by side in one grave. one hundred wounded. some are dying & some recovering. One of my finest Lieuts. was killed—Kendall. & Capt Billings very severely wounded. 5 other officers wounded not seriously.

Poor Vincent fell early in the fight & died a day or two after.

I grieve for him much. The Pres. made him a General before he died, but he was unconscious. I am going to write Mrs.V. & I wish you would.

Fanny I took several officers in the fight prisoners—& one of them insisted on presenting me with a fine pistol as a reward of merit I suppose. Swords &c plenty.

What fighting that was. 1000 dead horses lay on the field torn

by shell, & half as many men, in one small field. These prisoners of
mine were fierce fellows from Texas. & Alabama—they said they
had never before been <u>stopped.</u>

But New York! I am sorry you are there. It is not safe to try to
get away is it? I wish you were at home. You should have been
there before.

I have been very danger-[letter ends abruptly.][80]

The regiment continued its march from Lovettsville, Virginia, south to
Goose Creek between July 18 and 20. The men encamped on the creek
that runs out of the mountains near Aldie, Virginia, for two days.

Head Quarters 20th Maine Vols
In the field July 21st 1863

To His Excellency Abner Coburn
Governor of Maine
Dear Governor,

I embrace a rare opportunity—namely, a days halt within a few
miles of our baggage—to write you in reference to the affairs of
our Regt. in which, I am well aware, you feel the deepest interest.

In the first place, allow me to thank you for the honor you have
done me in entrusting to my care this noble Regiment. I trust I
shall be always worthy of the confidence you have thus placed in
me. I consider it an officer's first duty to look after the welfare of
his men. To this he is bound no less by the responsibility which the
arbitrary nature of his power imposes, than by the regard he should
have to the interests of the service in which he is engaged. My
experience in several trying campaigns has taught me that the way
to ensure the efficiency of the army is to keep the <u>men</u> in the best
possible condition, physically & morally.

Within a month this Regiment has been engaged in the most
active & honorable service—taking a conspicuous part in three
fights in as many different states, within that time; & in all of them
doing as well as the best. At the great battle of Gettysburg, however, the Regiment won distinguished honor. We were assigned to
the <u>extreme</u> <u>left</u> of our line of battle, where the fiercest assault was
made. A whole Rebel Brigade was opposed to this Regiment,
charging on us with desperate fury, in column of Regiments, so

that we had to contend with a front of <u>fresh</u> <u>troops</u> after each struggle. After two hours fighting on the defensive, our loss had been so great, & the remaining men were so much exhausted, having fired all our "sixty-rounds" & all the cartridges we could gather from the scattered boxes of the fallen around us, friend & foe, I saw no way left but to take the <u>offensive</u> & accordingly we charged on the enemy—trying "cold steel" on them. The result was we drove them entirely out of the field, killing & wounding one hundred & fifty of them & taking <u>three</u> <u>hundred</u> <u>&</u> <u>eight</u> prisoners & two hundred & seventy five stand of arms. The prisoners taken were from five different Regiments from Alabama & Texas—twelve of the number were officers—some of the staff of the General commanding their Brigade. They admitted that they had charged on us with a Brigade, & said that they had fought a dozen battles, & never had been stopped before.

We were afterward ordered, or asked, to carry a height which afforded the Rebels a very advantageous position, & was considered by our Generals a strong point to carry; and exhausted as we were, the <u>one</u> <u>hundred</u> <u>&</u> <u>ninety</u> <u>eight</u> bayonets I had left after that days fighting, charged up that hill & carried every thing before them—taking many more prisoners & arms, but what is better taking the <u>heights</u> & holding them—the darkness which had now come on deceiving the enemy as to our numbers.

Our services have been officially acknowledged, though no partial friend has published our praises in the state whose name we are proud to bear, & which, we believe, we have not dishonored.

I protected my men in every possible way, but I grieve over the loss of thirty two gallant fellows who fell on that field which their courage helped to make a "field of Honor," & I regret to lose the services of the 102 who were wounded there. Besides this, in our other fights we had a loss of three killed & sixteen wounded & missing. I fear I have written too freely but this is not an "official" letter, & I know you desire to be informed reliably of the service rendered by your Regiments.

I am sorry to say that Lieut. Col. Gilmore was obliged to leave us on our march through Maryland, & is now in Baltimore not yet fit for duty. We all suffered for want of <u>medical</u> <u>attendance.</u> Our toilsome & hurried marches broke down a great many, & I had to be Surgeon & father as well as Colonel, to such an extent that I fell sick myself & came near dying, but was providentially able to lead my gallant fellows into the fight. The surgeons recently appointed have reported & we are highly gratified with their appearance.

I should be glad to have Rev. Dr. Brown whom you recommended with Hon J. J. Perry & others, appointed Hospital Steward & ordered to report at once. I very much need a field officer. I had to go through the fights alone. Is there any objection to following the suggestions of Col. Ames in the appointment of Major? I should heartily endorse that.

very Respectfully your obdt. Servt & friend
J. L. Chamberlain, Col. 20th[81]

On the afternoon of July 22, the 20th Maine continued its march southward for ten miles to Rectortown, Virginia. Early in the morning of July 23, the 20th, with the 5th Corps, supported the 3rd Corps as it was supposed to attack Lee's army through Manassas Gap. On July 24 the 5th Corps did reconnaisance to the right of the 3rd Corps at Wapping Heights near Manassas, but withdrew in the afternoon two miles behind the lines. Early the next morning the troops marched toward Warrenton, and contin-ued on July 26 to within three miles of Warrenton, where they encamped.[82]

Chamberlain rewarded men who performed their duties and requested punishment for those who refused. As he might with disruptive students in a classroom, he simply had them removed.

Head Quarters 20th Maine Vols
near Warrenton Va. July 26th 1863
Lieut.

I have the honor to request that no further action be taken in the case of certain privates of this Regt. against whom charges have been preferred for refusing duty viz:

John Lynes Jr. Company "D"

John Conway Company "E"

These men went on duty at Gettysburg, and have since conducted themselves well. Thomas Townsend, who was also awaiting trial took his gun & his place in the ranks, & was killed in a fight on the Sharpsburg Pike.

I would however earnestly request that privates Charles C.

Brown & William H. Wentworth against whom charges have been preferred be brought to trial at the earliest moment practicable, as their persistent refusal to do duty, when all other prisoners have consented so to do, aggravates their case.

I would also request that, if it be practicable, the prisoners last named, Brown & Wentworth, together with private Henry H. Moor, a prisoner awaiting sentence of Court Martial, be taken into the custody of the provost Guard, as their continued presence here "off duty" is unfavorable to "good order & military discipline," & our numbers are so reduced, that it is a burden to keep these prisoners (who have never done duty here) for so unusually long a time, "under guard."

> Very resfy,
> Your obdt. servt
> J. L. Chamberlain
> Col. 20th Maine Vols.
> Lieut. Jno M. Clark
> A. A. A. G. 3rd Brigade
> 1st Div. 5th Corps.[83]

The troops marched again on July 27, passing through Warrenton, and encamped three miles beyond.[84]

As July drew to a close, Chamberlain was still suffering from the effects of the long campaign and perhaps also what his surgeons described as "malarial fever."

> Head Quarters 20th Maine Vols
> Near Warrenton Va. July 27th 1863

Lieut. Col. F. T. Locke
Assistant Adjutant General,
Colonel,

I have the honor to request leave of absence for twenty (20) days, for the benefit of my health.

I would respectfully state that I had a severe attack of illness during the recent campaign; but unwilling to leave the command of my Regiment while in the face of the enemy, I went on duty before I was able without detriment to do so, & have since been constantly engaged in the most active duties.

I am convinced that I cannot longer continue these duties without the most serious consequences.

> Very respectfully
> Your obdt. servt.
> J. L. Chamberlain
> Colonel 20th Maine Vols.[85]

To Governor Coburn, Chamberlain reported some casualties and mentioned the effect on the reputation of the regiment in the army that the fight at Gettysburg produced.

> Hd. Qrs. 20th Maine Vols
> Warrenton July 29, 1863

Hon. A. Coburn,
Governor of Maine,
Governor,

In regard to the case of Verano G. Bryant, I have the honor to state that he left us on the march to Gettysburg & is now in some hospital, whence he will readily obtain his discharge if he is entitled to it.

I regret to say that his Capt. (Billings) & 1st Sergeant (Estes) have both died of the wounds so honorably received in that terrible battle.

> I am very respectfully
> Your obdt. servt
> J. L. Chamberlain
> Col. 20th Maine Vols.

(over)
I regret to add that our loss at Gettysburg has reduced the Regt. below the <u>minimum</u> so that Hospital Steward <u>Baker</u> commissioned as asst. surgeon cannot be mustered in until the drafted men join us; until that time there can be no legal vacancy of Hospital Steward. Rev. Dr. Brown therefore will do well to wait till the drafted men come, when he can be mustered in at once.

We are expecting to cross the Rappahannock tomorrow.

The 20th gained a great reputation in the army for its conduct at Gettysburg.

> C.[86]

At the end of July, Chamberlain went to Washington for medical treatment and was given fifteen days' sick leave. He then traveled to Brunswick. Home must have been a delight, because he applied for a longer leave. But Colonel Rice requested that he take over the brigade while Rice visited his own wife. Before leaving to rejoin his men, Chamberlain wrote to the governor. Shortly afterward, he returned to the brigade headquarters at Beverly Ford on the Rappahannock River.[87]

Brunswick Aug 7th 1863.

Hon Abner Coburn
Governor of Maine
Governor

I regret to learn indirectly of the death from wounds of Capt. Billings of Company "C"—& Lieut. Linscott of ["I."] I do not propose to make any recommendations to fill those vacancies at present. It is of such importance to the interests of the Regiment & the service to have <u>good</u> officers, that I wish to exercise the greatest care in recommending any to your favor.

I have only to name at present Lieut. Elisha Besse of Company "I" as Captain of Company "A". Lieut. Lewis now in command of "A" forfeited all claim to promotion by overstaying a leave of absence a few months ago, in consequence of which he was ordered before a military commission, & would have been dismissed [from] the service without doubt, had not the battle of Gettysburg cut the proceedings short. I released him from arrest to enable him to take part in the battle. His conduct was so good that I sent off a request to have no further action taken in the case of his unauthorized absence, & he may perhaps be allowed to retain his <u>present rank,</u> but cannot expect to be promoted. Moreover, he lacks energy & promptness in the ordinary routine of military life. Lt. Besse has had charge of that company a good deal, & he would be just the man to make up for the deficiencies of Mr. Lewis. The company needs a captain, & I hope Mr. Besse may receive the appointment.

Mr Lewis is a man of excellent character & I should be sorry to have him resign, but he has not yet come up to the ideal of a captain. It would give me much pleasure to recommend him, whenever I can with conscience.

I am at home a few days, having been ordered north on account of my health.

I left the Regiment in good spirits. Am much pleased with Drs. Benson & Shaw.

With much respect
Your obdt. servt.
J. L. Chamberlain
Col. 20th Maine Vols[88]

It is apparent in this series of letters regarding the promotion of men in the regiment that Chamberlain, upon reflection, began to find in that inscrutable domain of combat, some answers to soldiers' universal questions about their very selves. Beginning within him can be seen the germination of understanding that battle was a crucible in which the essences of manhood boiled, an all-refining fire wherein duty and honor and love of country roiled with cowardice, abject fear, and love of self. Peering into the remains in that caldron revealed the answers to men's characters. The dead, of course, to Chamberlain, were the most noble and courageous, as were the wounded. Those who stood their ground though frightened were also worthy of Chamberlain's respect. Those who shirked their duty to country and to one another were worthy neither of Chamberlain's respect nor promotion. Some things were obscured in the haze of mortal combat; others were clarified.

One must wonder if Chamberlain, when writing down the name of Lieutenant Linscott, recalled the letter he wrote in August 1862 recommending Linscott for the military service: "I think he has especial qualifications in that line, & am quite sure he would do himself honor. . . ."

Head Quarters 20th Maine Vols
Beverly Ford, Va. Aug. 25th 1863

To His Excellency Gov. Coburn
Governor,

Upon returning to the Regiment & carefully considering its condition & wants, I deem it for the interest of the Regiment to recommend the following appointments & promotions.

William E. Donnell of Portland to be 1st Lieut. & Adjutant, vice Brown promoted.

1st Lieut. Rufus B. Plumer of Co. "C" to be Capt. Co. "C" vice Billings died of wounds received in battle.

1st Lieut. Thomas D. Chamberlain of Co. "G" to be Captain of Co. "G", vice Spear promoted.

2d Lieut. James H. Stanwood of "C" to be 1st Lieut. of "C" vice Plumer promoted.

1st Sergeant John M. Sherwood of Co. "E" to be 1st Lieut. of Co "G" vice Chamberlain promoted.

1st Sergeant Hiram Morse of Co. "I" to be 2d Lieut. of Co. "I" vice Besse promoted.

The other vacancies I do not propose at present to fill; as I am very desirous that all candidates for commissions should be thoroughly tried, & I only recommend when I feel sure of the worthiness of the person proposed.

Commissions for Capt. Spear as Major, & Lieut Besse as Capt. were received at these Head Quarters in my absence.

During this absence the Regiment was in command of Capt. A. W. Clark, the senior officer on duty (Capt. Spear not having been mustered in as Major), & who, I am gratified to believe, spared no exertion to discharge his duties with fidelity.

It gives me great pleasure to say that Lieut. Col. Gilmore, of whose services & society we have been for a long time deprived, is with us again.

As I have been assigned by Gen. Griffin to the command of the 3d Brigade of the Division, the command of the Regiment will devolve upon Lt. Col. Gilmore, or Major Spear, in whose hands its interests, I think, will not suffer.

I regret being thus obliged to leave even temporarily, the noble Regiment with which I have shared so many hardships & perils, & not a few honors too; but I shall have it still under my eye, & in any case, I shall spare no effort to maintain its high & deserved reputation.

Any suggestions which, in the mean time, I may take the liberty to make, as holding myself responsible for the Regt., will be prompted by a regard solely to its welfare, & the good of the service.

Very respectfully,
Your obdt. servant
J. L. Chamberlain
Colonel. 20th Maine Vols.[89]

On August 26 Chamberlain, after Rice's promotion, received command of the 3rd Brigade.[90]

> Head Quarters 3rd Brigade, 1st Div. 5 Corps
> Camp at Beverly Ford, Va.
> Aug 31st 1863

To His Excellency Governor Coburn,
Governor,

I am well acquainted with Lieut. Adelbert B. Twitchell of the 5th Battery Maine Vols., & my knowledge of his character as a man & his high reputation as an officer, enable me to say with pleasure that he is a most deserving officer.

I know of no one from our State, in the Artillery service, whose character, conduct, experience & gallant services, better entitle him to promotion.

[Ill.] such appointment which might be [ill.] your gift would be deservedly bestowed & creditable to our state.

> Very respectfully
> Your obdt servt.
> J. L. Chamberlain
> Col. 20th Maine Vols. Comdg. Brigade[91]

That evening, Chamberlain found an opportunity to write to Fanny.

> 3d Brigade Aug 31st [92]

Dearest,

The bugle has just sounded before my door on this hill. "<u>3d Brigade, Extinguish lights</u>"! Your sleepy head is tired—but the dear letter just received must have a word of answering love before any lights are extinguished in these quarters.

I am happy to think of you as at home again—now my little dear ones are all nestled together—"<u>all</u>"— I paused over that word—the tears filled my eyes—a dull heavy pain flowed over my heart. I could not have spoken then. But it is all well—well & bright with <u>her,</u> whose sweet face still shines in my heart. Come & let me kiss your dear lips—precious wife—sad mother—let our hearts worship together God's love & wisdom & mercy.

Yes all is well—well with us, darling—well, if we can only meet at last, as I pray God we may, never to part.

I overheard you & dear Daisy making your prayer for me, & I thought how many a night when I was out on some perilous duty, or in some fierce storm & hardship, that gentle prayer has gone up for me. Then too on other nights not outwardly so dangerous. I dare say I have been in peril of forgetting God & his goodness, & that prayer has been heard for me.

How I wish I could sit with you & Daisy at some communion table, if we could only get rid of the associaton of formality, & factitious if not forced feeling—lugubriousness instead of solemn joy— How happy such a season would make me.

I would not let Daisy go to church on communion days, if they will not receive her into the church, which I hope they will do. For their own sakes as well as for hers—& you too—dearest—you must be there too.

You were in "two moods". So I am, always, when I write you. Especially last night when I wrote you. You would not miss it at all if you were to tell me of the "dreamy love". If you are tempted to write of "facts"—write about that fact. I do not have much of the beautiful & spiritual said or done to me here.

Oh ho! You want to be liked. Well, that will do—a girl that is loved so much that she longs to be liked! But there's sense & logic in that too. And did you ever think of that word like—it carries an idea of things reciprocally befitting—of a certain agreeableness—of similarity—likeness in fact. Yes, wife, Fanny I like you if I may pay myself that compliment after the analytical definition. If I might be so bold, I do like you for I am like you. Sufficiently unlike for all practicable purposes—(& some impracticable ones!) & all the more "like" for being not the same. I suppose you think you are a pretty likely girl intrinsically & absolutely & it was doubtless my opinion to the same effect which set me to liking you.

I told you about the "two eyes" didn't I. Don't you get my letters? On yes it hadn't time to reach you by the 27th. Well you will see how they struck me. I had no business staring in a girls face, but I could not help just stepping out to take a nearer view of that one somehow. But where is the picture—the card picture of you? And can you send me a "proof" of mine? Love & liking.[93]

Chamberlain and his brigade spent the first half of September on the Rappahannock River guarding Beverly Ford. His next existing letter to

Fanny is typical of Victorian prose and style. He explains how he came to lose some sweet pickles she apparently had preserved and given to him when he was returning to the army, and then goes on to tease her about her spelling and her hair curls. Perhaps his thoughts on the death and commemoration of his comrade Strong Vincent—since Chamberlain now holds Vincent's old position in command of the 3rd Brigade—caused his openness to his wife, which began to be seen in the last letter, but had not come out quite this much in previous letters. His thoughts on the war coming soon to an end are almost tragically ironic. Another twenty months of some of the bitterest fighting lie ahead.

Head Qrs. 3d Brigade
Beverly Ford Sept. 12, 1863

Are the cheeks pale or rosy this hot noontide? I hope the Darling of my home is happy. How I think of you sitting here evenings under the shelter of the "fly", in front of my tent, looking out upon the waterfall foamy & misty, & farther upon the broad spreading river reflecting the trees upon the banks & winning my gaze & almost my feet like the "Green River" of my school boy days.

I dreamed last night that many ladies were coming to camp, & I was all excitement to have <u>you</u> come. But I suppose we shall have something else upon our hands before a great while.

This war, I suppose you can see, is rapidly coming to a close issue, & the <u>heavy</u> <u>fighting</u> is nearly over. <u>We</u> may see one or two battles more like Gettysburg though many doubt even that.

I did not tell you about Mrs. Vincent's present from the staff.

It was an oval breast pin nearly two inches long. The stone was <u>onyx</u>—an emblem of mourning I believe. Inlaid—cut in—was an exquisite oval wreath of <u>forget-me-nots</u> in <u>diamonds.</u> The border (outside edge of setting) was of little <u>pearls,</u> close-lying, & each riveted with a gold pin, the head of which projected slightly & seemed to add beauty even to the pearly beads. On the reverse was written—(<u>inscribed</u> somehow is a better word) in ornamental characters (the name at least was)

His Staff
in remembrance of
Gen. Strong Vincent

The back was hinged making a locket inside of which might

be placed any gentle memento such as a lock of hair—How sad—
sad—sad—& yet could any thing be more exquisite in taste & sig-
nificance?

To me it was a poem unutterably sad—yet darkly beautiful. I
have set, or lain, dreamily gazing with an inner sense, on that wonderful memento hours together.

We rough soldiers have at least some remnants of feeling &
taste—dont you think so—or else such a gem as that never could
have been conceived of.

It is hot noon, my precious one; but I love you even at <u>noon!</u>
Before dinner too ———

Ah. rogue you scold me about losing the sweet pickles, but the
logic was poor. You are too kind surely to imply that I shouldn't
have taken them & having resolved to do so, would you have
bought a new box-valise? or would you have me "lug" that big
heavy thing all the way to the Rappahannock, weak as I was?
Moreover if you were late in getting in to Boston & had to drive
like John to reach the New York Depot, would you have dragged
that great pack into a coach already crammed full of men, or
would you have just told the driver to take it on the box where he
was, & take care of it? Then if another man asked him to do the
same for him, could you help it if he <u>banged</u> <u>a</u> <u>big</u> <u>box</u> <u>right</u> <u>on</u> <u>top</u>
<u>of</u> <u>your</u> <u>valise</u> & slambanged through Boston?

Fan., you pretty butterfly, how you do spell. "<u>advise,</u>" you ask
for—"<u>bussiness</u>" inadvertent no doubt. And then—don't think I
would care how an angel spelled a loving word to me—
"<u>dreamyly</u>"— you darling, sweet girl, it is dream<u>i</u>ly. How are your
pretty roly-poly horns, or "rats"—or whatever you call the puffs of
hair I plague you about. <u>Good</u> <u>day!</u>

[The following is written upside down at the top of the first
page.]

It is all the same whether you direct "20th Maine", or "3d
Brigade". All the letters are sorted here for the Brigade. L.[94]

On September 16 Chamberlain and his brigade left their Beverly Ford
camp, crossed the Rappahannock with the rest of the 5th Corps, and
marched nearly to Culpeper, Virginia. The next day they marched
through Culpeper only about 2 miles and camped. There they stayed for

the next few weeks, outside of Culpeper, where other armies of both sides had camped numerous times before. They were encamped near the battlefield of Cedar Mountain, site of the August 9, 1862, fight.[95]

Along with his official military paperwork, Chamberlain found it important to keep the governor informed of the regiment's needs and the officers' desires in filling certain positions. And he still had to deal with the problem of the men of the 2nd Maine.

Head Qrs. 3d Brigade, 1st Div.
Sept. 19th 1863.
Near Cedar Mountain.

To His Excellency
Governor Coburn,
Governor,

I have the honor to acknowledge the receipt of your favor of the 12th instant in reference to the appointment of surgeon of the 20th Maine Vols.

I have consulted with the officers of the 20th, & find that they would prefer (so far as I can discover) <u>Dr. Shaw,</u> our present assistant surgeon, to any stranger or any other person except, perhaps, Dr. Martin.

I have not the slightest objection to Dr. Wescott, but I believe the Regiment would be better pleased with Dr. Shaw. He deserves promotion I think, although he has been with us but a short time. His promotion would also allow Hospital Steward Baker to be mustered in, & consequently make a vacancy in that office, which you desired to fill by the appointment of Rev. William Brown—at present we are only entitled to one asst. surgeon.

This arrangement would suit us all very well.

But I know how you must be embarrassed in making appointments, & beg that you will not give yourself too much trouble merely to <u>please</u> us. I am confident you would send us none but competent & worthy surgeons.

The Regiment is in good health & spirits, & has won the high respect & esteem of those whose opinion is of value in the Army.

Col. Gilmore & Major Spear are performing their duty with great faithfulness & credit.

I learn that our conscripts are to be here by the 25th inst. & I trust we can manage them with enough skill & prudence to save them from desertion & its inevitable consequence—shooting. I don't want any of that business with Maine men. I obtained the release of those men of the 2d Maine against whom charges had been preferred for mutiny, & they are on duty, & are good soldiers.

I trust it may be agreeable to your views & your convenience to commission the officers I had the honor to recommend in my last, as it requires some time to get "mustered-in" now, & we need more officers to assist in managing the drafted men.

> I have the honor to be
> Your Excellency's most
> obdt, servant & friend
> J. L. Chamberlain
> Col. 20th Maine Vols.
> Comdg. Brigade [96]

Early on October 13, Chamberlain's 3rd Brigade sleepily struck camp in the dark and joined the Army of the Potomac on the march. Robert E. Lee's Army of Northern Virginia, minus Longstreet's detached corps, was on the move northward again. By evening there were some minor clashes, not involving the 5th Corps. But on the fourteenth near Bristoe Station, Virginia, some Confederate artillery found the range of Chamberlain's brigade while they cooked dinner in bivouac. Up and into line went Chamberlain's men, but word came from Gen. Charles Griffin, Chamberlain's division commander, to keep moving and not engage the enemy. It was one of the rare times these men had actually avoided a fight. [97]

Chamberlain apprised the governor of certain changes in the regiment and recommended some officers for promotion.

> Head Quarters 3rd Brigade
> 1st Divis.n 5th Corps.
> Army of Potomac
> Auburn Oct. 28 1863

To His Excellency
A. Coburn
Governor of Maine
Governor,

I have the honor to acknowledge the receipt of your favor of the 23d inst. in reference to the promotion of officers in Company "K" of the 20th Regt.

We have been on the point of recommending Lt. Nichols once or twice for the captaincy of that company, but an unfortunate occurrence growing out of drinking intoxicating liquor to excess each time interrupted the recommendations, & the vacancy has been left in hopes that Lt Nichols would overcome his habit to such a degree that he could consistently be promoted.

Mr Nichols is a brave & energetic officer, & these good qualities have made us more lenient with him than we should otherwise have been.

I gave him a strong commendation for Cavalry service in the belief that a new sphere of duty might give him a better opportunity to reform, & with the conviction that his peculiar <u>dash</u> & fearlessness fitted him for that arm of the service.

Lt. Col. Gilmore now comdg. the 20th says he is not prepared at present to recommend Lt. Nichols or Lt. Fuller for promotion. If they prove themselves fit, in the respect referred to, they will be recommended at the earliest moment.

I think there will be some other changes suggested before long.

Dr. Shaw is giving the best of satisfaction—few surgeons within my observation have been so faithful & have won the general good will of the Brigade, to the degree he has.

I trust it may be convenient to you without embarrassment, to promote them.

I do not expect to be able to resume command of the Regt. for a long time at least—but I never lose sight of its interests.

I sincerely hope its ranks so honorably thinned may be filled as soon as possible.

I am having a careful sketch of the history of the Regt. prepared for the convenience of Genl. Hodsdon in the preparation of his report.

I am
very respectfully
your obdt. servt.
J. L. Chamberlain
Col. 20th Maine Vols.[98]

The 3rd Brigade went into camp three miles from Warrenton Junction for more than a week in November, during which time Chamberlain was able to complete his report on the fighting at Gettysburg.

> Head Qrs. 3d Brigade.
> 1st. Division, 5th Corps.
> Near Warrenton Junction
> Nov. 4th 1863.

Brig. Genl. John L. Hodsdon
Adjt. Genl. of Maine
General,

I have the honor to enclose to you, by permission from Corps Hd. Qrs. a copy of my official report of the battle of Gettysburg.

Had it been written for you I would gladly have given you some particulars which would have made you proud of our noble fellows from the State of Maine. But ever since that report was written I have had so much to do in all ways, that I could not prepare such a particular account of individual good conduct on the part of some men as I wished & intended to do. If we remain quiet a day or two I may be able to send you additional particulars. You may find this of service however in making up your report. In some statistics it may differ slightly from the first letter I wrote. This I think is correct.

Maj. Spear has been assisting me in preparing an account of the various actions in which this Regt. has been engaged, & we hope to send it by tomorrow's mail.

I was assigned to the command of the Brigade in August & papers which have come to me from your office, have gone directly to Lt. Col. Gilmore who I suppose has acknowledged their receipt.

I will do all in my power to render your information in regard to the 20th as full as possible.

> I remain
> with high respect
> Your servt. & friend
> J. L. Chamberlain
> Col. 20th Maine Vols.[99]

On November 7 Maj. Gen. George G. Meade attacked Lee's fortified position north of the Rappahannock at Rappahannock Station. At three that afternoon, Chamberlain's men of the 3rd Brigade, moving as a strong picket line, advanced from about two miles away from the river on the left of the Orange and Alexandria Railroad, with the right flank—

consisting of the 20th Maine—moving along the railroad. Advancing and keeping in touch with the 6th Corps, which was supposed to make the main attack on the right of the tracks, they were led by Capt. Walter G. Morrill. Some of the 20th found themselves touching the flank of the 6th Maine boys and, without orders, assisted them in their attack upon the Confederate works. They overran the Rebel position in a hand-to-hand affair, and Morrill won the Medal of Honor for his role.[100] Chamberlain's horse Charlemagne took another wound under him in the foreleg.[101] After the fighting, the 3rd Brigade returned to where they had been bivouacked before the attack.

On November 9 to 10 Chamberlain and his brigade were involved in a reconnaissance across the Rappahannock at Kelly's Ford and extending three miles downstream. From the balmy weather of a few days previously, the Virginia countryside had turned into a snowy freezer. On the reconnaissance, Chamberlain and his men slept on the ground without fires in the freezing sleet and snow. Chamberlain, who had never fully recovered from his illness before the Battle of Gettysburg, again became ill with what the surgeons called "malarial fever." In mid-November he was sent on a cattle car to Washington accompanied by a doctor. He was in and out of consciousness during the rough, cold journey. He arrived in Georgetown at the Seminary General Hospital on November 19, 1863.[102] On the same day that Chamberlain entered the hospital, President Abraham Lincoln addressed the crowd at the dedication of the new National Cemetery at Gettysburg. He spoke his imperishable phrases over the graves of many of the men Chamberlain had commanded there.

The next letter is not in Chamberlain's handwriting, and his signature appears scrawled. He was so ill that he was not able to write his own correspondence and could barely sign his name. It may very well have been the last correspondence he wrote before being sent to the hospital unconscious.

Hd. Qrs. 3d. Brigade,
1st Div. 5th Corps.
Kelly's Ford, Va.
Nov. 15th, 1863.

Lieut. Col Locke,
A. A. G. 5th Corps.
Colonel:

I have the honor to request leave of absence for fifteen days on account of sickness, on Surgeon's Certificate enclosed.

> Your obedient servant,
> J. L. Chamberlain
> Col. 20th Maine Vols.
> Comdg. Brigade.

The following was enclosed:

I hereby certify on honor that Col. J. L. Chamberlain 20th Me. Vols. has been ill of Malarial Fever for the last four days and is still dangerously sick. I moreover state my opinion that said officer's life will be much jeopardized by moving him in an ambulance or by his remaining in this locality that he will not be able to resume his duties in a less period than fifteen {15} days and that a Surgeon should accompany him as far as Washington.

> M. W. Townsend
> Surg 44 N.Y.V.
> Surg in Chief
> 3 Brig 1 Div 5 Corps.
> Kelley's Ford, Va.
> Nov. 15, 1863.[103]

⇜ 1864 ⇝

Do not grieve too much for me. We shall all soon meet Live for the children
                                    —Maj. Gen. Joshua L. Chamberlain

CHAMBERLAIN SPENT DECEMBER and January of 1863 to 1864 recuperating from his "malarial fever," which had afflicted him so severely at Gettysburg and was exacerbated by his having slept out in the freezing cold in November. While he recovered, the army engaged in the Mine Run Campaign. He was well enough in December to travel to his home in Brunswick for the holidays. In February he drew court-martial duty in Trenton, New Jersey, and Washington, D.C.; the responsibility would last three months. During Chamberlain's absence, winter encampment for the 20th Maine was at Rappahannock Station, Virginia, with Maj. Ellis Spear in command.[1] Still, however, Chamberlain was involved in some of the administration of the regiment.

> Washington D. C. Jan'y 24th 1864
> The one hundred & nineteen screw drivers and cone wrenches referred to in my Return for the 4th Quarter of 1863 as on hand to be accounted for were "turned over" to me by Col. A. Ames 20th Reg't. Maine Vols, on the 20th day of May 1863. They were not & have never been actually received by me—the understanding being at the time & until now that the said articles were stored in Washington.
> They were sent from the vicinity of Antietam Battlefield (with

116

other surplus stores for which we had no transportation) Sept 17, 1862 with verbal order from the Brigade Commander to Washington D. C. to be there stored. I now after the most careful ["& strict" written, then crossed out] search find that the box containing the said one hundred and nineteen (119) screw drivers & cone wrenches was lost and cannot be recovered.

I certify on honor that the above statement is correct and true.

J. L. Chamberlain
Col. 20th Maine Vols.[2]

While on detached duty, he continued to apply his influence to help friends from the army or from his hometown to gain the appointments they wished or to secure for his old regiment qualified appointees.

Washington D.C.
February 10th, 1864

I consider Mrs. Fogg one of the most faithful, earnest and efficient workers in the humane cause in which she has been engaged for the last three years, that I have ever seen in the field. My opportunities for observing her efforts have been the most favorable, and I think it may safely be said that she is peculiarly qualified for such a service, and that her success is greater than of many more assuming agencies.

I consider her services are too valuable to be dispensed with and trust that she may receive such countenance and support as may suitably recognize her past success and the high character she has sustained.

J. L. Chamberlain
Col. 20th Maine Vols.[3]

Washington D.C.
March 10th 1864

I cheerfully give this testimonial to Mr. James H. Nichols late 1st Lieut. in the 20th Regt. Maine Vols, who intends to apply for a position in the Cavalry service.

Mr Nichols was at considerable personal expense in raising his company in the 20th Regt. and failed to receive the appointment he expected. He has shown himself an earnest and brave officer. I have often been obliged to notice his especial service and gallantry.

As he has now left the Infantry service & wishes to enter the Cavalry, I cordially wish him success. On many accounts I think him peculiarly fitted for the Cavalry Arm, where his personal courage and enterprise would have more scope.

Justice to a brave man demands this testimonial.

J. L. Chamberlain
Colonel, 20th Maine Vols.[4]

To Chamberlain, it seems, Nichols's indiscreet drinking habits are out-weighed by his "personal courage and enterprise." Then again, perhaps this glowing recommendation is Chamberlain's way of helping to get rid of a troubling soldier. But the testimonial is given "cheerfully" and carries those words that Chamberlain applied to his definition of manhood: earnest and brave, and imbued with gallantry.

General Court Martial
Washington D. C
March 15th 1864

To His Excellency Gov. Cony
Governor,

Mr. Thomas M.[?] Giveen of Brunswick writes me that he is making application for the position of Lieutenant in one one [*sic*] of the Batteries about to be raised in Maine.

I know Mr. Giveen very well; he is a young man of character and capacity. I am glad he desires to enter the service, and have no doubt that, should you be pleased to grant him the position he wishes, he will fully meet all the requirements of the office, and do honor to his state & the service.

I feel an interest in Mr. Giveen as a deserving young man, & trust he may receive an appointment suitable to his abilities and education.

Very respectfully, your obdt. servt.
J. L. Chamberlain.
Colonel 20th Maine Vols.[5]

While Chamberlain was in Washington listening to testimony and writing letters of endorsement, the men of the 20th Maine were preparing, with the rest of the army, for a new spring campaign under a new commander, Gen. Ulysses Grant.

Court-martial duty was not all boredom for Chamberlain, especially since Fanny managed to spend some time with him. He took her on a battlefield tour of Gettysburg in early April—just ten months after he had fought there.[6] What visions must have risen before him as he stood on Little Round Top and described the fight to his wife. And even *in absentia,* between visits and tours, Chamberlain still found time to see to the proper spiritual care of his men.

> Trenton N. Jersey
> General Court Martial
> April 25 1864

To His Excellency Governor Cony
Governor,

Understanding that Rev. Mr. Mitchell recently appointed Chaplain of the 20th Maine Vols. declines the appointment, I respectfully endorse the recommendation by the officers of the Regiment of Rev. Mr. Godfrey for the position of chaplain of the 20th Regiment Maine Vols.

I trust he will be directed to report without delay.

> I have the honor to be
> Very respectfully
> Your obdt. servt.
> J. L. Chamberlain
> Colonel 20th Maine Vols[7]

Spring brought the time for active campaigning, as the muddy Virginia roads began to dry. New to the Eastern Theater of the war was Ulysses Grant, brought in by Lincoln from his successful campaigns in the West. His ability to utilize every aspect of the huge Northern war complex—manufacturing, transportation, and communication, as well as the virtually limitless manpower—would dictate a relentless kind of war to be waged upon the Confederates. Grant's life would soon intertwine with Chamberlain's. The connection nearly cost Chamberlain his life, eventually brought him recognition and great glory, and would last a lifetime.

On May 1, 1864, the men of the 20th Maine struck tents at Rappa-

Samuel Cony, governor of Maine in 1864 and 1865. Maine State Archives

hannock Station and began a march that would take them across the Rapidan River. There would be no turning back until victory was secured.

On May 4 the 20th Maine and the rest of the 5th Corps, with flags flying and bands playing beneath a bright spring sky, crossed the Rapidan over pontoon bridges laid at Germanna Ford. But the next day the air was filled with a darker, more hideous cacophony.

The murkiness came from the eerie, tangled mass of undergrowth known as the Wilderness, the area to the west of Fredericksburg, across part of which the Battle of Chancellorsville had been fought exactly one year before. The strange sound came from that jungle too; the men remembered it as a sound deeper and more hollow than that of other battles. The smoke wreathed itself among the overhanging branches and produced an almost impenetrable haze.

Familiar men from the regiment became casualties or performed heroically. Capt. Walter Morrill, leader of Company B's flank attack at Little Round Top, was hit in the face by a minié ball and carried off the field, blinded and nearly strangling on his own blood. Sagacious, compassionate Holman Melcher, who had been near the colors on Little Round

Top, led a small group of men from his Company F who had been cut off into the rear of the Confederate lines and, by ruse, got them back again to the 20th Maine's lines. And Capt. William W. Morrell, who had once worked so hard in Brunswick recruiting, lay dead after the battle.

The haze in the Wilderness grew thicker when the muzzle flashes of the muskets caught the dry leaves on fire, and soon helpless, wounded men were roasting alive in the inferno. The Wilderness must have seemed very close to hell that night. The living listened to men dying by fire under a sky made lurid by the flames.

On May 6 the fight had moved down the line from the 20th and, with the exception of some skirmishing, passed them by on the seventh as well. But there were more than one hundred casualties among the Maine men in the two days of fighting.[8]

After what many considered a defeat in the Wilderness, the men in the Army of the Potomac expected, as always before, to turn around and head back north of the Potomac River, regroup—probably under a new commander—and try yet another invasion. But as Grant left the Wilderness, he turned his horse's head not northward, but to the south, to attempt to cut Lee off from Richmond at a vital road matrix near which a few houses and a courthouse had been built: Spotsylvania.

During all of this, Chamberlain was still in Trenton, and he wrote a letter to the adjutant general at the War Department asking to be returned to his unit at the front. It apparently got mislaid or lost, so he wrote another.

Washington D. C. May 9 1864
Colonel E. D. Townsend,

Asst. Adjt. General,
Colonel,

Understanding that my application to be permitted to rejoin my command dated Trenton N. J. April 25th 1864, has not been received, I beg leave respectfully to renew my request to be relieved from duty on the General Court Martial convened by Special Order No. 41, War Dept. AGO. dated Janry. 27th 1864, and to be ordered to the field.

At the time I was placed on duty, I was under medical treatment in Georgetown D. C. My health will now, in my opinion, permit my resuming active duty, and never before having been absent from my command in time of an active campaign my anxiety to be in the field is very great.

I beg therefore to be permitted to rejoin my command as soon as communications with the front are re opened.

I have the honor to be
Very respectfully Your obdt. servt.
J. L. Chamberlain
Colonel 20th Maine Vols.[9]

By the second week of May, Chamberlain had rejoined the men of the 20th Maine and took over its command since Gen. Joseph J. Bartlett had been given command of the 3rd Brigade in Chamberlain's absence. Maj. Gen. Gouverneur K. Warren was now in charge of the 5th Corps.[10]

On May 8, before Chamberlain had returned, Warren's corps ran into entrenched Confederates at Laurel Hill near Spotsylvania Court House, Virginia, and after a fight that lasted all day, was driven back. This was one of the actions that opened the Battle of Spotsylvania.[11] That battle would last until May 21, when Grant marched once again to the east and south to attempt to get around the Army of Northern Virginia.[12]

The day after he returned to the army, Chamberlain was back in action.[13] He took over command again of his old 3rd Brigade when Bartlett fell ill, and continued bouncing back and forth from brigade commander to regimental commander while Bartlett's health failed him several times over the next few weeks.[14]

At Spotsylvania, Chamberlain wrote to his governor while under artillery fire.[15]

Before Spotsylvania C.H.
May 18 1864

To His Excellency
Gov. Cony
Governor,

I have the honor to recommend the following officers for promotion. I do this at the present time to secure to deserving men positions which the casualties of this Campaign may otherwise prevent their receiving.

I would recommend

1st Lieut Weston H. Keene of co "D" to the Captain of co "A" vice Morell [Morrell] killed in battle.

2d Lieut. William K. Brickford of "H" to the 1st Lieut. of co "H" vice Morell [Morrill] promoted.

2d Lieut. Hiram Morse of "I" to the 1st Lieut. of co. "I" vice Linscott killed in battle.

Our chaplain has not yet reported.

We advanced our line half a mile last evening with little loss.

I write this as we are lying in line of battle behind our rifle-pit works not more than 600 or 800 yards from the enemy's works. We have been exposed to a heavy cannonading all the morning, but the 20th has as yet lost only one man—Augustus Ellis of Co "D"—severely wounded in head. We are expecting a warm engagement. I had a hard time to get relieved from that court martial duty & rejoin my command. The week of active operations when I was kept out of the field was one of the most unhappy of my life. I am making up for it now however.

Major Spear is in actual command of the 20th still, as on my return I was placed temporarily in charge of the Brigade, Gen Bartlett being sick.

The artillery fire is very hot now. Shells are bursting over us every second. The Brigade is losing men fast.

Lee is holding us very stiffly. We are not pushing him in front, but are moving to turn his right & that of course brings us nearer to Richmond.

There is no discount on your Maine men.

Very respectfully
Your friend
& servt.
J. L. Chamberlain
Col. 20th Mne.Vols.[16]

Along with the rest of the army on May 21, the 5th Corps left the trenches around Spotsylvania and marched toward the North and South Anna rivers and Hanover Junction. The troops crossed the Po River at Guiney's Bridge and camped, then were off again the next morning.

Again General Bartlett was sick, and Chamberlain led the 3rd Brigade. They traveled south on the Telegraph Road and a road parallel to it.[17]

On May 22 Chamberlain's men crossed Pole Cat Creek in an attempt to take a Rebel battery. The creek was deeper than expected, so Chamberlain ordered his men to dismantle a nearby fence and reconstruct it as a makeshift bridge. The enemy saw the ruckus, opened fire, then escaped.[18] The next day the 5th Corps waded the North Anna near Jericho Mills, with Griffin's division establishing a bridgehead, advancing nearly a mile. Chamberlain and the 20th Maine were in reserve at center rear of the division when the Confederates attacked. The fight became heated, and three regiments of Bartlett's brigade entered the fray. Chamberlain and his men were sent to the left, but darkness, along with stout Yankee resistance, persuaded the Confederates to break off the engagement.[19]

As other Union corps crossed along the North Anna, they found the Confederates well entrenched on the south side—so well, in fact, that Grant decided to sidle to the east and south again. The men of the 20th Maine marched all night on May 26 and all the next day until they crossed the Pamunkey River, where they found Lee between them and further advance toward Richmond. Contact with the Rebels was almost constant for the next several days while they crossed the Virginia peninsula between the York and the James rivers, made famous by the Seven Days Battles in the summer of 1862.[20]

By the end of May and the beginning of June, the division was at Bethesda Church. This was the area of Virginia where McClellan got bogged down during the 1862 campaign; Grant decided to take his army as rapidly as possible through it.[21] But once again Lee stood in his way, this time at a place called Cold Harbor.

There was fighting on June 1. The next day the Union army planned an attack, but it never got under way. Meanwhile, the Confederates used the time to fortify their entrenchments.

On June 3 at 4:40 A.M., after a ten-minute cannonade, Grant launched several attacks on the well-entrenched Confederate positions near Cold Harbor. By 5:15 the attacks were over, and Grant had lost between fifty-six hundred and eight thousand men.[22] Grant, normally *sangfroid* about military matters, wrote later, "I have always regretted that the last assault at Cold Harbor was ever made."[23] The 5th Corps for the most part did not participate in the slaughter, except for Griffin's division, which coordinated an attack with the 9th Corps successfully against

Maj. Gen. Henry Heth's and Maj. Gen. Robert E. Rodes's Confederate divisions.[24] The 20th fought that day near Bethesda Church and took twenty-six casualties.[25] It was the last time Chamberlain would command the men of his old regiment in battle.

The 5th Corps was reorganized after the fighting at Cold Harbor. Warren pooled some Pennsylvania regiments from the veteran 1st Corps (the 121st, 142nd, 143rd, 149th, 150th) and a green one, the 187th Pennsylvania, and created a new brigade. Chamberlain, already experienced in handling a brigade, became its commander.[26]

To emphasize his being placed in command, on June 6 Warren glowingly recommended Chamberlain for promotion to brigadier general.[27] By June 9 Meade had Chamberlain's name on the list of promotions.

By June 12 Grant had begun his move to cross the James. Chamberlain's 1st Brigade started its march that evening. The next morning the men crossed the Chickahominy River, which bisects the peninsula, on pontoon bridges at a place called Long Bridge.[28]

The advance forces of the Army of the Potomac arrived at the James River and prepared to cross. Early on June 16 the 5th Corps was ferried across the James at Windmill Point, landing at the old colonial plantation called Flowerdew Hundred.[29]

Suddenly, that week Chamberlain began having premonitions—those haunting flashes of doom that appear in Civil War literature—of being shot in the abdomen. He removed his blanket roll from the cantle of his saddle and brought it around to the front. It would not have stopped a minié ball or a piece of shrapnel, but perhaps it gave him peace of mind.[30]

After crossing the James, the 5th Corps marched all night toward Petersburg and took position on June 17 to the left of two other corps remaining in reserve.[31] The men of the rank and file may not have realized it, but a number of foul-ups conspired to deny the Union army a bloodless march into Petersburg, cutting Lee's supply lines from the Deep South. For one newly appointed brigadier general from Brunswick, Maine, it would lead to the most disastrous occurrence in his life, and to his worst premonition coming true.

Meade realized that time was of the essence, that Confederate troops from south of Richmond and Cold Harbor were rapidly filling the lines circling Petersburg. He ordered an early morning assault.

At 4:30 A.M. on Saturday, June 18, an advance along the Union lines

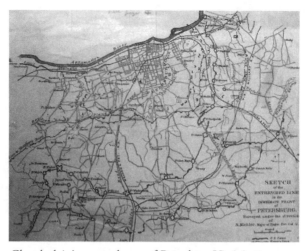

Chamberlain's personal map of Petersburg, Virginia. LIBRARY
OF CONGRESS

to take Petersburg began. The first enemy works the men struck in their
advance they found empty; the Confederates had pulled back from the
forward lines into a more compact position closer to the city. Chamberlain's 1st Brigade was moved to the left of the 5th Corps.[32] When the
men got into position, they came under the fire of Confederate artillery
to the south near the Jerusalem Plank Road, left there in the advanced
position when the rest of their army pulled back.[33] The shells killed and
wounded some of the men in the corps, and at about 10:30 A.M., General Warren rode up to Chamberlain and asked him almost off-handedly
if he thought he might be able to silence the battery. Chamberlain took
it as either an order or a challenge.

    The brigade moved out in columns of fours, and by the left flank
marched along the cut of the Petersburg and Norfolk Railroad. The men
crossed the railroad south of the cut, and Chamberlain formed them into
two lines of battle in some woods on the south side of the railroad.
Emerging from the woods in battle lines, the front line consisted of all
the veteran Pennsylvania regiments, and the rear line the green 187th
Pennsylvania. This maneuver enabled Chamberlain's troops to drive the
artillerists from their position by advancing on their flank and peppering
them with musketry. It was, as Chamberlain would recall later, a "sharp
and hot, but short, encounter . . . we carried everything."[34]

Chamberlain and his staff were riding between the two lines as they advanced. Suddenly a shell burst overhead and dismounted them all. Chamberlain's horse was wounded "severely through the haunch," [35] and three men were killed and seven wounded. Among the wounded was Corp. James A. Stettler, whom Chamberlain would meet later in less frenetic but more horrifying circumstances. [36] The brigade's color bearer also went down, but Chamberlain seized the triangular brigade flag and continued the charge with it. [37]

Though they drove the battery off, the men found themselves too close to the Confederates' main works and under "a storm of shot and shell." Chamberlain pulled his men back to the shelter of the crest he had just carried and prepared for an expected enemy counterattack. [38]

It was a bad position by Chamberlain's reckoning. The jutting breastwork before him was called Rives' Salient and commanded his position. In addition to Rives' Salient, three to four hundred yards ahead of him were "several strong earthworks with twelve or fifteen guns so disposed as to deliver a smashing cross-fire over the ground between us." Across the Jerusalem Plank Road was a fort whose heavy guns could enfilade any assault upon the earthworks. Chamberlain estimated three thousand entrenched infantry in the enemy's lines. He had already accomplished Warren's wishes and chased away the annoying Confederate cannons. But no word had come to withdraw, so he called up the three batteries of artillery given to him and began placing them behind the crest on slight "platforms" to level them with their "muzzles lying in the grass." Recoil would send them back farther behind the crest so that the gunners could reload in relative safety. [39]

Chamberlain got his men partially out of danger by half wheeling them first to the right, then to the left, then moving them forward to the backside of a ridge upon which an old rail fence ran. The fence was overgrown with briers and brush that obscured the men from the enemy. He had them lie down there. [40]

The maneuvering and placement of the guns took some time, and the prostrate men had an opportunity to observe the fine effort the Rebels had made in creating defensive works. Chamberlain moved about with what was left of his staff and spent some time sitting on the extreme right of his line. He asked his staff for some water and was offered some by Sgt. Patrick DeLacy of Company A of the 143rd Pennsylvania, but Chamberlain turned him down, not wanting to consume the precious water of an enlisted man who may soon do some fighting and might need it. [41]

Meanwhile, Chamberlain continued to see to the placing of the batteries on the crest he had just won from the Confederate battery. He was waiting for orders, but the ones he got were not what he wanted or expected. A lieutenant colonel from staff rode up and gave him an order "in the name of 'the general commanding' to assault the enemy's main works in my front with my brigade."[42] Astonished, Chamberlain decided to risk being relieved from duty and wrote, in the field, a note for the staff officer to carry back to his commander.[43]

Lines before Petersburg
June 18, 1864

I have received a verbal order not through the usual channels, but by a staff-officer unknown to me, purporting to come from the General commanding the army, directing me to assault the main works of the enemy in my front. Circumstances lead me to believe the General cannot be perfectly aware of my situation, which has greatly changed within the last hour.

I have just carried a crest, an advanced post occupied by the enemy's artillery supported by infantry. I am advanced a mile beyond our own lines, and in an isolated position. On my right a deep rail-road cut; my left flank in the air, with no support whatever. In front of me at close range is a strongly entrenched line of infantry and artillery, with projecting salients right and left, such that my advance would be swept by a cross-fire, while a large fort on my left enfilades my entire advance, (as I experienced in carrying this position.) In the hollow along my front, close up to the enemy's works, appears to be bad ground, swampy boggy [*sic*], where my men would be held at a great disadvantage under a destructive fire.

I have got up three batteries and am placing them on the reverse slope of the crest, to enable me to hold against expected attack. To leave these guns behind me unsupported,—their retreat cut off by the railroad cut,—would expose them to loss in case of our repulse.

Fully aware of the responsibility I take, I beg to be assured that the order to attack with my single Brigade is with the General's full understanding. I have here a veteran Brigade of six regiments, and my responsibility for these men warrants me in wishing assurance that no mistake in communicating orders compels me to sacrifice them.

From what I can see of the enemy's lines, it is my opinion that if an assault is to be made, it should be by nothing less than the whole army.

Very respectfully,
Joshua L. Chamberlain,
Colonel comdg. 1st Brigade, 1st Division, 5th. Corps[44]

Chamberlain's men continued their preparations for the defense of their isolated position. Soon the staff officer returned with the information that the attack was to be made with the entire army, led by Chamberlain's brigade. Preparations then began for the assault.

Other brigades were moved into supporting positions: Col. Jacob Sweitzer's brigade from the 1st Division to Chamberlain's right and Gen. Lysander S. Cutler's 4th Division on his left. Chamberlain went over to see Cutler to make sure all orders were understood and that he would be supported on that flank. "I shall know what to do when the time comes," was Cutler's only response.[45]

The "hollow" across which the attack was to be made was not as steep as some contemporary accounts make it seem. Rather, it was a gently sloping plain down to a deep-cut, crooked rivulet, remembered thus by Sergeant DeLacy, who saw it from the same point of view as Chamberlain: "After crossing the old fence, the ground sloped toward the enemy. We had to move down this slope through an old field partly covered with shaking asp, brush and briers."[46]

Chamberlain called his regimental commanders together and explained the details of the assault. Because of the proximity of the Rebel line and the deadliness of the crossfire, there could be no stopping to fire a volley and reload. Their men would move quickly down the slope; ranks broken while crossing the rivulet would re-form once across; then they would rush toward the enemy and breach their line so that the follow-on troops could exploit it.[47]

When the officers returned to their regiments, the men of the rank and file found out that they were to assault the formidable Rebel position before them across the sloping plain with its little creek at the bottom. At least half the brigade were veterans. With combat experience came two things: the moral knowledge that one's duty must be done, and the tactical knowledge that the task before them would be horrifyingly deadly. From that moment until the assault began, there suddenly seemed to be both too much time and not enough.

Chamberlain walked before the prone men behind the old fence. He stopped at least once to deliver a brief speech. Maj. M. L. Blair commanded Company E, the center or color company, of the 143rd Pennsylvania Volunteers. He remembered Chamberlain stepping leisurely along the front of the company and speaking kindly to the men:

> Comrades, we have now before us a great duty for our country to perform, and who knows but the way in which we acquit ourselves in this perilous undertaking may depend the ultimate success of the preservation of our grand republic. We know that some must fall, it may be any of you or I; but I feel that you will all go in manfully and make such a record as will make all our loyal American people forever grateful. I can but feel that our action in this crisis is momentous, and who can know but in the providence of God our action to day may be the one thing needful to break and destroy this unholy rebellion.[48]

The five veteran regiments, averaging about 250 men apiece, were again in the front lines, and the green 187th—more than 1,000 strong, according to Sergeant DeLacy's estimate—made up the rear lines. They formed up thusly:[49]

   121st PA   142nd PA   150th PA   149th PA   143rd PA

———————————187th PA———————————

There was an interval of about fifty yards between the front lines and the lines of the 187th. Normal attack procedure, according to *Hardee's Tactics,* would place all the regiments in double ranks—a front and a rear rank— with thirteen inches between the first rank's knapsacks and the rear rank's chests. (In an assault like this, however, the men usually piled the knapsacks in a safe spot until their hoped-for return.) Officers and sergeants not given a specific place became file closers marching two paces behind the rear rank, using fixed bayonets and drawn swords to encourage those ahead of them to do their duty.

But in combat everything changes. No doubt the men did things automatically by now; that's what all the drilling was for. *Hardee's* called for the colonel to be thirty paces to the rear of the file closers. Chamberlain, however, would lead the battle lines on foot, in the center of the brigade. The brigade front would extend, if DeLacy's estimates of troop strengths were correct, about 425 yards, and the 187th Pennsylvania's line a little shorter, about 340 yards.

The general assault was planned for 3:00 P.M. Tension and uncertainty wove through the ranks and up the chain of command. The men of the 187th, in their naivete and inexperience, probably feared most that they would run. The veterans knew of the dreadful consequences of the coming charge over a killing ground, knew that they would not run, and that was a fearful thing. Chamberlain saw that he was unsupported on his left and that Cutler was nowhere to be seen. He knew that he had cause to fear.

Chamberlain looked at his watch and it was nearly three. He stepped out, turned to his men, and drew his saber. The time for premonitions was past. *Most likely I shall be hit somewhere at sometime, but all "my times are in His hands."*[50] He called the men to attention. "Trail Arms! Double-quick, march!"[51] The bugler called the advance. As the men crested the ridge and passed over the old fence and briers, from their throats came a low, hoarse, rolling yell, as old as men moving to battle, like that heard at Waterloo, or Cannae, or Jericho. DeLacy writing to Chamberlain later recalled,

> First, quick march; soon after, double quick, and finally we went on the run with our brigade commander, yourself, in front carrying the brigade flag, rushing on until we reached the bottom of this slope which was filled with brush and running sweet briars, alder trees, and part of the ground was composed of marsh, swamp and deep mud. On the other side a small rivulet or stream ran down right along our front and washed out three to five feet deep and from four to six feet in width at the top with banks perpendicular. From this point the ground gradually ascended to the point or ridge on which the Confederate line of breastworks and fortifications were erected with numerous lines of rifle pits covering every approach. This ground was soft and sandy, with a dwarfish crop of grain or corn in it.[52]

As they topped the crest and headed down the slope, it seemed that every Confederate gun that was trained on them opened. They were within long-musket range, and almost any Rebel volley was bound to hit someone. Case shot exploding overhead hammered men with concussions and showered them with hot, hissing iron fragments and lead balls;

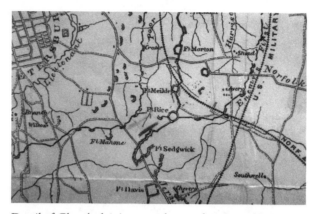

Detail of Chamberlain's personal map of Rives' Salient show-
ing his hand-drawn battle lines of the fighting in which he
took part on June 18, 1864. LIBRARY OF CONGRESS

percussion shells striking the ground and detonating tossed men and fragments of men into others, causing further injury; canister, like giant shotgun blasts, ripped the ranks apart as they ripped men apart; and the incessant small-arms fire staggered individual soldiers and dropped them with fearful rapidity. As DeLacy later wrote to Chamberlain:

> The moment the brigade started for the front in the charge, that moment it seemed as if all hell broke loose, a perfect cyclone of all the furies in the Confederate lines opened upon us. The brigade was in plain view of every gunner in the confederate forts and the guns on our immediate front, with at least 5000 muskets playing upon us. But nothing daunting, the boys rushed on in the wake of their commander amidst the terrible hail of iron and lead until nearing the bottom of the slope, heretofore mentioned, where you directed the line to oblique to the left. The swamp and brush was hard to get through, as it was forty or fifty yards across at many places,—it really was an obstacle like the sunken road at Waterloo, that you did not observe until we were mixed in it and then we had the deep gully made by that small stream to cross. Many of the boys jumped across it and fell back into the mud and water and clambered up its steep sides and rushed on up into the field and nearly reached the enemy's breastworks when the troops off to our

left broke back. I heard it was Cutler's Division, but as to that I am not clear. However, I saw troops go back, a great mass of them, which permitted the rebel line to our left to turn all their attention to your brigade. Inasmuch as the rebel line of works ran down so that we seemed to charge into a crescent shaped position strongly intrenched, after we left the stream in our rear and pushed on up the hill towards the rebel works, we stopped the fire of several of their guns, our whole line was enfiladed heavily from the left and right by the rebel fire. If the brigade had been well supported, we would have cleared the works of the enemy.[53]

Strange as it may seem, the safest place for Chamberlain's brigade was closer to the Rebel lines. The Confederate artillerists could only depress the muzzles of their guns so far down; the closer Chamberlain's men got to the Confederates, the less artillery fire they would have to endure. The morass slowed the men down and made them easy targets; they had to get through it quickly. Apparently seeing an easier way through the swamp, Chamberlain turned his right side to the enemy and motioned with his saber for the men to oblique to the left. *I am in the right place, & no harm can come to me unless it is wisely & kindly ordered so. I try to be equal to my duty & ready for anything that may come.*[54]

From the top of the rise in the breastworks, a Confederate soldier fired too low. His bullet hit a rock somewhere under the swampy ground of the gully, ricocheted upward, and struck Chamberlain in the low side of his right hip, just in front of the hipbone. It missed the bone but passed through his lower abdomen, traveling diagonally backward, nicking the bladder and urethra and doing more damage inside than the entrance wound would indicate. Soft lead minié balls sometimes became misshapen when they struck flesh; surgeons of the day noticed that interior human organs tended to evacuate rapidly from a minié ball's hot path, literally tearing themselves apart. The ball came to rest just under the skin at Chamberlain's other hip, behind the bone.[55]

Chamberlain felt the dull electriclike shock to the nervous system from being struck. The pain hit him first in his back. Blood gushed from his hips and began its sticky course down the inside of his pant legs. Afraid that if he fell his men would lose heart for the charge or halt to help him, he jammed his saber into the ground before him as a makeshift cane. He continued to stand rigid as the men broke ranks around him

*This Confederate minié ball struck Chamberlain at Rives'
Salient.* PEJEPSCOT HISTORICAL SOCIETY

and moved toward the Rebel lines. Watching them, Chamberlain sank to
one knee from the shock and loss of blood. Then he fell to the other
knee, then sagged to the muddy quagmire in a heap.[56] *You need not worry
if you hear of a battle, until you know that I was in it; If I am injured, you will
hear at once. I expect to get some sort of a scratch when we "go in," but the
chances are it will not be serious if anything.*[57]

DeLacy wrote:
   I am not clear as to the spot where you fell and received your terrible wound; it has always been my impression that it was near the
gulch washed out by that small stream on the top of the bank. You
directed us through that swamp or swale and for that reason you did
not see the break and recoil of the 187th regiment under the terrific
fire. However to the everlasting credit of the officers and men they
were rallied and brought back under the same galling fire, which
accounts for the fearful loss of that regiment, but it spoiled the effect
of the main charge. The old regiments were unsupported, but they
clung to their position with great tenacity nearly all night, or until
after I had been sent back for orders by Col. Glenn who appeared to
be the only commanding officer of any note on the front line at the
time that had not lost his head; but cool and collected that brave
officer formed us in a little depression in the ground in a half circle,
and let the boys use their muskets as best they could.

Chamberlain was wounded near this small stream and gulch.
AUTHOR PHOTO

The rebel gunners depressed their guns all they possibly could in our front and continued the fire until their infantry and a lot of batteries opened on our left which swept the entire field with an enfilading fire that was terrible to encounter.[58]

Two of Chamberlain's aides—Lt. West Funk and Lt. Benjamin Walters—spotted him down in the muck. Into the maelstrom they ran and dragged the seriously wounded Chamberlain out of relative danger. But there were no safe places on that field. Chamberlain immediately had orders for the two officers: inform the senior officer in the brigade that he was now in command, and get support for Capt. John Bigelow's artillery on the ridge behind them for the anticipated countercharge by the Confederates. The officers left and Chamberlain lay there alone, bleeding into the Virginia clay, for nearly an hour. "I am not of Virginia blood," he would pun darkly nearly a half century later, "she is of mine."[59]

Bigelow found out that Chamberlain was wounded and sent some of his artillerists to retrieve him. Chamberlain, however, thought he was dying and that the gunners should go after other, more hopeful cases that lay scattered about. But the men had their orders from Captain Bigelow. They loaded him on their stretcher and carried him through a sudden artillery bombardment that covered them with more mud and dirt. They put him behind the guns of Bigelow's 9th Massachusetts Battery.

The rest of the brigade lay huddled in whatever sheltering swales their officers could find until about 3:00 A.M., then made their way back to the ridge where the charge started. They were "almost completely worn out," remembered DeLacy, "after having passed through the most terrible ordeal of their lives in the past twenty-four hours. The men who were there, can never forget it."[60]

The division hospital where Chamberlain was taken was three miles back from the lines. Lying on the amputation table when they brought Chamberlain in was Corporal Stettler, who had been wounded in the shell burst that had dismounted Chamberlain. Stettler was quickly laid to the side for the officer, an action that brought rebuke from Chamberlain and everlasting admiration from Stettler. According to DeLacy, Stettler "well remembers, and he has so stated to me several times what you said to the surgeon at the time: 'Lay me one side; I am all right. Go and take care of my dear boys.' But the doctors went in and laid James Stettler one side and placed you on the table in spite of your protests. Comrade Stettler says he can never forget the incident."[61]

It had been several hours since Chamberlain's wounding.[62] In the interim, word of the incident had reached the 20th Maine and Chamberlain's brother Tom. The younger Chamberlain rounded up two surgeons he respected and made his way through the night, past hospital after hospital brimming with wounded from the day's fighting, until he found his brother. The surgeon who had initially examined Chamberlain's wound—probably with the twelve-inch steel probe common to the surgeon's kit—gave his brother the heartbreaking news: He saw no chance of recovery. The ball had torn up too many internal vessels, and the bladder and urethra were involved. Civil War–era surgeons could amputate arms and legs in their field hospitals, but internal operations were practically impossible under the conditions. Normally they just left a gut-shot soldier until he died.[63]

But Tom had brought along two more pairs of skilled surgeons' hands, Dr. Shaw from the 20th Maine and Dr. Townsend from the 44th New York, and they would do what they could. Halfway through the operation, the pain became sheer torture, and the surgeons laid down their instruments, thinking that the agony had gone on long enough. But the patient himself encouraged them to go on, and they did, reconnecting severed organs and removing the minié ball that had done so much damage. Still, hope for recovery was nearly nonexistent.[64]

Generals Warren and Griffin looked in on their suffering subordinate and sent word up the chain of command requesting a promotion to brigadier general for the dying volunteer officer.[65] Grant got word of the request, remembered the numerous other times Chamberlain had been recommended, and "promoted him on the spot," as Grant recalled in his *Memoirs*.

The day after his wounding, still suffering physically, he put at least his mind to rest.

June 19th 1864

My darling wife

I am lying mortally wounded the doctors think, but my mind & heart are at peace Jesus Christ is my all sufficient savior. I go to him. God bless & keep & comfort you, precious one, you have been a precious wife to me. To know & love you makes life & death beautiful. Cherish the darlings & give my love to all the dear ones Do not grieve too much for me. We shall all soon meet Live for the children Give my dearest love to Father & mother & Sallie & John Oh how happy to feel yourself forgiven God bless you evermore precious precious one

Ever
yours
Lawrence[66]

Chamberlain did not know it, but Fanny was carrying another child. If Fanny herself did not know it then, she certainly knew soon enough, perhaps by the day she received his letter or in the ensuing weeks when the doctors determined that he would not recover. What a horrible burden this brief, seemingly last note brought with it.

He was sent to City Point the next day and placed on the hospital ship *Connecticut*. Via the James River, then the Chesapeake Bay, he was transported to the Naval Hospital in Annapolis, Maryland.[67]

For more than two weeks, Chamberlain hung on tenaciously. Maj. Charles D. Gilmore, still stationed in Washington, where he had served with Chamberlain on court martial duty, hand delivered Chamberlain's commission as brigadier general from Secretary of War Edwin Stanton, along with a copy of a resolution passed by the Senate confirming it.[68] The response from Chamberlain was written in a different hand and signed by Chamberlain.

Annapolis Md July 4th 1864

Brig. Gen. L. Thomas
Adjt Gen U.S.A.
General;

I have the honor to acknowledge the receipt this day of a Commission as Brigadier General of Volunteers. I hereby respectfully tender my acceptance of the same.

My Age is thirty five (35) years.
Native State, Maine
Present Residence, Brunswick, Maine
Full name, Joshua Lawrence Chamberlain

I have the honor to be,
Very Respectfully
Your obedient Servant
J. L. Chamberlain
Col. 20th Maine Vols[69]

The promotion to general had been long in coming. When it came, it was almost too late. After Gilmore visited Chamberlain, he wrote a letter on July 5, 1864, to General Hodsdon, adjutant general of Maine, describing Chamberlain's condition.

His wound is a very severe one and a very dangerous one, the surgeons are by no means certain of saving his life, the ball passed through the lower part of the abdomen and severed the Uretha [*sic*] so near the bladder that by no artificial means can all the urine be conducted from the bladder without some of it escaping and passing out through the wounds at the opening, which is on the right side of the right leg, two inches below the hip joint. It is feared that ulcers will form in the Abdomen & terminate his life—[70]

But Chamberlain began to recover. His brother John wrote to Hodsdon on July 22, 1864, from Annapolis. Hodsdon had given John a letter that expedited his passage to visit Lawrence. After thanking Hodsdon for his help, John wrote:

In my dispatch from Bangor I stated that Gen Chamberlain was worse. It seems there was a crisis in his case about that time. I am happy to inform you it turned favorably, and on my arrival here last Saturday I found him in a comfortable condition. Since then he has gained perceptibly every day, and everything has worked as favorably as possible. The most excruciating of his pains have ceased, and his wounds have healed greatly; on the left side entirely. His internal difficulties, which are the most serious, have so far adjusted themselves, under his skillful treatment, that we feel quite assured of his recovery.

The General holds his strength wonderfully, both of body and mind. He bears his sufferings with patience and calmness, in full confidence he shall soon be able to resume his duties in the field....

The Surgeon who has just come in tells me I can assure Gen Chamberlain's friends in Maine that his danger is considered passed, and his recovery certain.[71]

Chamberlain's recovery, as indicated by the following letter, was coming along slowly but optimistically. After receiving a glowing letter from his governor, Chamberlain characteristically limits his discussion of his own recovery to one small paragraph and spends most of the letter lobbying for a fellow officer in the 20th Maine and expressing hope that his health will not prevent him from returning home to vote. Until then, he will do his best to assure that every solid Union man who is able, will be sent home to participate in the election. If he could not participate in saving the country on the battlefield, Chamberlain would do it from his hospital bed.

The last paragraph fairly sums up Chamberlain's patriotic feelings for his country in a symbolism typical of the Victorian era.

U. S. General Hospital
Annapolis, Md. Aug. 31st 1864

Dear Governor,

Capt. P. M. Fogler of the 20th Regt. has written me expressing some grief that he was not appointed Major of the Regt. and asking me to recommend him to you for appointment in some new organization.

I am not aware that any such organizations are proposed, but I cheerfully (as in duty bound) bear testimony to the merits of an officer who has endeavored to honor his profession.

Capt. Fogler has taken pains to acquaint himself with the duties of his position. He is a thorough tactician & takes excellent care of his men, and I have never known him to fail under fire. Sometime ago he was examined before Genl. Casey's board, & passed for a first class Major of colored troops. He has been in daily expectation since, of receiving his assignment. Other things being equal, he was perhaps entitled to expect promotion in his own Regiment.

In view of peculiar circumstances, however, connected with our Regimental history, it was feared he would be wholly unable to exercise proper command over some of the other officers, and for this reason he was not recommended.

But there is no objection that I am aware of to his appointment to a Field position in a new organization. On the contrary he is so conversant with all that is required in the organization & drill of troops, that he would no doubt be an efficient and valuable officer, in such a place.

In response to your inquiry as to a brother of the late Capt. Keene, I doubt if I am acquainted with him, but if he is as good a man as the rest of the family he must be deserving of the place he seeks.

My recovery is going on slowly. I am able to sit up a good part of the day & am assured that time only is needed to complete my restoration to health.

I am trying to get on fast enough to go to Maine in season for the coming election, but I am afraid I shall fail in that. However I have been doing what I could here, looking up soldiers in the hospital who are true to the Country's cause in order to have them sent home to vote.

I hope the prospect is good for us, but I feel that every one should do all he can to keep old Maine steady in the front rank of patriots.

Allow me to thank you for your letter—hearty and affectionate beyond the custom of epistles of condolence or congratulation, even among friends. I assure you I place this among my treasures and trophies—kept for my children—& not the least (if you will permit me) among the "laurels" of which you so kindly speak.

I long to be in the field again doing my part to keep the old flag up, with all its stars.

Your friend & servant

J. L. Chamberlain[72]

One of the most revealing of all of Chamberlain's writings is a fragment of a letter, probably written in the fall of 1864, possibly around the time of his birthday, September 8.[73]

. . . yet, I confess. Not a selfish ambition: for I assure you not all the honors & titles that can be given or won, would tempt me to hazard the happiness and welfare of any dear ones at home, nor would they be any equivalent whatever, for these terrible wounds as must cast a shadow over the remainder of my days, even though I should apparently recover.

But what it is, I cant tell you. I haven't a particle of fanaticism in me. But I plead guilty to a sort of fatalism. I believe in a destiny—one, I mean, divinely appointed, & to which we are carried forward by a perfect trust in God. I do this, & I believe in it. I have laid plans, in my day, & good ones I thought. But they never succeeded. Something else, better, did, and I could see it as plain as day, that God had done it, & for my good.

So I am right, be sure of that, happen what may. Not for any merit of mine, but for divine & loving mercy all is bright with me, in this world & beyond.

So dear mother, with a more appreciative love and a growing gratitude towards my Parents, as I recount their faithful care & unfathomed kindness & the trust that I may never do dishonor to their name, I am your obedient & loving son,

Lawrence.[74]

While continuing to recover, Chamberlain wrote a letter to the governor in behalf of a comrade.

Officer's Hospital,
Annapolis, Md.
Sept 22 1864

His Excellency,
Samuel Cony Gov. of Maine,
Governor,

I have the honor to address you in behalf of Capt. A. B. Twitchell of the 7th Maine Battery, who writes me that he is proposed as Major of the Light Artillery Regt. from our State.

I am well acquainted with Capt. Twitchell and know what his reputation is in the Army, and I can conscientiously and cordially say that I know of no officer in that arm of the service whose ability, experience, and services are so worthy of your favorable notice as his.

I am sure his promotion would be deserved on his part, and creditable to the State and Service. I take a particular interest in Captain Twitchell on account of the high character which he every where so nobly maintains. He is a true man.

> I have the honor to be
> Very respectfully
> Your friend & servt.
> J. L. Chamberlain
> Brig. Genl.[75]

Shortly after writing this letter, Chamberlain returned home to Brunswick on furlough. Certainly there was some wonderful tonic in spending time at home with his family. By November 18, 1864, in spite of the serious nature of his wound and the continual pain and discomfort, Chamberlain had—incredibly—returned to active duty in the field.[76]

His new command, officially designated the 1st Brigade, 1st Division, 5th Army Corps was smaller than the brigade he had last commanded at Petersburg. It consisted of only two large regiments, the 185th New York Infantry, commanded by Col. Gustavus Sniper, and the 198th Pennsylvania, under Brig. Gen. Horatio Sickel.[77]

Three weeks after he returned to the army, the 5th Corps began a campaign against a major supply route of the Confederate army now solidly ensconced in and around Petersburg. On the morning of December 7 the 5th Corps—supported by artillery, a division of cavalry and additional infantry from the 2nd Corps—began a raid on the Weldon Railroad.[78]

On December 8 they began destroying the railroad below the Nottoway River. The next day they destroyed the tracks all the way to the Meherrin River—a distance of twenty-five miles—until they found the railroad fortified by the enemy. A dispatch from the field transmitting Chamberlain's orders—one of few in existence—shows the difference between terse field orders dictated and scribbled against the pommel of a saddle and often flowery, verbose after-action reports.

> Head Qrs 1st Brig
> Dec 8, 1864
> 9:30 P.M.
> The skirmish line will at once commence moving by the left flank on its present line to cover the Division which is now working

below Jarrets Station. The line will move at least <u>one mile.</u> The Reserves will move near the Rail road, & will pass 100 yards below Jarrets. The movement will commence <u>on the right</u> so as to bring the men together, instead of separating them. Battalion commanders will execute this movement, & report when it is completed by note or otherwise, to the Gen Commanding at Jarrets Station. The officer on the right will give notice of this movement to Genl Crawford's officer with whom he connects.

By Comd of
Brig Genl Chamberlain
John F. Farrons
AAG[79]

During the advance, the men were allowed to forage. Many of them found stores of liquor in private houses and began to indulge. March discipline broke down, and a number of men (from brigades other than Chamberlain's) disappeared from the ranks. It was dangerous for individual soldiers to be alone in hostile territory, wintertime notwithstanding.[80] The night of December 9 it began to snow, turning into freezing rain. Stragglers were at the mercy of the elements, as well as in danger from the locals. On December 10 the column began the march back.

The men were miserable, many hung over from the sweet apple and peach brandy they had drunk. Marching was very difficult on the icy roads. Then they found the first of the Union stragglers, stripped naked and their throats slashed by bushwackers, civilians extracting revenge on the invading army.

In retaliation, the soldiers burned the homes, barns, and outbuildings of civilians for a half mile on either side of the Union march route, possibly punishing the miscreants, but doubtless punishing many more innocents, leaving them without shelter for miles around in the dead of winter.[81] Chamberlain expresses his distress over the incident in a letter to his sister.[82]

Wednesday Eve. [possibly December 14, 1864][83]

My Dear Sae,

Thank you for your valuable anti[ill.] & & [*sic*] hints. A woman knows so much more than a man, after all. I wrote you another letter almost exactly the same night totally different in the turn &

bearing of it. You would be much amused to see how the same words could be made to do such different duty.

We have just returned from a "raid," (I suppose it would be called,) towards the North Carolina line for the purpose of destroying the Weldon Rail Road. We had a hard time, but were perfectly successful in our object. I'll tell you how we destroyed the road.

The roads are very perfectly laid here, & you cant tear them up rail by rail. Not only are these securely fastened to the "chairs" as they are called but the rails are riveted together by strong wrought iron bars which connect the joints passing under the hollow—for the rail is in this shape, seen endwise—[drawing inserted]. So you see the rail is one continuous whole. Well now you take a Regt. or Brigade & form them along the track. Select a spot where the rail is easiest to get at, & all hands in that vicinity take hold & raise it up—up—until over it goes, upside down with the sleepers or "cross ties" still attached & on top. Mind you the rail does not break, but as it goes over of course it lifts a portion from the ground & as this comes up it is seized by the men & passed along, so there will be one successive & unbroken roll for perhaps a mile—just as a plough share turns a furrow—and it is very quickly done too. The next thing is to pry the rails off the ties; break the joints by 20 or 30 men taking hold & swaying to & fro. The ties are piled up to a sharp ridge & the rails laid across the top, balanced so that the weight of the ends will bend the rail nearly double when heated. Then set fire, & you see a grand sight. The next morning you see a ruin. [drawing inserted] This is the shape of the pile [drawing inserted] This is what you are left in the morning. The bent & useless rails. Well, we left 20 miles in that shape. The Rebels sent a large force to cut us off, but we out marched, & out witted them. Our stragglers fared hard when caught by the enemy's scouts & guerrillas. In fact they were murdered—their throats cut from ear to ear. Several of our men were found in this condition who had straggled a little from the column to cut a corner or something of that sort. In retaliation our men on our return burnt almost every house on the road. This was a hard night. Our men got very much exasperated & one day when I brought up the rear, I saw sad work in protecting helpless women & children from outrage, when the Rebels had been firing from their houses on us, & the men were bent on revenge. I invariably gave them the protection which every man of honor will give any woman as long as she is a woman. But I have no doubt they were all "burnt out" before the whole army got by. It was sad business. I am willing to fight men in arms, but not <u>babes</u> in <u>arms.</u> [ill.] Lawrence.

The questions will be answered next time [inserted at the top of the first page, but obviously the last thing he wrote in this letter.][84]

The burning of civilian homes affected Chamberlain deeply. Nearly a week later, in a letter to his brother John, he mentions the depredations again, and also reveals the state of his health.

> Head Qrs. 1st Brig. 1st Div. 5th Corps.
> Dec. 19th 1864

Dear John,

I was very glad to find out exactly where you are. I think it was a good move on your part, to go to New York. It is vexatious to know that nobody in Bangor took any pains to make friends for you in New York. However you will find them, & I have no doubt can afford to dispense with testimonials from anybody. I am not at all anxious for you to get into the traces of a minister's drudgery at once. It is better to take time & prepare a good pile of sermons in advance. The "two sermons a week" routine would kill you. So I would write one a week now, & finish them by retouching after preaching them once or twice, so that you may have confidence in them whenever you have to fall back on them.

I should like it if you could go to Washington, though I suspect that is a pretty difficult post to take charge of, on account of the loose way in which things are done there. I think better of those towns in the vicinity of New York City, for your present circumstances: as a pastoral change there would not be so trying. However strike as high as you can.

For me, I am managing to do full duty without much injury, & not a great deal of suffering. Still I "was not fit" to return to field duty, & it is very hard to take such chances as we had on the "Weldon raid."

By the way, we never intended to go to Weldon. Our task was to destroy the Railroad as far as Hicksford, & we did it pretty thoroughly, & with very little loss. Our stragglers were the chief sufferers. Those who went aside from the column, or fell behind it were murdered without mercy, and that unfortunately roused a spirit of retaliation & the result was the burning of all the houses on our road back. It was a sad sight, & showed war in its most disagreeable aspect; for my part I had rather charge lines of battle.

I ride some, too much, probably & to tell the truth, I don't feel right yet, though the "Herald" proclaims my "perfect recovery" & all that. I shall have to take to the knife again, & am making up my mind where to have it done, that is, the "knifing."

Tom is well. Somehow his Brevet didn't come with the rest. It is no doubt some mistake & will be rectified. They are managing those Brevets, so that they don't amount to anything. Gen. Bartlett is going away & I am to have the old 3rd Brigade of 8 old Regts. That will make me the Senior General officer of the Div. Six months ago I was not even the Senior Colonel of my Brigade, & was assigned to command over the heads of three or four others. If I only didn't have to go away this minute, I should stand a good chance among Brigadiers. And as it is, I am well enough off. Gen. Griffin won't let anybody come & rank me. I trust all your affairs are prosperous.

With much love,
Lawrence.[85]

⇥ 1865 ⇤

The winnowings of life and death must go on till the troubles be sifted to the core.
—Maj. Gen. Joshua L. Chamberlain, *The Passing of the Armies*

By January 15, 1865, Chamberlain still had not completely recovered from his wound of the previous summer. He went to Philadelphia for additional surgery, then to Brunswick for recuperation.[1] While there, he received some offers for civilian positions. In addition, Fanny had given birth to another daughter, giving him more incentive—even an excuse—not to return to the mortal danger he would face in the warfare being waged in Virginia. But in spite of both the added responsibility and the pain he was daily enduring, his feelings of patriotism remained.

Brunswick, Feby. 12th 1865.

Dear Father,

Though still confined mostly to my room, I am fast recovering, and by proper caution think I shall be able to get away by the first of next week. I am anxious to be back with my command; if I am to hold my position there I want to be at any post. The campaign will soon open, & it will open strong.

I have been considering the past week whether to accept the office of Collector of Customs in the District of Bath, which has been offered me. I believe it is considered a very good position, second only to the similar one in Portland held by Governor Washburn.

I do not at present encourage the idea, preferring, if possible, to continue my duties in the Field, where my services were never more needed, or more valuable than now. I shall probably resign my professorship here this summer, and be ready to throw myself on the current of affairs, & either remain in the military service (as is most congenial to my temperament) or strike into some other enterprise of a more bold & stirring character than a College chair affords. I take no steps at present, waiting to see how my wounds are going to turn.

I enjoyed your letter much, but was sorry to hear, both from you & from Mother, that Thomas was so restless & roving while at home. However, I think you need have no fears of his indulging any incorrect habits whatever.

He annoys me chiefly by being too sensitive, & allowing a few cowardly fellows disturb his peace of mind. It is more creditable and more safe to have such men enemies than friends, & in my opinion it will be a good thing for him to have to stand his hand away men just as they come [*sic*].

Fanny & the baby are doing well. We should all be glad to see Mother, if she will make us a visit, though we are in no particular need of her care & attention. We have a warm house, which she will appreciate, & plenty of things in it, & I think she might enjoy a visit well, if disposed to come. I do not think it advisable for me to go to Brewer this time, as I am so much over my time of leave for the army.

Your aff. son

Lawrence.[2]

Chamberlain's parents seem to have been fairly adamant about their desire for him to return to civilian life.[3] It certainly would have made sense for him to withdraw from active field service to take care of his young family, to sleep every night in a warm house, and to allow his health to recover. But his next letter to his father shows his strong patriotism and adherence to duty.

Brunswick Feb. 20th. 1865.

Dear Father,

I appreciate fully the view you & Mother take of the Collectorship offered me. It is natural and proper advice, & such as I certainly expected. But my own consideration of the subject has not, as yet, brought me to favor the proposal any more than at first.

I owe the Country three years service. It is a time when every man should stand by his guns. And I am not scared or hurt enough yet to be willing to face to the rear, when other men are marching to the front.

It is true my incomplete recovery from my wounds would make a more quiet life desirable, & when I think of my young & dependent family the whole strength of that motive to make the most of my life comes over me.

But there is no promise of life in peace, & no decree of death in war. And I am so confident of the sincerity of my motives that I can trust my own life & the welfare of my family in the hands of Providence.

And then as far as these human probabilities go, my position & prospects in the Army were never better. I am now among the Senior officers of my rank. And after all I have gone through, I am not willing to back out just at the decisive moment, & leave the rewards & honors of my toil & sufferings to others. I had a great deal rather see another man in that Custom House, than see another next commander of the 1st Division. Nor will my claims be any less for an honorable post in civil life after still longer & better service in the Field, nor for having declined advantageous offers for myself personally, rather than to abandon our cause in the hour of its need.

At all events I must return to the army, and if I find I cannot stand it I shall not be foolish about it but shall take proper care of myself.

I shall leave tomorrow. Have not yet been out of the house, but think I can bear the journey. Am sorry not to have seen you before leaving. Will write as soon as I reach the front.

Your aff. son,
Lawrence.[4]

On February 21, 1865, Chamberlain began his last journey to rejoin his beloved Army of the Potomac. He would receive the command of a new brigade consisting of two new regiments, the 185th New York and the 198th Pennsylvania. He would lead additional assaults, would be in mortal danger again and again, would be wounded two more times, and would be offered perhaps the greatest honor of any officer in the Army of the Potomac.

But before the honor came the mundane routine of military life. A clerical misunderstanding prompted Chamberlain's letter to the assistant adjutant general of the division.

> Head Quarters 1st Brig. 1st Div. 5th Corps.[5]
> March 2nd 1865.
>
> Captain:
>
> I respectfully ask permission to state in regard to furloughs this day returned by order of the Major General Commdg. Division, that the number of applications pending, together with furloughs already granted, in this Brigade, is not in excess of the per centage allowed in Special Orders No 11—Hd. Qrs. Army of the Potomac. The maximum there fixed is 5 pr. cent.
>
> The 198th Regt. has present for duty, 1050 enlisted men, which would allow 52 furloughs.—The 185th 700—which would allow 35 furloughs.
>
> The furloughs returned were all forwarded previous to my resuming command of the Brigade; but while the urgency of some of these cases may not have been made sufficiently apparent, I am unwilling to have it appear that there has been culpable inattention and negligence at these Head Quarters in forwarding papers in violation of orders. (Over)
>
> I have the honor to be
> Very Respectfully
> Your Obdt. Servt.
> J. L. Chamberlain,
> Brig. General
> Commdg.
> Capt. William Fowler
> AAAG. 1st Div. }[6]

These last frenetic weeks in the army would eventually be recorded in the only book Chamberlain wrote about his experiences in the war, *The Passing of the Armies.*[7] The book, which covered only his last two and a half months in the service, was one of the most moving and eloquent pieces written on the war. In Chamberlain's eyes, his own impressive role in the conflict was merely a reflection of who and what really won the war: the men; the army.

Before he wrote his book, he delivered numerous speeches before his old veterans. That helped him hone his historical facts and his wording. But the work as a whole is woven through with a sort of spirituality, a recognition of the other world to which so many of his comrades had passed. It was an appropriate tone for a man who was approaching his own death in 1914 and who had nearly touched it many times in his younger years.[8]

The genesis of a few of the phrases that appear in his book can be seen in his last letters of the war period.

> Head Qrs. 1st Brigade
> Hatcher's Run
> March 9, 1865

My dear Sae,

I have been back about ten days now, and find the change very agreeable so far as my health is concerned. I was detained in Philadelphia by the state of my wounds; but that misfortune proved a good fortune; for besides the warm courtesies & compliments I received from every body there, I found the services of Dr. Pancoast—the most skilful [*sic*] surgeon in the United States—not only relieved my existing disabilities, but put me in the mood of a more rapid recovery.

You cannot imagine how favorable this kind of life is to my health. One would not think me fit to walk a half mile if I was home; but here I ride as fast & far as the best, and ask no favors. I have no doubt that my recovery will be greatly promoted by my return to the field, and I do not in the least regret my choice. I shall not feel obliged to lead any more charges, unless it becomes necessary, & hope to escape any further injuries. I have no insane desire to deprive my little family of any protection & support I assure you. On the contrary, I look forward with delight to a speedy return to the happiness and affection of my little home.

No man's ever was dearer or more blest. And to no man could it be a greater sacrifice to leave them far away and face the dangers which in threatening me threaten them tenfold. Still let me say the course I take is not only that which honor & manliness prompt, but the one which will prove best for <u>them</u> & for all who belong to me or to whom I belong.

Please understand that my wounds are now doing finely, and I am encouraged to hope I may not have to leave the field again till we finish the campaign. I was sorry indeed to lose the pleasure of visiting you, but you know I did not set foot out of doors while I was at home.

Give my dutiful love to Father & Mother, & my undiminished regards to all. Tom is finely. He has been making a great dash with his horsemanship today at a grand Review in the presence of distinguished spectators, ladies &c. His horse "slumped" into the treacherous ground while he was going on the "wings of the wind," & fell & rolled over & over; but Tom alighted on his feet as light as a cat & won great praise from all. Ask Aunt Hannah if I do not owe her a years interest? Hoping to hear from you soon & that you are well.

Your afftc. [*sic*] brother,
Lawrence.[9]

In February there had been a fight near Hatcher's Run, a small stream running in a broad west-to-east semicircle eight miles north of the small village of Dinwiddie Court House, Virginia, and a junction called Five Forks. Chamberlain's brigade was there with the rest of the 5th Corps. The brigade was again called in support of two Union divisions caught up in a battle on March 25.

No. 94

Report of Brig. Gen. Joshua L. Chamberlain, U. S. Army, commanding First Brigade, of operations March 25.

Hdqrs. First Brigade, First Division, 5th Corps,
    Near Hatcher's Run, Va, March 28, 1865.

Captain: In compliance with orders this day received, I have the honor to submit a report of the operations of this command on the 25th instant.

The First Brigade moved out at about 8 o'clock a.m. (following the Third Brigade) in the direction of Third Division headquarters. Remaining massed in that vicinity for a few hours, we then moved to our left, passed the line of works occupied by the Second Division, Second Corps, and massed near a house known as Mrs. Warren's. Soon after, we moved to the right and massed in rear of General Miles' division of the Second Corps. At about 3 p.m. I was ordered to return to the Warren house and report to Major-General Mott. Arriving there I received the order from Major-General Humphreys to move directly to the front. I moved by the right flank along a narrow road through the slashing, and on reaching the thin belt of woods in front of which General Mott's line was formed and in a position to overlook this line, I was directed by General Humphreys to halt. In this position I remained for about two hours, during which there was some skirmishing along the line, with some artillery firing from the right and left and from a battery directly in our front. I could distinctly see the men working at one of their guns.

At about dusk there was very heavy firing to the right of our position, and in the midst of this an advance was made by the enemy in our front with great vigor and boldness, though not in heavy force. Our skirmishers were driven back in confusion, and the enemy were close upon the main line and advancing with spirit. As I feared they might follow up their attack with sufficient force to break through the main line, I immediately ordered Brevet Brigadier-General Sickel to form "forward into line" at a double-quick with his two battalions of the One hundred and ninety-eighth Pennsylvania Volunteers, and to occupy the edge of woods close in rear of General Mott's line, and in full sight of the enemy, which was promptly done. At the same time General Humphreys requested me to strengthen General Mott's right, which was then very hard pressed. I directed Colonel Sniper, commanding the One hundred and eighty-fifth New York Volunteers, to move up rapidly to the front line and occupy the space between General Mott's and General Miles' divisions, which he did, his center being nearly in front of the Watkins house.

Simultaneously with these movements of General Sickel and Colonel Sniper, the troops of General Mott opened a vigorous fire on the enemy's advancing line, followed by a gallant charge, in which the rebels were handsomely repulsed, with considerable loss on their part in killed, wounded, and prisoners.

My regiments remained in the position last indicated until 9 p.m., when I was ordered to withdraw and to report to Major-General Griffin in camp.

The casualties in my command were as follows: Wounded, 2 privates One hundred and ninety-eighth Pennsylvania Volunteers. The captures from the enemy, 1 lieutenant-colonel, 1 sergeant, 8 privates. These were turned over to the provost-marshall of General Mott's division. The lieutenant-colonel (who was wounded) stated that he was in command of the portion of the attacking party in Colonel Sniper's front, and that it consisted of the Forty-third, Fifty-ninth, and Sixtieth Alabama Regiments.

I have the honor to be, very respectfully, your obedient servant,

J. L. Chamberlain,
Brigadier-General.
Capt. William Fowler,
Assistant Adjutant-General, First Div., 5th Army Corps.[10]

Besides his new brigade, there were a few other changes Chamberlain found when he returned to the army by March 1865. Perhaps the one that would most affect the role of the 5th Corps was the arrival from the Shenandoah Valley of Gen. Philip Sheridan, the hyperactive little cavalryman who, upon his arrival at Grant's headquarters, stated unequivocally, "I'm ready to strike out to-morrow and go to smashing things."[11] Unfortunately, one of the things he smashed was the reputation of 5th Corps commander Maj. Gen. G. K. Warren, an event that would haunt Chamberlain for the rest of his life.

On March 29 the 5th Corps moved out before dawn, marching to its assigned position on the extreme left of Grant's line, extending it to the junction of the Vaughan Road and the Boydton Plank Road near Dinwiddie Court House. The movement was part of Grant's general campaign plan to continue to stretch the Confederate line toward the west as the Southerners attempted to cover the Rebel supply and rail lines leading from the southwest. With its left flank anchored covering Petersburg, the Confederate line grew thinner every mile westward that Grant forced it.

By March 25 Confederates were entrenched from the junction of the White Oak Road and the Boydton Plank Road west along the White Oak Road (which led to Five Forks), roughly paralleling Hatcher's Run.

Chamberlain's personal map of the White Oak Road battle-ground. LIBRARY OF CONGRESS

From here they could cover Claiborne Road leading to Sutherland Station on the South Side Railroad, a supply route into Petersburg. Grant had gotten word from Sheridan that he was near Five Forks on the White Oak Road and decided that there should be an additional push toward that road to the east.[12] Under orders from General Meade (who still technically commanded the Army of the Potomac, though Grant traveled with it), General Warren began moving his 5th Corps about noon on March 29, in column north on the Quaker Road toward the Confederate entrenchments.

Chamberlain and his brigade were leading the march that afternoon when word came back that the bridge on the Quaker Road over Gravelly Run had been destroyed and the Confederates were entrenched on the opposite bank.

Gravelly Run in some places was just a few yards across. But at the Quaker Road crossing, the run was wide and swampy on the west side of the road, and recent rains had made it more so. Chamberlain formulated a plan and got the go-ahead, along with some supporting troops, from Gen. Charles Griffin, his division commander.

Sickel would take eight companies to the right, downstream from the wrecked bridge, and deliver a large volume of fire into the enemy position. Meanwhile, Chamberlain would take the rest of the brigade upstream to ford Gravelly Run where it was waist-deep, and they would come in obliquely on the Confederate right flank.[13]

Quaker Road at Gravelly Run, where Chamberlain crossed to attack the Confederate right flank on March 29, 1865. AUTHOR PHOTO

Chamberlain wrote in later years that the encounter was hand-to-hand, the attack impetuous. The entire brigade swept across the stream, then pushed the Confederates from their works and drove them a mile or so back to some buildings on a farm owned by the Lewis family. The Confederates were reinforced there and had the additional protection of breastworks thrown up along the edge of a wood behind them, to which they could retreat and re-form. As Chamberlain's brigade reached the Lewis farm, the men took what the general called a "withering" volley and recoiled, but they still maintained the discipline to carry off their dead and wounded.

The Confederates took advantage of this backward movement and rushed to attack Chamberlain's retreating line. The fight turned again into scattered hand-to-hand encounters, and the Confederates were repulsed. The Confederate line was reinforced, which made it wider and deeper than Chamberlain's, but the Union troops attacked the line vigorously and cleared the field. Chamberlain re-formed his lines on each side of the Lewis farm buildings.[14]

Griffin was there and was anxious about moving on the White Oak Road and Boydton Plank Road juncture. Chamberlain formed his new line with the right commanded by General Sickel and the left by Colonel

Sniper. Chamberlain went to the center with Maj. Edwin Glenn and the six companies under his command. They were to charge straight up the Quaker Road. So much for Chamberlain's reflection to his sister Sae just twenty days before: "I shall not feel obliged to lead any more charges, unless it becomes necessary, & hope to escape any further injuries."[15]

A steam-powered, portable sawmill had stood next to the road in the center of the Confederates' advance line. Near the site remained a large pile of sawdust that gave the Confederates some cover. Chamberlain's men advanced in spite of heavy fire from the enemy line and from sharpshooters nested in the trees, then stopped to deliver their own fire. During this fight, Chamberlain received his second wound. He recalled nearly fifty years later:

> In the full crescendo of this, now close to the sawdust pile, my horse, wild for the front, all his pulses aglow, was exceeding the possible pace of the men following and I gave him a vigorous check on the curb. Resenting this, he touched his fore feet to the earth only to rebound head-high to the level of my face. Just at that instant a heavy blow struck me on the left breast just below the heart. I fell forward on my horse's neck and lost all consciousness. The bullet at close range had been aimed at my breast, but the horse had lifted his head just in time to catch it, so that, passing through the big muscle of his neck (also I may say through a leather case of field orders and a brass-mounted hand-mirror in my breast-pocket—we didn't carry towels in this campaign), demolished the pistol in the belt of my aide Lieutenant Vogel, and knocked him out of the saddle. This, of course, I only knew afterwards.[16]

Chamberlain described his wound: "The bullet had riddled my sleeve to the elbow and bruised and battered my bridle arm [the left arm] so that it was useless, and the obstructions it met had slightly deflected it so that, instead of striking the point of my heart, it had followed around two ribs so as to come out at the back seam of my coat."[17]

Chamberlain, covered with his own and his horse Charlemagne's[18] blood, recovered consciousness, still mounted but supported by General Griffin, who had ridden up. Griffin, thinking Chamberlain was mortally wounded, said, "My dear General, you are gone." But through the foggy consciousness, Chamberlain heard the Rebel yell and turned to see the right of his line tumbling back. He took Griffin's meaning differently:

"Yes, General, I am," he said and, to Griffin's surprise and shock, galloped off to the danger point.[19]

He found Sickel attempting to rally his men; in a minute, Sickel was shot through the arm. The regiment re-formed and went back at the Confederates with a yell. Chamberlain returned to the center to a greeting of cheers from the men as he passed. Strangest of all, as the Confederates saw him riding back to the center, they cheered him as well.

Charlemagne was spent from loss of blood, and Chamberlain dismounted. He elbowed his way to the front of the mass of men near the sawdust pile, nearly being captured in the confusion as he did, and looked to the left to see Sniper's men slowly falling back and being pursued by the Rebels coming out of their breastworks. Someone loaned Chamberlain a horse, and he rode to the endangered left.

Chamberlain found Sniper, sent for reinforcements, and got word from Griffin that a battery would be up in ten minutes. He shouted to Sniper so the men would hear: "Once more! Try the steel! Hell for ten minutes and we are out of it!"[20]

At his words, Sniper's men surged and drove the Confederates back into their breastworks. Chamberlain saw Battery B, 4th U.S. Artillery, come dashing up, the horses steaming and earth flying off the wheels. He rode to the battery, helped place it in position, and made sure it could fire over the heads of his men without inflicting damage to his brigade.

The battery poured fire into the woods around the Confederate breastworks and destroyed an attempted flank attack. The commander of the battery leaped onto a gun carriage after recoil to view the effect of his fire, but the enemy shot him off the gun.

Reinforcements came up and the Union troops regained the momentum, driving the Confederates from the woods and trenches, sending them running up the road to their main works on the White Oak Road.

Years later Chamberlain realized that with 2,700 men, including artillery, he had been fighting four brigades numbering 6,277 officers and men.[21]

The battle was over and the adrenaline subsiding. Chamberlain suddenly felt so weak and sore that he could hardly stand up. But gathering some strength from his deep sense of duty and compassion, he saw to his wounded horse and walked out onto the dusky battlefield. He stopped now and then, speaking tenderly to the wounded. He came upon Sickel, weak from loss of blood, his arm shattered. Sitting down next to him, he tried to cheer him up with a few words, but Sickel was the one who was eloquently inspiring to Chamberlain: "General," he whispered, smiling, "you have the soul of the lion and the heart of the woman."[22]

Chamberlain made his way back to the Lewis farmhouse. There he sat at a "rude kitchen box" and by candlelight wrote a letter that was to break a family's hearts. In the letter he addressed "dear, high-souled Doctor McEuen of Philadelphia, remembering his last words commending to my care his only son, with the beseeching, almost consecrating hands laid on my shoulder," and told him of the death of his heir: "To tell him how, in the forefront of battle and in act of heroic devotion, his noble boy had been lifted to his like, and his own cherished hope merged with immortal things."[23] Hundreds of Chamberlain's letters exist in numerous archives. This one too may still exist, tucked between the pages, perhaps, of an old family Bible, describing the end of a young life and, sadder still, perhaps even the end of a lineage.

After several days of clear, road-drying weather, torrential rain began on the evening of March 29, and by the next evening, the roads below Petersburg became like quicksand. Spirits dropped and frustration rose in the ranks. "Men lost their tempers," recalled Grant's staff member Horace Porter, "and those who employed profanity on such occasions as a means of mental relaxation wanted to set up a mark and go to swearing at it."[24]

On March 30 the 5th Corps marched to the Boydton Plank Road and established lines facing the enemy on the White Oak Road. Early the next morning the troops advanced north, beyond the Boydton Plank Road to the Confederate main lines along the White Oak and Claiborne roads. Chamberlain's brigade was on the extreme left of the 5th Corps line.

Though the active campaign kept Chamberlain from writing his reports, he made certain that the men received this congratulatory order.

Head Quarters 1st Brig. 1st Div. 5th Corps[25]
Camp in the field Boydton Plank
March 30, 1865.

General Orders
No. 2}

The General Commanding congratulates troops of the Brigade on their admirable conduct in the engagement of yesterday. The steadiness of their advance, the gallantry of their attack, the courage with which they withstood the repeated assaults of a far superior force of the enemy for nearly two hours, without support, undismayed by the heavy cross fire of the enemy or their own severe losses, the good order which it maintained when compelled to yield ground due to the exhaustion of their ammunition, the handsome manner with which they formed to cover the Artillery have given a character to this Brigade of which the General is proud.

By Command of
Brig. Gen. Chamberlain
Thos. Mitchell,
Actg. Asst. Adjt. Gen.[26]

Chamberlain later wrote that the men were disappointed that Sheridan, for all his aggressiveness, failed to take the vital crossroads of Five Forks at the west end of the White Oak Road when he had the chance.[27]

The Union attack on March 31 began with Gen. Romeyn Ayres's division moving three brigades forward in an inverted V formation. By happenstance, the Confederates had launched an assault at almost the same time. Also by happenstance, one of the Rebel brigades got on the left flank of Ayres's leading brigade and smashed it, causing his entire attack to falter, then retreat in disorder. In retreating, the men broke through the reserve line of Crawford's division and headed for the Boydton Plank Road, where Chamberlain's men waited in reserve with artillery. Warren and Griffin rode up just then and saw the rout. There was an exchange about the honor of the 5th Corps—now in doubt—and a query whether Chamberlain thought he could save it. Warren, the engineer, said he could have a bridge built within the hour across the small, swampy branch of Gravelly Run lying in front of Chamberlain's brigade. With Griffin's comment about the honor of the 5th Corps in mind, Chamberlain said they did not have time to wait for a bridge, and ordered Major Glenn and his 1st Battalion of the 198th Pennsylvania into the chest-deep branch, covered by another battalion beating down resistance with their firing. Once Glenn secured the far bank, Chamberlain followed with his brigade, then another.

More Union brigades followed, including Ayres's re-formed division, and they pushed the Confederates back. There was more sharp fighting when the Rebels stopped to make a stand at the top of a ravine, then a halt on the part of the Union troops when the Confederates retreated into their prepared works. Chamberlain found shelter for his men behind a crest—much like he had done at Rives' Salient—and prepared for a charge. Warren sent word to hold off.

Chamberlain rode back to remonstrate, and after outlining his plan, Warren granted him permission to continue the attack.

Behind a diversionary attack, Chamberlain's men would advance quickly with an open front—no ranks or alignment—to lessen losses. They began the advance, and when they got to three hundred yards— killing distance for rifle-muskets—they rushed the Confederates, leapt their breastworks, swung to the right, and drove them back to their entrenchments on the Claiborne Road. Halting, they planted themselves directly across the White Oak Road facing northeast.

The battle took three hours and cost the Union attackers about one hundred men, but as Chamberlain said, "It was to cost us something more—a sense of fruitlessness and thanklessness."[30]

Firing was heard near Dinwiddie; it sounded like Sheridan was in trouble. A large brigade was sent from the White Oak Road to help him. After dark Chamberlain reconnaissanced the enemy, crawling on his hands and knees with Warren, and discovered exactly where the Confederate line was entrenched. He had his men prepare to stay for the night, and then readied himself to spend all night awake on the picket line.

His plan was to entrench along the White Oak Road to secure a pivot point for Sheridan's troopers to swing around their left and strike the South Side Railroad. But suddenly confusing and contradictory orders began pouring in to Warren from Meade and Grant, all instigated because Sheridan needed help against the Confederates near Five Forks. There would be no sweep by him to the railroad to cut Petersburg's supply line. The final orders were that the 5th Corps was to pull out of its hard-won lines, report to Sheridan immediately, and fall under his command. At daylight the movement commenced.[29]

On the morning of April 1, Griffin and Crawford had massed their divisions near the J. Boisseau house by the juncture of the Crump Road and the road from Dinwiddie Court House to Five Forks. Behind them was Ayres's division. The men rested about four hours.[30]

By one that afternoon Warren had received his orders for attack from Sheridan. His 5th Corps would move north to the Gravelly Run Church Road. There, Crawford's division was placed to the front, with

Detail of Chamberlain's personal map showing part of his route from the White Oak Road to Five Forks, where he was headed to aid Sheridan's forces on April 1, 1865. LIBRARY OF CONGRESS

Griffin's just behind it. When Ayres came up, he went into line to the left of Crawford.

In Griffin's division, Bartlett's brigade formed the left wing and Chamberlain's the right, deployed in triple battle lines. Griffin's other brigade, Gregory's, was used by Chamberlain to extend his right, to cover Griffin's right flank, and to act as skirmishers.[31]

Just before four o'clock all were in position, and Sheridan called his commanders together. He was surly, impatient that the sun would go down before his chance to fight. He pulled his saber and drew for his commanders his battle plan in the sandy Virginia soil, carving into the very land of the enemy a plan that might end the war.

His cavalry was to occupy the enemy with a "demonstration" on the left nearer Five Forks, while the 5th Corps was to swing wide to their right and come in on the Confederates' rear and left flank along the White Oak Road. There was a bend in the Rebel breastworks—a "return"—that ran north from the road for about 150 yards. As Chamberlain recalled the plan later, "Ayres should strike the angle of the 'return,' and Crawford and Griffin sweep around Ayres's right, flanking the Confederate 'return' and enfilading their main line."[32]

The troops formed the assault lines, with Ayres to the left of the Gravelly Run Church Road, two brigades wide with one brigade in reserve; Crawford on the right of the road in a similar formation; and Griffin (in the battle order described above) behind Crawford. At about four o'clock they stepped off.

Chamberlain was concerned because he had just received a map from Warren showing a different route for the attack. Griffin eased Chamberlain's mind: "We will not worry ourselves about diagrams. We are to follow Crawford. Circumstances will soon develop our duty."[33]

As they approached the White Oak Road, Chamberlain heard some firing to his right and rode away from Griffin toward the sound. He discovered Gregory's men fighting some Rebel cavalry on the end of his line at the junction of the White Oak and Gravelly Run Church roads. They drove off the cavalry, and Crawford's and Griffin's lines crossed the White Oak Road—without finding the Confederate entrenchments.[34]

Worse, Ayres's division, which was supposed to strike the Confederate "angle," also crossed the White Oak Road without hitting its objective. The whole wheeling movement, two divisions wide, was supposed to hinge on Ayres when he struck the enemy. Finally, the Federal column drew fire from their left, and the Union officers discovered that the Confederate lines had not extended as far east on the White Oak Road as they had thought.

Ayres wheeled his division to attack the Confederate "return," and in so doing left the rest of Warren's assault to continue without him on its left.

Chamberlain and his men had been gaining ground toward the left and had gotten past Crawford's left flank and almost in line with his division. He heard firing from his left, which was Ayres, and halted his line to reconnoiter. He rode out into an open area called Sydnor Field and could see Crawford to the north skirmishing and Ayres to the south "in a confused whirl of struggling groups." Seeing Griffin near where Ayres was fighting, Chamberlain knew where he should be, and he marched his men by the left flank, "pushed across a muddy stream and up a rough ravine towards Ayres. Half-way up, Griffin came to meet me . . . and without coming near enough for words waved me to follow up to the head of the ravine and to attack on my right where, hidden by brush and scrub, the enemy had a line perpendicular to their main one on the White Oak Road, and were commencing a slant fire in Ayres's direction."[35]

The moment Chamberlain's men emerged from the ravine they became engaged at close quarters with the Confederates. An exchange of volleys and a rush stopped the Rebels from firing on Ayres.

Chamberlain met the impulsive Sheridan near the angle of the "return." "By God, that's what I want to see!" the cavalryman shouted. "General officers to the front." Not seeing any other officers near Chamberlain, he gave him command of all the infantry in the area and ordered him to break the Confederate line. Chamberlain gathered up everyone he could, from a single man cowering behind a stump to an entire brigade of Ayres's, standing in line with no orders.

Sheridan suddenly rode up again and rebuked Chamberlain for firing into his cavalry. "Then the cavalry have got into the rebels' place," was Chamberlain's observation. Ayres came up, his men driving on the "return" and along the White Oak Road. Sheridan repeated his caustic comment about Ayres firing into his men, but Ayres replied heatedly that he was firing at the men who were firing at him. "These are not carbine shot," Chamberlain recalled Ayres saying, speaking from vast experience under fire. "They are minié balls. I ought to know."[36]

But the lines, converging upon the Confederates, were firing into one another and, at the same time, catching the Rebels at the "return" in a crossfire. Chamberlain had to hold up his advance for fear of marching his flank in front of Ayres's firing line.

As Chamberlain swung his left flank forward to get out of the way, a large group of Confederates rushed him from behind. As cool as if on parade, he faced his left battalion about, placing the men's backs to the Confederates in the trenches, and had them lower their weapons for a volley. Even though the charging Confederates outnumbered Chamberlain's men, the sudden precision maneuver convinced the Rebels that a lot would die if they continued, so the group immediately surrendered.[37]

Chamberlain saw that the "return" had been carried, but the Confederates in the trenches were still resisting. Two of Bartlett's regiments had gotten tangled up with Crawford's men and ended up on the Ford Road to the west of the rest of the fighting but directly north of the Confederates at Five Forks.

Chamberlain was having trouble pushing his left center through the Rebel line. He turned to his friend Major Glenn, who had led the assaults across Gravelly Run and the fight at the sawdust pile on the Quaker Road. "Major Glenn," he challenged, "if you will break that line you shall have a colonel's commission!" Chamberlain would regret the offer. He watched as Glenn's 1st Battalion of the 198th Pennsylvania charged into the fiery maelstrom before it and broke over the enemy

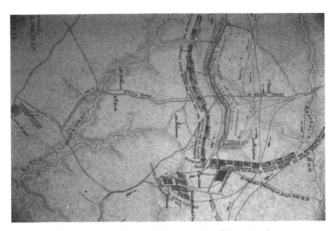

Chamberlain's personal map of the Battle of Five Forks.
LIBRARY OF CONGRESS

breastworks like a wave. He saw the battalion's flag go down in the fury three times, only to be raised again each time. One of those times it was Glenn who raised it.

Chamberlain rode over to congratulate him but found Glenn being carried to the rear on a stretcher, his blood making a trail behind him in the sandy Virginia loam. Chamberlain leaned down in his saddle and Glenn looked up and recognized him. "General," he said, "I have carried out your wishes!"

Chamberlain felt as if he had been struck by a bullet, and his head whirled at the consequences of his order. Choked with emotion, Chamberlain could only answer, "<u>Colonel,</u> I will remember my promise; I will remember <u>you</u>!" He would carry the burden of having singled Glenn out for death for the rest of his life.

Though Glenn received a deathbed promotion from major to colonel, Chamberlain said that the title, "so costly won, so honorable then, made common since, has seemed to me ever after, tame and something like travesty."[39]

Crawford had marched a wide, counterclockwise wheel northward and to the west and ended up on the Ford Road near the Hatcher's Run crossing. Chamberlain's route took him and his men in that westerly direction as well, and when he struck the Ford Road, his men mingled with Crawford's, who were attacking the Five Forks from the north.

About this time, Chamberlain received word that the impetuous Sheridan had relieved Warren of command of the 5th Corps and put Griffin in his place. This action began a long, heartbreaking chapter in Chamberlain's life, as he attempted to right the wrong for years to come. But for the present, there was more fighting to be done.

As Chamberlain rode toward Five Forks on the Ford Road, he emerged into a clearing. To his astonishment, there appeared Sheridan riding next to him. They exchanged pleasantries as if Sheridan's earlier, stormy rebuke had never happened. But Chamberlain got a taste of Sheridan's changing moods when another officer rode up and proudly announced to Sheridan, "We are on the enemy's rear, and have got three of their guns!"

"I don't care a damn for their guns," was Sheridan's hot reply, "or for you either, sir! What are you here for? Go back to your business where you belong! What I want is the Southside Road." The officer galloped off, no doubt happier to be in the Confederates' range of fire than in Sheridan's.

A group of other officers had gathered near Sheridan, wide-eyed at the scene, and Chamberlain wondered whether he would be the next target of Sheridan's wrath. But Sheridan stood in his stirrups, waving his hat, and roared, "I want you men to understand we have a record to make, before that sun goes down, that will make hell tremble!—I want you there!"[40]

As they approached the Confederate breastworks, Griffin galloped in from Chamberlain's right and leapt the works. Charlemagne was going over a lower section near a Confederate cannon when he was shot again, this time in the left hind leg.[41]

The Confederates were being driven back now, before the Union assaults from the north and the east. Chamberlain recalled that the Confederate lines looked like they were in the ancient "hollow square" formation, with men fighting on several sides facing outward against the foe. The Northerners had overrun the Confederate guns on the Ford Road, and now they overran those at the forks as well. The infantry fighting broke down into small but tenacious knots: a group of desperate men proudly defending their flag, or a few brave soldiers clustered around some courageous officer.

The Federal troops were disorganized as well from their rapid and circuitous advance, and Chamberlain had his bugler sound the brigade calls for the division. As the men followed the calls, Chamberlain took them to the left.

He came upon Warren, who told him of his being relieved of command. Chamberlain tried to soften the blow by explaining how Sheridan had been placing everyone in command of everybody, but it did no good. He watched as Warren approached some serious fighting that was still going on at the White Oak Road. Lt. Col. Hollon Richardson of the 7th Wisconsin picked up his regimental colors and rode forward toward a particularly stubborn line of Confederates firing hotly. Warren grabbed his corps flag from its bearer and rode quickly to Richardson's side, and the two of them, yards ahead of their troops, rode right into the fire and lead of the Confederate line and over the breastworks.[42] Warren's horse went down, and a Confederate took aim at the Yankee general. Just as the Rebel pulled the trigger, Richardson leapt in front of Warren and took the bullet for him, falling on his own regimental flag and soaking it with his blood.[43] It may seem strange today that a man would offer his own life for a superior officer's. But it happened then, and as recently as World War II, when Marines leapt on grenades to save their comrades. It remains one of those mysteries of war and of brave men facing death. *Greater love hath no man than this.*

Shortly thereafter, official orders relieved Warren of his command.[44]

Griffin took over Warren's command and had the 5th Corps pursue the Confederates until darkness brought the operation to a halt.

As soon as Grant heard about the victory at Five Forks, he ordered his 9th and 6th Corps to assault the Confederate defenses at Petersburg early the next morning.

At noon on April 2 the 5th Corps, with Chamberlain's brigade leading, moved north on the Ford Road. They ran into stout Confederate resistance at the crossing of Hatcher's Run, but Colonel Sniper and the 185th New York attacked and drove the Rebels from the Run.

As they pushed toward the South Side Railroad, they could hear a locomotive coming. Chamberlain rushed the 32nd Massachusetts foward to act as a strong skirmish line, and they managed to capture the last train flying the Confederate flag out of Petersburg.

Approaching the Cox Road, Chamberlain discovered what he estimated as fifteen hundred Confederates before him, dismounted troopers of Fitzhugh Lee's cavalry division. He established a battle line and advanced rapidly against them. The troopers retreated slowly along the Cox Road. Chamberlain realized that the Confederate retreat from Petersburg would have to come this way and determined to hold the road. Meanwhile, the rest of the 5th Corps tore up the South Side Railroad track for several miles to the rear of Chamberlain's lines.

A battle to the east of Chamberlain's position and behind Fitz Lee's lines at Sutherland Station ended in a Confederate defeat, with the fugitives escaping to the northwest. Sheridan came up with the cavalry to pursue them, and Chamberlain marched to bivouac for the night at the junction of Namozine Church Road and the River Road.

On April 3 the 5th Corps moved out at daylight along the south side of the Appomattox River, with Sheridan's cavalry in the lead. During the march, Chamberlain heard that the Confederate government had fled from its capital, Richmond, and that Lee's army was in full retreat. Grant had ordered a general assault all along the Petersburg defensive lines for April 3, but by the time it got under way, the lines had been abandoned. Petersburg, the long sought prize that had almost cost Chamberlain his life, had fallen.

The Federals were now in pursuit of Confederates also moving along the south side of the Appomattox River. At the crossing of Deep Creek, Fitz Lee's cavalry and two Confederate infantry brigades made a stand, but Sheridan drove them off before the 5th Corps could get involved.

Sheridan had gathered the information that Robert E. Lee was headed to Amelia Court House. Before morning on April 4, he ordered the 5th Corps on an all-day march to Jetersville to cut Lee's communications and supplies from Danville. By evening they were entrenched across the Richmond and Danville Railroad, nervously expecting an attack by Lee's whole army the very next morning.

But Lee never attacked the lonely 5th Corps. By 2:30 on the afternoon of April 5, the 2nd Corps arrived at Jetersville to reinforce the 5th; soon the 6th Corps joined them on their right flank.

Chamberlain's men had been called out of the lines at one that afternoon to support the cavalry on the left, which had just captured a large number of wagons, prisoners, and artillery pieces. Their support was not needed, however, and Chamberlain was amused to see that the cavalrymen had raided the wagons before burning them and had strapped incongruously to their rough army saddles silver sugar bowls, coffeepots, and "favors" of the boudoir.[45]

Sheridan had told Grant that Lee's army was at Amelia Court House, and so on April 6, Grant on the strength of that report, ordered the 5th Corps to head to Amelia. But Lee had pulled out at eight the night before. The 5th Corps marched five miles toward Amelia before they were faced about and sent westwardly, via Paineville, Ligontown, and Sailor's Creek. Somehow, Lee had gotten ahead of Grant.

Lee was trying to get to Farmville, where he hoped to find rations for his hungry men. Here and there they burned a bridge in their wake to slow the pursuing Yankees. And the pursuers still marched cautiously, with skirmishers and flankers before and beside their columns. The Confederate army was hungry, tired, and hunted, and because of that, still a very dangerous animal. As Chamberlain wrote later, "There was blood at every bridge and ford."[46]

After encamping near Sailor's Creek at Shepherd's Farm overnight on April 6, the 5th Corps marched at daylight on the seventh, and by 9:50 A.M. was passing High Bridge, a massive structure built across the Appomattox for the South Side Railroad. By 7:30 P.M. the men had marched to Prince Edward Court House.

That night from Farmville Grant sent a note to Lee: "The result of the last week must convince you of the hopelessness of further resistance on the part of the Army of Northern Virginia in this struggle. I feel that it is so, and regard it as my duty to shift from myself the responsibility of any further effusion of blood, by asking of you the surrender of that portion of the C.S. Army known as the Army of Northern Virginia."[47] Lee replied that he did not agree with Grant that his cause was hopeless, but he too wanted to avoid spilling more blood and asked Grant what terms he would offer.

Chamberlain and the 5th Corps knew nothing of this at the time. Instead, by six on the morning of April 8, they were marching again, trying to edge in front of Lee. Crossing the Buffalo River, Charlemagne slipped off a submerged ledge and fell with his master into neck-deep water, soaking Chamberlain. The corps made it to Prospect Station on the South Side Railroad, finally drawing even in the westward race with Lee's column, then at New Store, eight miles due north across the Appomattox.

But Grant had orders for the 5th Corps to continue its march in the dark—twenty-nine miles of road that day and night according to Chamberlain—until the men practically collapsed six miles from Appomattox Station on the South Side Railroad.[48]

The men did not sleep much during the remainder of the night. They were up before dawn on April 9 and reached Appomattox Station by sunrise. A staff officer directed the officers at the heads of the columns to march northward toward the Appomattox River, and in this movement, they cut across the path of Lee's retreat. Chamberlain heard the horse artillery first—Sheridan's guns—then the deeper boom of the field artillery. He heard the sharp crackle of cavalry carbines and the rolling thunder of musketry from the infantry.

Union general O. C. Ord's troops led the march toward the sound of the guns. The 5th Corps came after, with Bartlett's division behind Ayres's; in Bartlett's division, Chamberlain's brigade followed by Gregory's; and Crawford's division behind all. Chamberlain rode in the middle of the 5th Corps column.

A cavalry staff officer rode up from some woods on the right with a request from Sheridan that Chamberlain bring his troops to his support. They followed the staff officer through the woods and came upon Sheridan beneath his guidon. A strong Confederate force was going to attempt to cut its way out of the closing circle of Federals, and Sheridan was holding them with his cavalry alone. As Chamberlain spread his infantry out in double battle lines Sheridan's cavalry broke off from their fight squadron by squadron and rallied to his right flank to help encircle the enemy. Chamberlain recalled years later that the Confederates "seemed astonished to see before them these familiar flags of their old antagonists"[49]—that they could hardly believe the Yankees could have marched as fast as cavalry to get across the Confederate escape route.

The Confederates were blocked to the south; the Federal 6th and 2nd Corps were closing in from behind. The Confederates before Chamberlain began to retreat. As Chamberlain later put it, "I try a little artillery on them,"[50] and they backed toward a crest behind them.

Chamberlain, obeying one of those maxims in the tactics books he had read back in 1862, decided he wanted the high ground too. In spite of a warning from one of his superiors, Chamberlain advanced to the crest, pushing the Rebels from it. Before him lay the valley of the Appomattox River, "a vast amphitheater, stretching a mile perhaps from crest to crest."

Moving his lines forward down the slope, he saw that Federal advance elements were already in the little village below, half-heartedly fighting an enemy who also was barely fighting. Chamberlain prepared

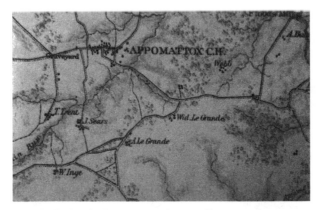

Detail of Chamberlain's personal map of his area of operations around Appomattox Court House. LIBRARY OF CONGRESS

tor an attack upon his flank from some Confederate cavalry he discovered there.

Suddenly, two horsemen rode across his front about a mile distant; then came a Confederate staff officer, above whom floated a white flag.

"Sir," the officer said, dismounting near Chamberlain, "I am from General Gordon. General Lee desires a cessation of hostilities until he can hear from General Grant as to the proposed surrender."

After two and a half years of fighting, after six wounds, after having read his own obituary, the word *surrender* left the former rhetorician momentarily speechless. "Sir," he finally responded, "that matter exceeds my authority. I will send to my superior."

He sent a message to Griffin and meanwhile watched as another flag of truce came in, though there was still some firing in the distance. One last cannon shot from the edge of town ripped into a young officer in Chamberlain's front line, Lt. Hiram Clark of the 185th New York. Chamberlain thought he was the last man killed in the Army of the Potomac, "a cruel fate for one so deserving to share his country's joy, and a sad peace-offering for us all."[51]

As word of the truce and possible surrender drifted down the lines, the celebrations began. Officers riding up to discover that Lee wished to surrender congratulated their men; the men broke ranks and climbed chimneys and haystacks to toss their dusty caps in the air. It was 10:00 A.M., April 9, 1865.

The truce was limited to three hours, however. As 1:00 P.M. approached, it looked as if the armies might start fighting again. Griffin told Chamberlain in a low voice, "Prepare to make, or receive, an attack in ten minutes!" As close as the two lines were, it would not be war, Chamberlain felt, but "wilful murder." Nevertheless, he mounted, and the men mechanically prepared to resume hostilities.

But then Chamberlain "felt coming in upon me a strange sense of some presence invisible but powerful—like those unearthly visitants told of in an ancient story, charged with supernal message." He turned in his saddle to see, riding between his lines, resplendent in his poise and control, Robert E. Lee.

A short while later there came another, less imposing, but more familiar form. Attired in a common private's blouse, unbuttoned but with general's stars showing on the shoulders, was Grant.[52]

An hour or so later, word went out that Lee had surrendered. It passed at first from soldier to soldier, then house to house, then along the wire to Washington, to Ohio and New York, Pennsylvania, Massachusetts, and Maine, and a dozen other Northern states, and nearly as many Southern ones, where people would rejoice at the prospect of their sons' return, or mourn bitterly for those who would not. But here, at quiet Appomattox, there were things to do yet.

Confederate general James Longstreet came to the Federal camps that evening and begged for food for his men. He did not know that the Yankees, after all the marching and fighting they had done, were just as hungry. Chamberlain later wrote of the immediate, unselfish compassion shown now that hostilities had ceased: "We were men; and we acted like men, knowing we should suffer for it ourselves. We were too short-rationed also, and had been for days, and must be for days to come. But we forgot Andersonville and Belle Isle that night, and sent over to that starving camp share and share alike for all there."[53]

That night Chamberlain was called to headquarters and told by Griffin that he was to command the formal laying down of the colors and weapons of the Army of Northern Virginia. The Confederates wanted to stack their arms where they were encamped, leave, and let the Federals come and collect them, but Grant felt that that was not respectful enough and that a formal surrender ceremony relinquishing all symbols and tokens of the armed and organized rebellion should occur. Chamberlain asked for command of his former brigade—the old 3rd—

during the ceremony. "This was to be a crowning incident of history, and I thought these veterans deserved this recognition."[54]

April 10 was filled with visits from those who were once friends, then enemies, now seeking friendship again. The Rebels wanted to see what manner of men these were who outmarched them. They wanted to trade mementos for food, but little was to be found even in the Union camps.

The formalities of a military surrender took up the rest of that day and much of the next: Paroles for the Confederate commands had to be printed, lists and muster rolls had to be arranged, and preparations made for the surrendered property. Chamberlain's men had lined up to receive the enemy weapons and flags on April 11 but returned to their camps when they found that the parole signing was taking all day.

Sadly, though only a few miles away, the 6th and 2nd Corps of the Army of the Potomac were not to be at the surrender ceremony. Chamberlain could not understand it, when so many longer marches had been made "for less cause and less good."[55]

Chamberlain continued his letter writing, even after the surrender was consummated, to secure the rightful praise for his subordinate officers. On April 10, 1865, he wrote a letter to Colonel Sniper of the 185th New York to assure recognition of Henry A. Kelsey of that regiment for his actions at the Lewis Farm, White Oak Road, and Appomattox Court House, where he rode ahead of the skirmish line to capture a number of officers and men. Perhaps this is the young man of whom Chamberlain recalled: "A young orderly of mine, unable to contain himself [on April 9 as they advanced to Appomattox], begs permission to go forward, and dashes in, sword flourishing as if he were a terrible fellow,—his demonstrations seemingly more amusing than resisted; for he soon comes back, hugging four sabres to his breast, speechless at his achievement."[56]

On April 11 Chamberlain officially took leave of the brigade he led last in battle.

> Head Quarters 1st Brig. 1st Div. 5th Corps
> Appomattox C. H. April 11th 1865.

General Orders
No. 3.}

The General Commanding having been ordered to another command hereby takes leave of this Brigade.

In this parting from troops to whom he had become attached by their soldierly behavior and gallant conduct in battle the General cannot forbear to express his satisfaction that the whole course of this brief Campaign found the First Brigade in the front line and at its triumphant close they exchanged the last shots with the enemy.

To the Officers of the Field, Staff and Line he tenders his thanks for their fidelity and courtesy and to the whole command the assurance of his deep interest in them and of the pride with which he will ever remember that he once commanded the First Brigade.

(sg.)J. L. Chamberlain
Brig. Gen. Comdg.

Official Copy

Thos. Mitchell
Lt. [ill.] & AAAG.[57]

The surrendering of some arms, particularly the Confederate artillery pieces, took place on the morning of April 11, with Turner's division of the 24th Corps of the Army of the James receiving the weapons until Bartlett's division relieved them. Mackenzie's Federal cavalry received the surrender of sabers of W. H. F. Lee's cavalry. By noon the Army of the James headed west to Lynchburg. Grant had left Appomattox for Washington; and Lee would soon depart for Richmond. The next day the Confederate infantry would surrender their arms.

Predawn on April 12, was gray and chilly, as depressing to the defeated Confederates as the occasion. The victorious Union soldiers must have felt something bittersweet as well in the laying down of arms by their gallant antagonists. It was like saying good-bye to a very dangerous but exciting habit. They would never again have the dubious thrill of facing a line of raised muskets and watching them disappear in a cloud of white smoke and fire. There had been something unreal about it, being only seconds or inches from the next world. Those who experienced it would never be the same, and they would never forget it.

Chamberlain had requested to have the three brigades with which he had been associated during the war under his command in the ceremony. The little 1st Brigade he placed in line behind his old 3rd Brigade. Across the street that led into Appomattox Court House he put the 2nd Brigade. They stretched from the bluff bank of the Appomattox River almost to the Court House itself.

From his vantage point where the Lynchburg Stage Road crested a small rise, Chamberlain could see the Confederates on the opposite slopes of the "amphitheater" taking down their ragged shelter tents and folding them for the last time. He watched as they formed their march columns and saw the rhythmic undulation of the columns as the men got into the old "rout step." Ahead of the column flew the Confederate ensign—a rectangular white flag with a red and blue miniature of the battle flag in the corner. Behind were the regimental battle flags, clustered thickly because of the thinning of the Rebel ranks.

For such an occasion as the surrender of "that great army which ours had been created to confront for all that death can do for life,"[58] Chamberlain decided to mark it with something only soldiers could appreciate. As the ragged remnants of the Confederate divisions moved between the Federal ranks, Chamberlain's bugler called the signal, and regiment by regiment, from right to left, the men shifted arms from "order arms" to "carry."

Confederate general John B. Gordon, riding with his head down, depressed at the proceedings, heard the sound of shifting arms as he had in battle many times before. He lifted his eyes and saw what Chamberlain had done, wheeled his horse, straightened, and returned the noble salute, dropping the point of his sword to his boot toe. He called orders to his men—some of the last he would ever give to them—and as each brigade passed, the men shifted arms into the same salute. "Honor answering honor," as Chamberlain recalled at the end of his life. The time for raucous celebration now was gone. Too much had happened between these two gallant bodies of men, "of near blood born, made nearer by blood shed." "On our part," wrote Chamberlain, "not a sound of trumpet more, nor roll of drum; not a cheer, nor word nor whisper of vain-glorying, nor motion of man standing again at the order, but an awed stillness rather, and breath-holding, as if it were the passing of the dead!"[59]

The Confederates lined up in the road facing Chamberlain's men just a dozen feet from them. They carefully aligned their ranks as if preparing for review, each officer particular that his men, though ragged and weak, were "soldierly." The men took special pains to do so, knowing that this would be the last time.

First came the bayonets, drawn by those who still had them, then fixed to musket barrels with that distinctive, metallic clatter that Chamberlain and his men had heard in desperation on Little Round Top. The men then stacked their arms in standing sheaves held together by the bayonets. They removed the cartridge boxes and laid them down. Finally, it was the color bearers' turn: "Reluctantly, with agony of expression,— they tenderly fold their flags, battle-worn and torn, blood-stained, heart-holding colors, and lay them down; some frenziedly rushing from the ranks, kneeling over them, clinging to them, pressing them to their lips with burning tears."[60]

Through the now peaceful gauntlet the Confederates marched. How odd it must have been for those men as they turned and aligned ranks, to look across the dozen steps that separated them from the Northerners and perhaps recognize a face that they once saw through the sights on a musket barrel. "What visions thronged as we looked into each other's eyes," wrote Chamberlain. "What shall we give them for greeting that has not already been spoken in volleys of thunder and written in lines of fire on all the riverbanks of Virginia?"[61]

Seeing, perhaps recognizing, men who had almost killed him, Chamberlain, uncharacteristically, personalized one small part of the mournful parade: "With what strange emotion I look into these faces before which in the mad assault on Rives' Salient, June 18, 1864, I was left for dead under their eyes! It is by miracles we have lived to see this day,—any of us standing here."[62]

All but one or two Confederate officers Chamberlain conversed with after the ceremony took the humiliation of defeat as a challenge, now that it was all over, to become as good Americans as any of the Northerners. "Brave men," Chamberlain was sure, "may become good friends."[63]

On down the road the Confederates marched to their dissolution, regiment after regiment, brigade after brigade, Chamberlain recognizing each by name as it crested the slope and stood before him.

Hours later it was over—the surrender, the laying down of arms at Appomattox, and essentially, the war in this part of the country. By Chamberlain's final reckoning, some seventeen thousand arms were collected, one hundred flags taken, and twenty-seven thousand paroles passed out at Appomattox. But was it really over?

A strange and somber shadow rose up ghost-like from the haunts of memory or habit, and rested down over the final parting scene. How strong are these ties of habit! How strange the undertone of sadness even at the release from prison and from pain! It seems as if

we had put some precious part of ourselves there which we are
loath to leave.[64]

And if indeed it was over, was it time to lay blame on those who started
the war and these men who had fought it and had cost Chamberlain's
generation the lives of more than 620,000 American men and boys?

> Nor blame them too much for this, nor us for not blaming them
> more. Although, as we believed, fatally wrong in striking at the old
> flag, misreading its deeper meaning and the innermost law of the
> people's life, blind to the signs of the times in the march of man,
> they fought as they were taught, true to such ideals as they saw, and
> put into their cause their best. For us they were fellow soldiers as
> well suffering the fate of arms. We could not look into those brave,
> bronzed faces, and those battered flags we had met on so many
> fields where glorious manhood lent a glory to the earth that bore
> it, and think of personal hate and mean revenge. Whoever had mis
> led these men, we had not. We had led them back, home. Whoever
> had made that quarrel, we had not. It was a remnant of the inher-
> ited curse for sin. We had purged it away, with blood offerings.[65]

And so, from one side of that gauntlet of noble, brave souls to the other,
across the flags and stacked arms, passed more than anyone there could
see, not only between those present but between the two sections of the
country. In part because of what they had suffered and accomplished,
something altogether mysterious and uniquely American was created at
that moment; it passed between them then and passes between Americans still.

> Forgive us, therefore, if from stern, steadfast faces eyes dimmed
> with tears gazed at each other across that pile of storied relics so
> dearly there laid down, and brothers' hands were fain to reach
> across that rushing tide of memories which divided us, yet made us
> forever one. . . .
> But slowly these lingering images of memory or habit are lost
> in the currents of a deeper mood; we wonder at that mysterious
> dispensation whereby the pathway of the kingdom of Love on
> earth must needs be cut through by the sword, and why it must be

that by such things as we had seen and done and suffered, and lost and won, a step is taken in the homeward march of man.[66]

Hdqrs. Third Brig., First Div., Fifth Army Corps,
April 13, 1865.

Capt. William Fowler,
Asst. Adjt. Gen., First Division, Fifth Army Corps:

Captain: Pursuant to instructions I have collected in the deserted rebel camp some 400 or 500 stand of arms, and stacked them near the road. There are also remaining in the camp 1 light 12-pounder brass piece of artillery, some 20 caissons, and a large number of wagons still uninjured.

I am, captain, very respectfully, your obedient servant,
J. L. Chamberlain,
Brigadier-General, Commanding.[67]

Head Quarters 3d Brigade
1st Div. 5 Army Corps
Appomattox Court House
April 13th 1865.

My dear Sae,

I am glad I was not tempted to leave the army this Spring. I would not for a fortune have missed the experiences of the last two weeks. It seems like two years, so many, & such important events have taken place, within that time. Father said in his last letter to me that "the glory of battles was over." But if he had seen some of these we have had of late, in which we captured the enemy by thousands & carried their positions by a dash, and at last at Appomattox Court House received the surrender of Genl Lee & his whole army he would think differently.

For my personal part I have had the advance every day there was any fighting—have been in five battles—two of them being entirely under my own direction and brilliantly successful—twice wounded myself—my horse shot—in the front line when the flag of truce came through from Lee—had the last shot & the last man killed, in this campaign; & yesterday was designated to receive the surrender of the arms of Lee's Army of Northern Virginia. The bare mention of these facts seems like boasting, but I assure you I do not feel any of that spirit. I only rejoice that I was here & bore my part in the crowning Triumphs of the war. It was a scene worthy of a pilgrimage, yesterday, when the old "Third Brigade" of the 1st Div. was drawn up to receive the surrender of the Rebel arms. My Brigade you know consists of 9 Regts. the remnant of the old 5th Corps. veterans of thirty battles. They number about six thousand men all told—on the right was old Massachusetts with the remnants of her 9th, 18th, 22d & 32d. Then Maine, her 1st, 2d, & 20th—Michigan 1st, 4th, & 16th—Pennsylvania—with the sturdy relics of her 82d, 83d, 91st, 118th, & 155th.—with my staff & the old flag—the red maltese cross on a white field with blue border. I took post on the right at 5 a.m., & received first Maj. Gen. Gordon with his corps—Stonewall Jackson's—then Longstreet's corps. with Hoods Andersons & Pickett's old Divisions—men we had faced a score of times & almost recognized by face. Pickett's [*sic*] splendid Div. only stacked 53 muskets & not a single stand of colors—we had so completely used them up at 5 Forks. Last came Hill's Corp.—by Divisions—Hill himself being killed. We received them with the honors due to troops—at a shoulder—in silence. They came to a shoulder on passing my flag & preserved perfect order. When the head of their column reached our left, they halted faced toward our line & close to it—say 4 or 5 yards—& stacked their arms & piled their colors. Poor fellows. I pitied them from the bottom of my heart. Those arms had been well handled & the flags bravely borne.

15,000 stand of arms & 72 flags were stacked before my line. I saw & conversed with nearly all the Rebel Generals, & shall have more things to tell you of by & by.

Your letter has just come. The first mail for two weeks. I thank you much. With great love to you all your aff. Lawrence.

[The following is written upside down at top of first page.]

I enclose this note just rec'd from Corps Hd. Qrs.[68]

Two days later, on Saturday, April 15, Chamberlain and his men, though still low on rations and without blankets or overcoats, began their march home. Passing Evergreen Station on the South Side Railroad long after dark, they bivouacked for the night. At six the next morning they were on the march again under a dark sky and a cold rain. That afternoon they reached Farmville, where they found brightening skies and rations and had an opportunity to wash up and rest in the warming sun. A band from Chamberlain's old 1st Brigade played some happy German music.

A little after four, a courier galloped up to headquarters and handed Chamberlain a yellow tissue-paper telegram: "Washington, April 15, 1865. The President died this morning. Wilkes Booth the assassin. Secretary Seward dangerously wounded. The rest of the Cabinet, General Grant, and other high officers of the Government included in the plot of destruction."

Chamberlain put his own emotions aside; he worried more about the effect this would have upon the men of the army, who had loved Lincoln and were armed and in the conquered land of the enemy. He began to secure the camp. But the men, after all they had endured, took the shocking news stoically.

Meade decided that the army should march on Washington in case the assassination was part of a coup attempt. But no news of that sort was forthcoming. Early the next morning came marching orders for Burkeville. The column marched down the wrong road, however, and encamped on the night of April 17 near Liberty Church by the Little Sandy River. The men arose early the next morning to march back to Burkeville to bivouac.

On April 19 orders came from Washington that the army was not to march while the president's funeral was occurring in the Capital. Chamberlain arranged services in camp for the day. The men draped tents, flags, and sword hilts with black rosettes. Each man wore a band of black crepe on the left arm—that arm closest to the heart. At noon was heard a distincive low booming as the artillery fired a mourning salute, then the band played the "Russian Hymn." Father Egan, senior chaplain of the division, began his sermon on the biblical text wherein Salome, after her sinful dance, requests as payment the head of John the Baptist. Salome, encouraged by her mother, represented the assassin; her mother, the Confederate government. Lincoln was John the just and innocent, brought to leadership by Providence. The fiery Irish chaplain warmed to his theme by reminding the men of Lincoln's love for them, then asked them whether they would endure this sacrilege. Should not such a foul spirit be ripped from the country forever?

Chamberlain saw the men tremble and begin reaching for their muskets, and he whispered to the chaplain not to incite them further.

Father Egan then evoked their pride and love for Lincoln, saying that it was better "to die glorious, than to live infamous. Better to be buried beneath a nation's tears, than to walk the earth guilty of a nation's blood." Chamberlain recalled afterward: "He gave us back to ourselves, better soldiers, and better men."[69]

> Head Qrs. 3d Brig 1st Div. 5th Corps
> Burkeville Apr. 19 1865

My darling wife, a good morning kiss for you, with big brown eyes & peach-bloom cheeks, and vol- no _vel_ vet lips!

That, I had written just three weeks ago, seeming like three months or years if you please—so much, & such momentous things have since transpired. That night I had fought a battle—the first of the campaign, and the fiercest—and more than four hundred of my men lay dead or wounded on the field—I too suffering from two wounds either of which was a miracle of an escape. Now I say the same thing to my dearest love, & if I could see her would have many many things to say. What tremendous scenes I have participated in within these three weeks. I told you I think that I fired the first & the last gun of this campaign—that I was present at that conference of officers—ever to be memorable—preliminary to the surrender of Lee's army. I had not then passed through the last & most intensely interesting scene. I happened to be designated to receive the formal surrender of the arms of that great Army of Northern Virginia. My Brigade you know is composed of the veterans of the old 5th Corps I have 9 Regts—representing two or three times that number which once made up the 1st 2d Divisions of this Corps—numbering in all some 7,000 men. It is the most magnificent Brigade in the Army, beyond all question. I can't describe this to you now. You can imagine what it was, when those veterans of a score of battles were drawn up to receive the surrender of the army they had faced so many times. They were met with the honors of war—Stonewall Jackson's old Corps, Longstreets, & Hill's—26,000 men surrendered—their arms were stacked, & their colors laid down—73 battle flags—in front of my lines. I shall have something to _tell_ you of this, as of other matters never to be forgotten. Since then we have marched in complete triumph everywhere. But, Fannie,[70] in the midst of all this triumph—in this hour

of exultation, in this day of power & joy & hope, when our starry
flag floats amid the stars of Heaven, suddenly it falls to <u>half-mast</u>—
"Darkness sweeps athwart the sky", & the President of the United
States, with his heart full of conciliation & charity & forgiveness is
struck down by the assassin's hand. Words will not tell the feeling
with which this Army receives this news.

I wish you could have been present to day at my funeral service
for the President—this field—the drooping flags—the dirges of the
bands—the faces of the men—the words of the chaplain from his
text—"<u>Give</u> <u>me</u> <u>here</u> <u>the</u> <u>head</u> <u>of</u> John <u>the</u> <u>Baptist</u> <u>in</u> <u>a</u> <u>charger</u>"!
<u>You</u> should have been here. <u>You</u> of all, I missed. The chaplain is an
Irishman, & the celtic soul took fire to day you may, be sure. I
ordered this service on my own responsibility, as it is the day of the
Presidents funeral, & all duties of a military character are sus-
pended. It will take a life time to tell you all I have to tell. These
are terrible times, but I believe in God, & he will bring good at
last. We march at 7 in the morning, to make a camp & rest for a little, when I shall write you more fully. God bless you, sweet love; I
thank you for your letters. I learn that some of the [ill.] commend
me. For your sake I am glad. I receive many congratulatory letters.
Give my love to Auntie, & all, especially to your dear Father. I
enclose $10 for you to give Helen.

[The following is written along the right edge of the first page.]

Sae speaks of your "most sweet & beautiful of letters." Thank
you darling. What is our baby's name?[71] With a good night kiss & a
<u>long</u> <u>one.</u> Your [ill.][72]

The next morning the 5th Corps was stretched out along the railroad
from Burkeville to Petersburg with Chamberlain's 1st Division assigned
to guard from Sutherland Station, near the site of Chamberlain's fight on
the White Oak Road, to Wilson's Station.[73] Chamberlain's duties consisted of protecting the unarmed and now undefended civilians. He did
that both by military presence and by seizing shops, stores, and mills and
getting them open, running, and distributing the goods to the people.
There were a number of violations of the law—both by civilians and by
soldiers—that had to be addressed. But, Chamberlain said, "We did not
undertake to settle questions of property, but only of conduct."[74]

The following note was found among Chamberlain's papers, addressed to no one in particular.

> Wilson's Station Southside R.R.
> April 21st 1865
> I am in command of the <u>1st</u> <u>Div.</u> <u>5th</u> <u>Corps</u> and have charge of the Rail road for 30 miles from Petersburg. My friends can come & see me if they want to look over the battle grounds of the campaign. L.[75]

> Headquarters First Division, 5th Army Corps,
> April 24, 1865.

Colonel Locke,
Assistant Adjutant General:

Colonel: My line extends to Petersburg, the lower end guarded by patrols. The First Brigade is at Wilson's, the Second at Ford's, the Third at Sutherland's. Prisoners taken at Five Forks: First Brigade, 1,054 men, 6 captains, 11 lieutenants, 2 colonels; Second Brigade, 475 men; Third Brigade 849 men, 3 captains, 5 lieutenants.

> J. L. Chamberlain,
> Brigadier-General Commanding.[76]

During this period, Chamberlain had an opportunity to write down details of the several battles and numerous marches that finally drove Lee to surrender at Appomattox. The following is his report from the Official Records.

> Camp of the First Division, Fifth Corps,
> April 24, 1865.

Captain: In compliance with orders just received, I have the honor to submit the following report of the operations of the First Brigade of this division from the 29th of March to the 9th of April, 1865:

The brigade broke camp on the morning of the 29th ultimo[77] and marched at 6 a.m., by way of Arthur's Swamp and the old stage road and Vaughan Road toward Dinwiddie Courthouse; turning to our right, we went into position near the Chappell house. Soon

after this we returned to the Vaughan Road and moved up the
Quaker Road in a northerly direction. On reaching Gravelly Run
Major-General Griffin directed me to form my brigade in order of
battle and advance against some works which were in sight on the
opposite bank. Crossing the run, I sent Major E. A. Glenn, commanding the second battalion of the One Hundred and ninety-
eighth Pennsylvania Volunteers, forward with his command as
skirmishers, and formed my lines, with Brevet Brigadier General
H. G. Sickel, One Hundred and Ninety-eighth Pennsylvania, on
the right, and Col. G. Sniper, One Hundred and Eighty-fifth New
York, on the left of the road. Major Glenn pushed forward vigorously and drove the enemy's skirmishers out of their works without any difficulty, and succeeded in pressing them through the
woods as far as the Lewis house. The enemy making considerable
show of force in the edge of woods beyond, I halted Major Glenn
and brought my line of battle up to supporting distance. Here I
was directed to halt. In a short time I was ordered by General Griffin to resume the advance. There being at that time no firing of any
consequence on the skirmish line I brought my line up to that
point, reformed it on the buildings, re-enforced the skirmishers by
a company from the One Hundred and Eighty-fifth New York,
and commenced a rapid advance with my whole command. The
skirmishers reached the edge of woods before the firing became at
all severe. I was exceedingly anxious that the troops should gain the
cover of the woods before receiving the shock of the fire, but the
obstacles to be overcome were so great that this could not be fully
accomplished, and my men were obliged to gain the woods against
a heavy fire. They advanced, however, with great steadiness and
drove the enemy from their position and far into the woods. It was
not long, however, before another attack was made upon us, evidently by a greatly superior force, and we became completely
enveloped in a withering fire. We replied with spirit and persis-
tency, holding our ground, taking rather the defensive at this stage
of the action. In the course of half an hour my left became so
heavily pressed that it gradually gave way, and at last was fairly
turned, and driven entirely out of the woods to a direction parallel
the road by which we advanced. This position could not be held
ten minutes, and nothing but the most active exertions of field and

staff officers kept the men where they were, the fire all the time being very severe. At this moment I sent a request for General Gregory, commanding Second Brigade, on my left, to attack the enemy in flank in their newly gained position. I was assured by Major-General Griffin, who was on the line, that if we would hold on five minutes he could bring up the artillery. Upon this I succeeded in rallying the men, and they once more gained the woods. Battery B of the Fourth U. S. Artillery now came into position and opened a most effective fire. By this assistance we held our line until the enemy fell heavily upon our right and center, and my men being by this time out of ammunition, many of them absolutely without a cartridge, began to yield ground. Seeing that this was inevitable I dispatched an aide to General Gregory asking him for a regiment, and at the same time Major-General Griffin ordered up three regiments of the Third Brigade. These regiments came promptly to our assistance. I was at that moment endeavoring to reform my broken line, so as, at all events, to cover the artillery. The line was falling back in front of the Lewis house when Lieutenant-Colonel Doolittle of the One Hundred and eighty-eighth New York, came up, gallantly leading his regiment, as also Colonel Partridge, Sixteenth Michigan; the One Hundred and fifty-fifth Pennsylvania and First Michigan came on in the most handsome manner, passing to my front, Brevet Brigadier-General Pearson, of the One Hundred and fifty-fifth, grasping his color and dashing straight against the enemy's line. This assistance and the admirable service of the artillery compelled the enemy to abandon their position; otherwise I must have been driven entirely from the field.

This action lasted nearly two hours before any support reached us. I need not speak of the severity of the engagement, nor of the conduct of my officers and men, inasmuch as it was all under the eye and direction of the major-general commanding, who shared the dangers, as well as the responsibilities, of that field; but I may be permitted to mention the fact that more than 400 of my men and 18 officers killed and wounded marked our line with too painful destructiveness. Nor can I fail to speak of the steadfast coolness and courage of Brevet Brigadier-General Sickel, whose example and conduct made my efforts needless in that part of the line, until he was borne from the field severely wounded; the unflinching tenacity of Colonel Sniper at his perilous post, and the desperate bravery with which he rallied his men, seizing his color after it had fallen from the hands of three color bearers and a captain, and bearing it into the very ranks of the enemy; the fiery courage of Major Glenn, which could scarcely be restrained; and of the heroic spirit of Major Maceuen, who fell dead foremost in the ranks of honor; nor shall I forget to name the young gentlemen of my staff—Lieutenants Walters and Vogel, my personal aides, both painfully wounded, but keeping the field to the last; Lieutenant Mitchell, my adjutant-general, and Lieutenant Fisher, pioneer officer—who rendered me essential aid in the hottest of the fire. Private Kelsey, my orderly, rode upon the enemy's line and captured, under my own eyes, an officer and five men, and brought them in.

Remaining on the ground that night and the next day, we buried our dead and 130 of the enemy's, and brought in the wounded of both parties.

On the morning of the 31st we moved up the Boydton plank road, and upon this nearly to Gravelly Run crossing, taking position on the left of the division and the corps. A sharp engagement commenced to our right, which resulted in the troops falling back through our lines in great confusion. I was desired by General Griffin to regain the field which these troops had yielded. My men forded a stream nearly waist deep, formed in two lines, Major Glenn having the advance, and pushed the enemy steadily before them. Major-General Ayres' Division supported me on the left in echelon by brigade, the skirmishers of the First Division, in charge of General Pearson, in their front. We advanced in this way a mile or more into the edge of the field it was desired to retake. Up to this time we had been opposed only by a skirmish line, but quite a heavy fire now met us, and a line of battle could be plainly seen in the opposite edge of woods and in a line of breast-works in the open field, in force at least equal to our own. I was now ordered by Major-General Warren to halt and take the defensive. My first line had now gained a slight crest in the open field, where they were subjected to a severe fire from the works in front and from the woods on each flank. As it appeared that the enemy's position might be carried with no greater loss than it would cost us merely to hold our ground, and the men were eager to charge over the field, I reported this to General Griffin, and received permission to renew the attack. My command was brought into one line and put in motion. A severe oblique fire on my right, together with the artillery which now opened from the enemy's works, caused the One Hundred and ninety-eighth to waver for a moment. I then requested General Gregory, who reported to me with his brigade, to move rapidly into the woods on our right, by battalion in echelon by the left, so as to break this flank attack, and possibly to turn the enemy's left at the same moment that I should charge the works directly in front at a run. This plan was handsomely executed by all that the result was completely successful. The woods and the works were carried, with several prisoners and one battle-flag, and the line advanced some 300 yards across the White Oak Road.

My loss in this action was not more than seventy-five, but it included some of my best officers and men.

It would be unjust not to mention the services of Major Glenn and Colonel Sniper in this affair, whose bravery and energy I relied upon for the successful execution of my plans. I would also express my obligations to General Gregory for his quick comprehension of my wishes and for his efficient aid. I may be permitted also to mention the gallantry of Captain Fowler, assistant adjutant-general of division, who rode into the hottest fire to bring my orders, having his horse killed under him in doing so, and who by his conduct and bearing showed an example worthy of all praise.

During the night we buried our dead and cared for our wounded, and bivouacked on the line.

The brigade left bivouac on the White Oak Road early on the morning of the 1st and moved, with the rest of the division, toward Dinwiddie Courthouse, until we met General Sheridan with his cavalry. We then moved in connection toward Five Forks. Arriving at a point near Gravelly Run Church we were formed on the right of the Third Brigade of this division in three lines. Brevet Brigadier-General Gregory, commanding Second Brigade of this division, reported to me with his brigade, by order of General Griffin, and was placed upon the right flank of our lines, one regiment being deployed as skirmishers in our front, one on the flank faced outward, and one held in reserve. Mackenzie's cavalry was on our right. In this formation we advanced in the order designated.

Our instructions were to keep closed [*sic*] to the left on the Third Brigade, and also to wheel to the left in moving, the design being to strike the enemy in flank. We advanced through an open wood with nothing but light skirmishers in our front for some time. The constant change of direction to the left made the march on the right flank exceedingly rapid. On coming out at a large opening it was discovered that the Third Division of the corps was no longer on the left of the First Division, as had been the order of movement, and the heavy firing was all concentrated at a point to our left and front, where the Second Division had struck the enemy's works. Seeing the division flag moving in that direction I immediately drew my brigade into the field by the left flank and formed them facing this fire, and General Griffin ordered me to move against the point. Brevet Major-General Bartlett advanced at the same time with three regiments of the Third Brigade immediately on my right. We moved up rapidly under the crest of a hill and charged the works, striking them obliquely in flank and reverse, the right of my line—the One Hundred and eighty-fifth New York (Colonel Sniper) and the first battalion of the One Hundred and ninety-eighth Pennsylvania (Major Glenn)—passing down to the rear of the works, and the left—second battalion of the One Hundred and Ninety-eighth (Captain Stanton)—passing in front of them. The regiments of the Third Brigade, striking farther up, met a very heavy flank fire on the right, which broke us up somewhat, the extreme right falling back and the remainder of the line showing strong disposition to swing to the left into the works from which we had driven the enemy, a position which would render them powerless against the flank attack which was then commencing. It required the utmost personal efforts of every general and staff officer present to bring our line to face perpendicularly to the line of works, and to repulse the attack. General Bartlett informing me of the imminent peril on his right, I directed my two right regiments to sweep down the rear of the Twentieth Maine and First Michigan and break the attack, General Gregory also pressing forward with his brigade in the same direction. In the attempt to do this the regiments of the several brigades became somewhat mixed, but a new direction was given to our line, and the enemy completely put to rout. In the meantime, with one staff officer and

Captain Brinton, of the division staff, I assisted General Bartlett in collecting the stragglers from all commands who were seeking shelter in the edge of the woods; these men, to the number of 150 or 200, were formed and pushed in. While engaged in this I saw in the open field in our rear the flag of General Gwyn, of the Second Division, and dispatched Lieutenant Fisher, of my staff, to request him to throw his brigade in as rapidly as possible in the same direction as had been given to the troops already in. This assistance was most cheerfully and promptly rendered, and contributed in a good degree to our success. The confusion of the battle at this moment was great; different commands were mingled, but our line was still good. The men of my own brigade were, for the most part, nearest to the line of works though many of them were mixed with those of the Twentieth Maine and of the Second Brigade. As the line all merged into one the right of our line, consisting chiefly of the Second and Third Brigade troops, struck a battery and wagons on a road running perpendicular to the works, while Colonel Sniper and Major Glenn, with their colors close together, came upon the flank of other guns in position in the works. Two battle-flags were taken here by the One Hundred and eighty-fifth New York Volunteers, and a large number of prisoners. The whole line then pressed on, three brigades of the division as one, and driving the enemy far up the road to the distance, I should judge, of a mile or more. At dark I received an order from General Griffin to collect the troops of the division, and afterward from General Sheridan, to gather all the infantry that could be found and reform them in an open field to the left of the road, which was done; and we then encamped for the night along the works.

The prisoners captured by my brigade who cannot be claimed by other commands were nearly 900. Four battle-flags were taken; all these were turned over and receipted for except one battle-flag, which was torn up and distributed among the men before it could be properly taken charge of. My loss was not heavy in comparison with that of previous days, but cannot be considered otherwise than severe, inasmuch as it includes the name of so excellent a soldier as Maj. Edwin A. Glenn, commanding One Hundred and ninety-eighth Pennsylvania Volunteers, who fell mortally wounded in the extreme advance. I have already recommended his promotion by brevet for distinguished gallantry at the battle of Lewis' farm and White Oak Road.

On the afternoon of the 2d we moved from the battle-field by the Church road, my brigade leading the advance. Colonel Sniper deployed six companies as skirmishers, holding four as support. Flankers were thrown out on the right and left. We advanced but a short distance when we came upon a strong skirmish line of the enemy who endeavored to oppose our crossing a small creek. Colonel Sniper, however, attacked them with a vigor which soon dislodged them, and drove them before him. At Church road crossing on the South Side Railroad we captured a train of cars, which happened to be passing, in which were some Confederate officers and men. Crossing the railroad, I was then directed by Major-General Bartlett, commanding the division, to push out, if possible, to the Cox Road, crossing our direction at nearly a right angle. The enemy here showed a disposition to make a stand, deploying a line in a single rank, composed, as I judged, of about 1,500 dismounted cavalry. I immediately formed the two battalions of the One Hundred and ninety-eighth Pennsylvania in line of battle, threw forward Lieutenant-Colonel Townsend's regiment, of General Gregory's brigade, which had reported to me, into a piece of woods to protect my right, and in this order pushed rapidly forward. The enemy fell back on Colonel Sniper's brisk fire, and, with a loss of only three men wounded, the road was secured. I was then ordered to make disposition to hold the road, which was done; the skirmish line being formed along a creek half a mile or more in advance. We remained in this position until General Sheridan came up, when we moved again down the Cox Road, with skirmishers and flankers as before, marching until night, and encamping on what is called the Namozine road. On the morning of the 3d we moved out the Namozine road toward Amelia Court-House; bivouacked that same night on the same road. Marched at 6 a.m. on the morning of the 4th, and after dark came upon the Danville railroad at Jetersville, and made preparations to attack the enemy's trains in that vicinity. As the enemy appeared to be in force we threw up works, and remained on the alert during the night. The next day, the 5th, we were under arms nearly all day prepared to receive or make an attack. At about 1 o'clock I moved out the Amelia Courthouse Road to support a portion of our cavalry who were bringing in a large number of prisoners, and were severely attacked on the road. Returned to camp and remained during the night. The next day, the 6th, we marched in pursuit of the enemy in a westerly direction, passing through Paineville, my brigade in advance; firing was heard on our left. The skirmishers captured about 150 prisoners and several teams and our pioneers destroyed, by order of the corps commander, a large number of army wagons, gun carriages, and caissons which had been captured by our cavalry or abandoned by the enemy. Our march this day was very rapid and tiresome. After dark we encamped near Sailor's Creek. On the morning of the 7th we moved up the road by Sailor's Creek, and crossing the Lynchburg railroad near Rice's Station, brisk firing was heard on our right. Marched to Prince Edward Court-House and encamped for the night. On the 8th we moved by way of Prospect Station up the Lynchburg pike, the Twenty-fourth Corps preceding. Our march was frequently obstructed and tedious. Bivouacked at midnight on the road. Information was here received that General Sheridan had met the enemy and captured several trains. Marched at 4 a.m. on the 9th to the vicinity of Appomattox Court-House, being but a short distance, and found the cavalry warmly engaged. My brigade having the advance was filed to the right, moved to the rear of the cavalry, and formed on the right of the division and corps, in two lines. A heavy skirmish line was thrown forward, connecting with the Third Brigade skirmishers on the left, and our lines advanced against the enemy, relieving the cavalry, who reformed on my right. The skirmishers drove the enemy rapidly before them, while our line of battle was opened on by a battery in the town, my right being exactly in the line of fire. My skirmish line had reached the town, its right being at the house of Mrs. Wright, and my line of battle was rapidly closing on them, when a flag of truce came in with an aide of the commanding officer of the opposing forces, who was referred to the major-general commanding. I soon after received the order to halt my lines and to cease the skirmishing. During the conference which ensued we remained as we had halted, and afterward went

into camp near the same ground. My loss this day was, 1 killed and
1 wounded, Lieut. Hiram Clark, of the One Hundred and eighty-
fifth New York being instantly killed by a cannon-shot just as the
flag of truce came in.

Respectfully submitted.

J. L. Chamberlain

Brigadier-General, Late Commanding First Brigade

Capt. William Fowler,

Assistant Adjutant-General, First Division, 5th Corps.[78]

After the tumultuous last few weeks, Chamberlain finally had a chance to
recognize some of the men who had assisted him in the virutally non-
stop combat since the end of March. Some who received promotions
bought them with a painful wound or death. Others were deserving of
promotion but had been passed over by the army bureaucracy for nearly
a year.

Headquarters First Division, 5th Corps,

April 27, 1865

Col. Fred. T. Locke,

    Assistant Adjutant-General, Fifth Corps:

    Colonel: In compliance with instructions from headquarters
Army of the Potomac of April 18, 1865, I have the honor to submit the following list of officers whom I recommend for promotion to the rank set opposite their names.

    Bvt. Brig. Gen. H. G. Sickel, colonel One hundred ninety-
eighth Pennsylvania Volunteers, to be brigadier-general of volunteers for meritorious services and distinguished gallantry at the
battle of Lewis' Farm on the Quaker road, to rank from March 29.
This officer has received a previous recommendation for promotion. Lieut. Col James A. Cunningham, Thirty-second Massachusetts Volunteers, to be brevet Colonel for gallant conduct at the
battles of Five Forks, April 1, and the Cox road, April 2. Bvt. Lieut.
Col. Ellis Spear, Twentieth Maine Volunteers, to be brevet colonel
for meritorious services at the battle of Lewis' farm, March 29.
Lieut. Col. Isaac Doolittle, One hundred and eighty-eighth New
York Volunteers, to be brevet colonel for gallant conduct at the

battles of Lewis' farm and Five Forks. Lieut. Col. J. G. Townsend, One hundred and eighty-ninth New York Volunteers, to be brevet colonel for gallant conduct at the battle of Five Forks. Maj. E. A. Glenn, One hundred and ninety-eighth Pennsylvania Volunteers, to be brevet lieutenant-colonel for distinguished services at the battle of Lewis' farm; also to be brevet colonel for conspicuous gallantry at the battle of White Oak road and Five Forks, in the latter of which he was wounded. This officer has received a previous recommendation for promotion by brevet. Capt. William Fowler, assistant adjutant-general, First Division, Fifth Corps, to be brevet major for meritorious service and gallant conduct at the battle of Lewis' farm, March 29, White Oak road, March 31, and Five Forks. Surg. R. W. De Witt, surgeon-in-chief, First Division, to be brevet lieutenant-colonel for efficiency and conspicuous bravery in discharging his duties on the field of battle, particularly at the White Oak road and Five Forks. Capt. T. D. Chamberlain, Twentieth Maine Volunteers, to be brevet major for distinguished gallantry at Bethesda Church, June 1, 1864, and at Peebles farm. This officer has received a previous recommendation for promotion by brevet. Capt. R. W. Jacklin, Sixteenth Michigan Volunteers, to be brevet major for distinguished gallantry at the battle of Five Forks, April 1, 1865. This officer has received a previous recommendation for promotion by brevet. Capt. E. S. Farnsworth, Thirty-second Massachusetts Volunteers, to be brevet major for good conduct during the late campaign. Capt. George F. Morgan, One hundred and fifty-fifth Pennsylvania Volunteers, to be brevet major for distinguished gallantry at the battles of Five Forks and Appomattox Court House. Capt. George P. McClelland, One hundred and fifty-fifth Pennsylvania Volunteers, to be brevet major for gallant conduct at the battle of Five Forks, in which he was seriously wounded. Capt. H. G. Denniston, One hundred and eighty-eighth New York Volunteers, to be brevet major for bravery during the campaign. Capt. A. M. Beman, One hundred and eighty-ninth New York Volunteers, to be brevet major for bravery during the campaign. Capt. Henry F. Sidelinger, Twentieth Maine Volunteers, to be brevet major for bravery during the campaign. Capt. William L. Guinther, One hundred and ninety-eighth Pennsylvania Volunteers, to be

brevet major for gallant conduct at the battle of Five Forks. Capt. I.
W. Kimbell, One hundred and ninety-eighth Pennsylvania Volunteers, to be brevet major for gallant conduct at the battle of Five
Forks. Capt. George R. Abbott, First Maine Sharpshooters, to be
brevet major for gallantry during the campaign. Bvt Capt. L. C.
Bartlett, to be brevet major for gallant conduct at the battle of
White Oak road, March 31. First Lieut. Benjamin F. Walters, One
hundred and forty-third Pennsylvania Volunteers, aide-de-camp, to
be brevet captain for distinguished gallantry at the battle of Lewis'
farm. First Lieut. T. K. Vogel, One hundred and ninety-eighth
Pennsylvania Volunteers to be brevet captain for gallant conduct in
all the battles of the late campaign. First Lieut. Lewis S. Edgar, One
hundred and eighty-fifth New York Volunteers, to be brevet captain
for gallant conduct in all the battles of the late campaign. Second
Lieut. Charles J. Rector, One hundred and eighty-fifth New York
Volunteers to be brevet captain for gallant conduct in all the battles
of the late campaign.

I am, colonel, very repectfully, your obedient servant,
J. L. Chamberlain,
Brigadier-General, Commanding.[79]

At the end of April, Chamberlain received orders to begin the march to
Richmond on May 2. Though they could hardly afford it, the people of
Dinwiddie County, where Chamberlain had administered, proposed a
formal dinner to thank him. Although Chamberlain appreciated their
sincere sentiments, he would not allow them to feed him when their
own families were going hungry.

At five o'clock on the morning of May 2, Chamberlain's men began
their march. By evening they had reached Sutherland Station. By six the
next morning they were heading along the Cox Road to Petersburg. The
march aroused stirring memories of battles fought just weeks before as
the men passed near the sites: Five Forks, the Quaker Road, the Boydton
Plank Road, the siege lines around Petersburg, and long-denied Petersburg itself.

Warren was in Petersburg, and the men—what was left of the once
massive 5th Corps that he had led across the Rapidan—passed him in
review. "One half the corps had gone," estimated Chamberlain, "passing
the death-streams of all Virginia's rivers; two hundred miles of furrowed

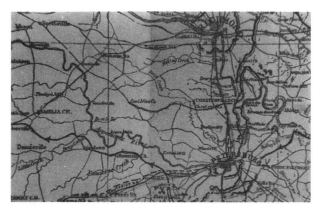

Detail of Chamberlain's personal map showing his march route from Appomattox Court House, through Petersburg, to Richmond. LIBRARY OF CONGRESS

earth and the infinite of heaven held each their own."[80] They had fought for nine months to capture it, but now they quickly passed through Petersburg and encamped five or six miles out on the road to Richmond.

By noon on May 4, they reached Drewery's Bluff on the south side of the James ten miles from Richmond. They were in Manchester that evening, just across the river from Richmond. A heavy rain prevented them from entering the capital of the former Confederacy on May 5.

Chamberlain and the men of the 5th Corps got a view of Belle Isle and Libby prisons as they crossed the James on the upper pontoon bridge. They saw the sections of Richmond that had been burned as the Confederate government fled a month before, and years later Chamberlain still remembered the houses of Robert E. Lee and Jefferson Davis. Furniture was piled outside of homes, and worthless Confederate money lay all over the place. Worse, they saw numerous residences draped with black crepe mourning a son or husband, possibly killed by the Federal soldiers that now marched in front of their homes.

For some reason they were ordered to continue to march—pressing on, Chamberlain thought, as if still in pursuit of Lee. They marched until ten the night of May 6, twenty miles in all, crossing the Chickahominy and encamping at "Peake's Turn Out" on the Virginia Central Railroad near Hanover Court House. Chamberlain regretted that the men did not have time to visit some of the fields upon which they had fought; he thought seeing those spots might have a healing effect upon them. "One day more for the whole march would have allowed our men the somber satisfaction of reviewing the fields of lost battles, which have their place, also, in making up life's full account. Broken threads are sometimes well worth picking up."[81]

Late that night, Chamberlain's horse was restive. As he walked to calm him, Chamberlain crunched through the moldering breastbones of a body that had been decaying for a year, undisturbed on this backwater battlefield. His horse, pawing at the ground, had uncovered two skeletons. In the morning, the men found some others as well. From marks the dead men had once carved in their belt plates, the men identified the remains as friends long believed missing. Chamberlain gave permission to gather them up, and the men placed them in cracker boxes and loaded them gently on the wagons to be shipped home.

They left at ten the next morning, passed through Hanover Court House, crossed the Pamunkey, and after twelve miles encamped at Concord Church near the battlefields of Jericho Mills and the North Anna. The next day's march got them to just below Bowling Green at Milford by five in the evening. On May 9 they marched twenty miles, passing through Bowling Green and nearing the battlefields of Fredericksburg. Though the men were tired, some walked a little farther to visit Marye's Heights, where they had nearly lost their lives.

They recrossed the Rappahannock on May 10 and marched through their old 1862 campground. That night they encamped at Dumfries, north of Fredericksburg. Chamberlain had an opportunity to write a glowing testimonial for Col. Gustavus Sniper, commander of the 185th New York.[82]

The next day they found the roads miserable, full of ankle-twisting ruts and holes from wagon wheels and horses' hooves. The men labored over steep hills and through swamps. In midafternoon a thunderstorm struck. From a hill he had just crested, Chamberlain could see the column toiling in front and behind with a space between divisions. Suddenly lightning cracked through the clouds and struck the column. He saw it first ahead of him, traveling along the muzzles of the muskets as it "leaped along the writhing column like a river of fire." It exploded like a "battery of shrapnel" between the columns, narrowly missing Chamberlain. One of the ambulances was struck. The bolt killed the horses and the driver and stunned those riding inside the wagons. Chamberlain gave orders to see to the injured men, and the column plodded on.

They crossed the Occoquan, marched another rain-soaked four miles, and encamped in the dark on the Orange and Alexandria Railroad a mile below Fairfax. Again the men wondered why they were being pushed so hard and blamed their officers. Chamberlain thought it might be attributed to economy: The army was costing the country millions every week, and the sooner it was disbanded, the less the final cost. "It seemed as if somebody was as anxious now to be rid of us as ever before to get us to the front."[83]

At nine o'clock on the morning of May 12, they were on the march again. They turned at Fairfax Court House onto the Columbia Pike, heading to Arlington Heights to encamp. The site near the home of Robert E. Lee was a familiar campground; it was from here they had departed for Antietam, their first battle. As they marched, the sun suddenly shone through, and they could see the White House and Capitol dome and, below them, "the river whose name and fame we bore, flowing in the darkness past us, as from dream to dream."[84]

After Chamberlain's men had been encamped for a week, they were joined by much of Sherman's army from the Western Theater of the war, whose campground was closer to Alexandria, a little below the Army of the Potomac's. At first the soldiers were cordial and intermingled. But soon jibes and jealousies arose about who had done the hardest fighting, and relations deteriorated.

The officers of the 5th Corps had sent to Tiffany's in New York for a specially designed memento for General Griffin. On the evening of May 22, the night before the armies of the Union were to pass in review through Washington, they held a grand ceremony and presented Griffin with a pin made in the image of their battle flag: a red Maltese cross on white enamel, all on a gold background. Small diamonds surrounded the cross, and a large diamond worth $1,000 was set in the center. Chamberlain delivered the presentation speech. Griffin responded by saying that he was reminded of the cost of the fame that had gained him this symbol. He referred to Chamberlain as an example of the fortitude and constancy that were inherent in the division. Whenever he would look upon the pin for years to come, he would "thank God for the manhood that has made it glorious."[85]

The next morning was the last grand review of the Army of the Potomac. Writing of it years after, Chamberlain admitted that it was difficult for him, because he felt such emotion for this group of men who, through trials and heartbreak, defeat and resurgence and finally victory, had become more than just an army to him.

Troops of other corps were to march before the 5th Corps. At four that morning, the 5th Corps marched over the Long Bridge and the bridge over the canal into Washington, then down Maryland Avenue to First Street. The troops, in a column of companies twenty men wide, with narrower intervals between the various units following, were to march down Pennsylvania Avenue. The reviewing stand stood in front of the White House.

By nine, with the sun shining brightly, the head of the Army of the Potomac moved out. General Meade and the officers of his headquarters led the procession, followed by the cavalry and other units essential to the functioning of a modern army: the Signal Corps, in charge of communication, which saw its duties modernized under Grant from simple wagging of flags to field telegraphy; the Engineer Corps, whose swift laying of the pontoons had aided Grant's rapid movements; and finally, the infantry.

The 9th Corps led, and behind it marched part of the 19th Corps; both contained Maine men whom Chamberlain knew. Next came Griffin's 5th Corps with Chamberlain's 1st Division. Riding between the buildings covered in flying bunting, flowers, and waving flags, Chamberlain felt like one of the children of Israel "walled by the friendly Red Sea."[86]

As he rode, a young woman rushed up to him with a victory wreath, but each time she lifted it, Charlemagne, unused to women, shied away. "Was this the soft death-angel—did he think?—calling us again, as in other days?"[87] Chamberlain never got the wreath. Instead, it went to a subordinate officer with a calmer horse.

The climax of the ceremony was when the army passed the reviewing stands, but to Chamberlain it was anticlimactic. The one weary face that should have been there was missing and sadly missed—Lincoln's. At the reviewing stands, Chamberlain, at the request of President Andrew Johnson, dismounted and joined the dignitaries and so was allowed to see his own division pass in review. He recalled:

> For me, while this division was passing, no other thing could lure my eyes away, whether looking on or through. These were my men, and those who followed were familiar and dear. They

belonged to me, and I to them, by bonds birth cannot create nor death sever. More were passing here than the personages on the stand could see. But to me so seeing, what a review, how great, how far, how near! It was as the morning of the resurrection![88]

Chamberlain watched as they passed and remembered, perhaps painfully, the men whom he had known throughout the past two and a half years. Some units and men he remembered more poignantly than others, as when he saw the United States Regulars, who lost so many of their number in the charge down the north slope of Little Round Top. The memories would rise again unbidden in his later years when he wrote about their commander Ayres, who had been badgered at the Warren Court of Inquiry by some impudent congressman. The elected official taunted Ayres about the U.S. Regulars at Five Forks: "Where were your regulars then?" "Buried, sir," Ayres replied, "at Gettysburg!"[89]

On and on they came, as those on the reviewing rostrum stood and whispered among themselves, "This is the 5th Corps!" "These are straight from Five Forks and Appomattox!"

Riding at the head of the 7th Wisconsin—of the famous, decimated Iron Brigade—was the calm figure of Hollon Richardson, who at Five Forks had stepped in front of his commander General Warren to take the minié ball meant for him.

And for Chamberlain, more were passing than just those before his weary eyes. He thought of the thirteen young colonels he had come to know especially, and of their fate: seven shot dead at the head of their men, the others wounded; all thirteen dead, disfigured, or dismembered by the surgeon's amputation knife. Wrote Chamberlain: "'Waes Hael!'—across the rifts of vision—'Be Whole again, My Thirteen!'"[90]

Memories both horrible and sublime filled his mind. Of the passing throng, now composed of the 2nd and the 6th Corps, he later said, "You could not say from what world they come, or to what world they go." One unit that had suffered, endured, and been resurrected a number of times by replacements and reorganization he called "the division which knows something of the transmigration of souls."[91]

Finally it was over. And in a few days, of the daily tumult and fear of imminent death, of the general confusion that is the day-to-day business of an army on campaign, and of the seemingly deathless friendships adversity makes, ripped apart by flying lead and steel, only memories would remain.

Head Quarters 1st Div. 5th Corps
June 6 1865

My dear Sae,

It is a long time since I have written. I doubt however, if I have had the pleasure of a letter direct from you since my last. You doubtless know very well that we are now reducing the army as fast as possible. What will happen next we do not know. I suppose the rest will be ordered into the interior of the Rebel states somewhere. My own affairs are in an exceedingly uncertain state. But I am by no means disturbed about them. I have plenty of "strings on my bow," or in better words, Providence will both open & guide my way.

You see I was right in sticking to the army to the last. I have now been recommended by all my superior officers for the rank of full Major General, besides the Brevet recommended at Five Forks. Whether I shall get the full appointment, I don't know. Anybody else would, if he had half the record or the recommendations I have. But the political gentlemen of Maine have not particularly interested themselves in me. It is only those who know me, & have seen me, <u>in the field</u> who take much notice of me. I can afford to be let alone however. It makes me perfectly independent. I am not much beholden to the State of Maine. I am far better known in New York or Pennsylvania than in my own State. Do not think I say this complainingly. I am not obliged to complain. My position is all I could ask—all I coveted—the command of 12,000 men whose record as soldiers never was surpassed. Of course I shall soon be reassigned. Where, I don't know. If I don't like it, I shall resign.

My wounds trouble me still. I tried to ride into Washington to night in my wagon & had to give it up. The saddle does not trouble me so much. I am in good spirits though, and ready to do anything I am called on for. Tom—the Major—is well & doing well. He is in luck too. By special order of Genl Meade he is retained in the service. He is now the senior captain of the new 20th Maine. Father & Mother I hope are well. They need not have a particle of anxiety about any of us now.

John has his place I suppose, as he sent me a security bond for $3000 to sign for him as Inspector &c. As for my own home I shall have to refer you to your own latest intelligence. I am not favored in that particular.

Dr. Adams has made me a visit. While he was here, Dr. Talcott dined with me. I enjoyed seeing them very much.

How is Mary now adays? I have not had any answer to my last letter to her. And how is Uncle [ill.]? Don't let Mother get low. I couldn't bear to lose Father or Mother any more than if I were a boy of 10.

> With a world of love
> your Lawrence.[92]

On June 28, 1865, special orders 339 came from the adjutant general's office, Headquarters of the Army of the Potomac, stating that "this army, as an organization, ceases to exist."

Chamberlain would obey, but as with so many other orders he had received in the last two years, he found it somewhat hard to believe.

Later he would write:

The War Department and the President may cease to give the army orders, may disperse its visible elements, but cannot extinguish them. They will come together again under higher bidding, and will know their place and name. This army will live, and live on, so long as soul shall answer soul . . .[93]

> Headquarters First Division, Fifth Corps,
> Camp at Arlington, Va [printed letterhead]
> July 1st 1865

Brig. Genl. L. Thomas
Adjutant General U.S.A.
General,

I have the honor to acknowledge the receipt of the notification of my appointment as Major Genl. by Brevet in the service of the United States, and to inform you of my acceptance of the same.

My age is thirty six years. My birthplace is Brewer, Maine, of which state I am a permanent resident.

> I have the honor to be
> very respectfully
> Your obdt. servt.
> J. L. Chamberlain
> Bvt. Maj. Genl.[94]

Brunswick, Me. July 31st 1865

Brig Genl. L. Thomas,
Adjutant Genl U. S. A.
General,

I have the honor to acknowledge the receipt of my appointment as Major Genl of Volunteers by Brevet dating from March 29th 1865, and to inform you of my acceptance of the same.

My age is thirty-six years; my birthplace Brewer, Maine, of which state I am a permanent resident.

Very respectfully
Your obdt servt.
J. L. Chamberlain
Bvt. Major Genl. Vols.[95]

When Chamberlain arrived home in Maine, he discovered that the man who gave him his battlefield promotion was also visiting his state. He sent him this invitation:

Portland, July 31st, 1865.

Lieut. General Grant,
General:

Learning that you are to be in town tomorrow, I respectfully solicit the honor of your presence at a reunion of the Graduates of Bowdoin College who have been in the war, on Wednesday Evening.

This would occupy but a small portion of your time, and would be exceedingly gratifying to all our citizens and especially to those on whose behalf I make this request.

Very respectfully
Your obedient servant,
(Signed.) Joshua L. Chamberlain,
Bvt Major General.[96]

Grant accepted Chamberlain's invitation. He was warmly welcomed to Brunswick, where he visited the Chamberlains in their home and was presented with an honorary doctorate from Bowdoin. A dinner and reception afterward brought forth poignant memories of the four-year conflict that had changed so many of those present.

It must have represented a closure of sorts for Chamberlain. But it was just one of many such moments he would experience over the next half-century of life left to him; just one of many times he would be called back to the days, as he would write in *The Passing of the Armies,* when "we questioned what life should be, and answered for ourselves what we would be!"

⇥ CONCLUSION ⇤

CHAMBERLAIN WROTE IN *The Passing of the Armies,* "It may be a trace of that curious paradox in the human heart which makes us love those who have been a care and trouble to us."

No doubt this is why Chamberlain grew to respect and love his men so much; why the 20th Maine, or the 1st Brigade or the army, for all the trouble they were, became so important to him. It is why all those they comprised—both living and dead—remained imperishable in his life and memory.

Yet that they were a care and trouble to him was partly his own fault. As many of his letters reveal, even upon his sickbed, Chamberlain cared and worried about his men. When individuals earned it, he wrote his superiors to praise them and request promotions or better assignments. When they died, he wrote of their deaths, sometimes painfully, to loved ones at the time, and then fifty years later, as they haunted his memory. "More were passing here," he wrote of the last review of the Army of the Potomac, "than the personages on the stand could see."[1]

Looking back over the war from the quiet of Appomattox, he was truly amazed that he was still alive—that any of them were still alive—after all they had been through. But he reached back into his religious training and Old Testament faith to find an answer to why the war had to be fought: "It was a remnant of the inherited curse for sin. We had purged it away, with blood offerings."[2]

General Griffin, who had a number of opportunities to observe Chamberlain under fire, noticed "his absolute indifference to danger . . . in the field his mind worked as deliberately and as quietly as it would in his own study."[3]

No doubt his scholar's mind and training enabled him to remain calm in tumultuous battle. But his faith helped too.

In his birthday letter to his concerned mother, written on September 8, 1864, can be read a serenity, a peace that seems to have been with him even in battle: "But what it is, I cant tell you. I haven't a particle of fanaticism in me. But I plead guilty to a sort of fatalism. I believe in a destiny—

one, I mean, divinely appointed, & to which we are carried forward by a perfect trust in God. I do this, & I believe in it. I have laid plans, in my day, & good ones I thought. But they never succeeded. <u>Something else, better, did,</u> and I could see it as plain as day, that God had done it, & for my good.

"So I am right, be sure of that, happen what may. Not for any merit of mine, but for divine & loving mercy all is bright with me, in this world & beyond."

Still ahead for Chamberlain lay his discharge from the army, then temporary reinstatement so that his wound could be operated upon again under the auspices of the War Department; his many years in public service and in civilian positions; and near the end of the century, his Medal of Honor, won on the slope of Little Round Top on July 2, 1863. And he would visit his old battlefields well into the beginning of the next century.

Through it all he would carry his experiences and memories of the war, his visions, his reminiscences, and the ghosts. And every time he began to forget the army and the men in it, the pain from his old Petersburg wound would remind him, again and again, until February 24, 1914, when infection from the wound finally killed him.

In his last wartime letter to his sister Sae, he seemed to understand that after all he had been through, he no longer belonged only to Maine: "I am far better known in New York or Pennsylvania than in my own State. Do not think I say this complainingly. I am not obliged to complain. My position is all I could ask. . . ." Although he did not write it, he certainly must have felt that after commanding troops from New York, Pennsylvania, Massachusetts, and Maine, and having fought against men from Virginia and Texas, North and South Carolina, Alabama, and Georgia, surely he belonged to all of the United States—North and South— and to everyone in it then and in the years to come.

Early in my research, I received a letter from Tom Desjardin, a historian from Lewiston, Maine, graciously offering his help in researching Chamberlain, a subject he had been working on for a number of years. One paragraph stood out:

"I would like to add one word of advice, if I may, about doing this research in Maine. To Mainers, the General has been one of 'ours' for a long time. This recent flurry of popularity has caused many an 'out of stater' to come up to Maine looking to make a fast buck on the story, and the products of some of these adventures have been pretty poor. You may run into a bit of skepticism because of this—and the fact that folks in Maine have always had a thing about people 'from away'—but if you can convince them that you intend to do the General justice, to neither exaggerate nor diminish what he did, you will do all right."

This I hope I have done.

⇒ NOTES ⇐

Because a number of sources appear with great frequency, the following abbreviations are used:

BC   Bowdoin College Library Special Collections, Bowdoin College, Brunswick, Maine
GNMP   Gettysburg National Military Park Library
LC   Joshua L. Chamberlain Papers, Collections of the Manuscript Division, Library of Congress, Washington, D.C.
MHS   Maine Historical Society
MSA   Maine State Archives, Augusta, Maine. "Records Relating to the Civil War Career of Joshua Lawrence Chamberlain."
NA   National Archives, Washington, D.C. Records of the Adjutant General's Office, 1780–1917, Record Group 94. Microfilm. JLC's papers are located under the designation "C411 CB 1866."
OR   U.S. War Department, *War of the Rebellion: Official Records of the Union and Confederate Armies,* 128 volumes (Washington, D.C., 1880–1901)
PHS   Pejepscot Historical Society, Brunswick, Maine
UME   University of Maine

INTRODUCTION

1. Interview with James Talbot of Turner, Maine, January 1995.

2. Nearly all of Chamberlain's official duties and correspondence ended with his active duty in August 1865, but because of his continuing troubles with his wounds and the necessity for more surgery, the state senators and representatives petitioned President Johnson to revoke his mustering out, at least until the operations were over. He was separated from the army for good in January 1866.

3. Trulock, 26–60.

1862

1. MSA.

2. MSA.

3. MSA. In a final paragraph marked "Private" in a letter from

Maine attorney general Drummond to Governor Washburn dated July 21, 1862, Drummond writes, "Have you app'td Chamberlain Col. of 20th? His old classmates here say you have been deceived: that C. is nothing at all: that is the universal expression of those who know him."

4. Oliver Otis Howard, Bowdoin alumnus and West Point graduate serving in the Federal army.

5. Chamberlain had been speaking at various recruiting meetings around Brunswick.

6. MSA.

7. MSA.

8. MSA.

9. MSA.

10. BC.

11. Pullen, 1–6.

12. MSA.

13. MSA.

14. John L. Hodsdon, adjutant general of Maine.

15. MSA.

16. Styple, 2. Some of the regiment apparently had already been issued the Enfield; Holman Melcher of the color guard wrote of receiving all his equipment at Camp Mason by September 1, 1862.

17. Trulock, 63–64.

18. Trulock, 64–65.

19. Styple, 5.

20. Trulock, 67–69.

21. Trulock, 69.

22. Trulock, 72–74.

23. Joshua L. Chamberlain Letterbook, PHS. Under heading Horse shot under me: "also Maj. Gilmore's black horse at Shepherdstown Ford Sept. 20/62 loaned me to avoid exposing my splendid white horse "Prince." in head near bit of bridle."

24. Trulock, 75.

25. If this letter begins the numbered series as the "6th," there must be at least five previous letters missing.

26. LC.

27. McClellan, 161.

28. Chamberlain spelled his daughter's name either "Daisy" or

"Daise." Perhaps the latter was a fatherly shortening of her name. The spelling appears from letter to letter as he wrote it.

29. "Aunty" is another nickname, along with "Cousin D," for Deborah Folsom, Fanny's adopted mother's younger maiden sister, who lived with the Chamberlains.

30. LC.

31. Hardee, 153.

32. Jomini, 167–69.

33. Trulock, 83.

34. Trulock, 83.

35. According to Julia Oehmig, curator of the Pejepscot Historical Society, Mr. Griffin owned a bookstore on Maine Street in Brunswick.

36. LC.

37. LC.

38. Trulock, 86–87.

39. Warrenton, Virginia.

40. MSA.

41. Pullen, 43–46; Trulock, 87–89.

42. Chamberlain Letterbook, PHS, newspaper article; Trulock, 90–92.

43. Trulock, 93–94.

44. Trulock, 95.

45. Trulock, 96–97.

46. Trulock, 98. Perhaps this is the genesis for the following letter to Chamberlain found in the Bowdoin College Library:

Rockville Aug 3rd 18/63

To J. L. Chamberlain Dear Sir

Your very kind and gentlemanly letter was received to night and in behalf of all our family friends, we deem it a very great kindness, that you, a stranger, should send us tidings, of so precious and yet so sad a memento.

We have never heard from my brother, since that terrible battle at F —g and have long since mourned him as dead, and it will be a kindness the memory of which death only can efface, if you will forward the book to C. H. Towne Esq. Rockville, Ct.

Very Respectfully, M. L. Morse

47. Chamberlain, 9: "My Story of Fredericksburg."
48. Ames, 122.
49. Trulock, 99–100.
50. Chamberlain Letterbook, PHS.
51. Trulock, 101.
52. Trulock, 102.
53. Chamberlain Letterbook, PHS.
54. MSA.
55. Trulock, 104–5.

1863

1. Trulock, 106–7; Pullen, 65–70.
2. PHS.
3. Trulock, 108.
4. MSA.
5. Trulock, 110.
6. NA.
7. LC.
8. LC.
9. Trulock, 110.
10. Furgurson, 94–97.
11. Trulock, 111; Pullen, 75–76.
12. Furgurson, 301–4.
13. Chamberlain Letterbook, PHS. Under heading <u>Horse</u> <u>shot</u> <u>under</u> <u>me:</u> "1863 Chancellorsville, May—'Prince' White Stallion. <u>Head</u> <u>'Grif-</u> <u>fin's</u> <u>Charge.'"</u>
14. BC.
15. MSA.
16. Trulock, 114.
17. MSA.
18. LC.
19. MSA.
20. MSA. (Not in Chamberlain's handwriting, but signed by him.)
21. MSA. (Not in Chamberlain's handwriting, but signed by him.)
22. Trulock, 116.
23. LC.
24. Trulock, 119.
25. Trulock, 120.

26. Trulock, 117–21.

27. Brig. Gen. James Barnes's report, OR, ser. I, vol. 27, pt.1, 595; Chamberlain, "Blood and Fire," 45.

28. Chamberlain, "Blood and Fire," 45.

29. Chamberlain, *Armies*, 308.

30. Elisha Coan Manuscript, BC.

31. Chamberlain, "Blood and Fire," 45; Coan Ms.

32. Coan Ms. Elisha Coan thought it was the gun Maj. Gen. Gouverneur K. Warren, of Meade's staff, ordered fired in the woods of Big Round Top to locate the Confederates as they rested before their assault on Little Round Top. But the timing is not quite right, since the Confederate cannonade prior to their stepping off occurred about this time. Perhaps what he heard was a signal gun from Longstreet's artillery signaling the opening of his cannonade.

33. Chamberlain, "Blood and Fire," 46.

34. Chamberlain wrote several reports on the action on Little Round Top. They all vary in detail somewhat, but pieced together along with Oates's report and both men's postwar writings on the subject—a fairly clear interpretation of the events can be reconstructed. In reconstructing these events, the most contemporaneous reports have been referred to first and letters and articles written later have been used to complete the narrative.

35. Coan Ms.

36. Chamberlain, "Blood and Fire," 48.

37. The exact wording, "at all hazards" or "at all costs," varies depending on which account is used. The meaning, however, is unequivocal.

38. Chamberlain Letterbook, PHS.

39. Oates's Report, OR, ser. I, vol. 27, pt. 2, 392–93.

40. Chamberlain, "Blood and Fire," 50.

41. Oates, 214. Oates's Official Report, written August 8, 1863, is merely an outline of what occurred from his point of view. His book, however, was produced after much correspondence with fellow combatants and contains more information. The historian must decide which account is more accurate. The OR accounts have been used but are supplemented with additional information from later accounts.

42. Oates's Report, OR, ser. I, vol. 27, pt. 2, 392–93.

43. Chamberlain's Report, OR, ser. I, vol. 27, pt. 1, 623.

44. Chamberlain, *"Bayonet! Forward,"* 186. Address presented by Chamberlain at the dedication of the Twentieth Maine Monuments at Gettysburg, October 3, 1889.

45. Unofficial report (n.d.), Chamberlain to Barnes, New York Historical Society, copy in GNMP.

46. Chamberlain, "Blood and Fire," 50. In 1913 Chamberlain, perhaps having read Oates's 1905 account, wrote that "ten minutes had not passed" before the artillery ceased and the infantry assault began.

47. Oates, 215: "The flanking party referred to . . . was mine."

48. Oates, 218.

49. Chamberlain's Report, OR, ser. I, vol. 27, pt. 1, 624.

50. Chamberlain, "Blood and Fire," 51.

51. Chamberlain, "Blood and Fire," 51.

52. Chamberlain, "Blood and Fire," 51.

53. Oates, 219.

54. Chamberlain, "Blood and Fire," 50. Chamberlain wrote in 1913 that he thought he had engaged all the companies.

55. Chamberlain, "Blood and Fire," 52. Interestingly, in a typescript portion of Ellis Spear's "Recollections" (GNMP, courtesy Abbott Spear, Warren, ME), Spear mentions going over to the center of the line but never receiving a direct order for a wheeling movement. Chamberlain never mentions in his account having given an order for a wheeling movement. Thus it seems that no order was given for this elaborate movement.

56. Oates, 220. Writing in 1905, Oates repeated three times on a single page that his retreat was ordered by him.

57. Oates's Report, OR, ser. I, vol. 27, pt. 2, 393; Oates, 220.

58. Though much has been made of a "textbook maneuver" performed by the 20th Maine—a right wheel by the left half of the regiment to bring it in line with the right wing, then an advance against Oates's men in the valley—there is no evidence that such a complicated wheeling maneuver had ever been ordered.

59. Chamberlain, writing after the war ("Blood and Fire," 55), remembered that Bulger "introduced himself as my prisoner." Oates denied that Bulger surrendered to Chamberlain, insisting instead that Bulger surrendered to Col. James Rice.

60. Chamberlain wrote at least seven contemporary accounts of the fight on Little Round Top, including a couple of unofficial reports. They

vary somewhat in minor details, and historians will continue to disagree on whether Chamberlain ordered the final charge and whether the right wheel was part of a complicated, preplanned maneuver. All of Chamberlain's known contemporary accounts are included here.

61. Trulock, 150–54; Pullen, 129–32.

62. Trulock, 156; Pullen, 133; Chamberlain's Report, OR, ser. I, vol. 27, pt. 1, 626.

63. Chamberlain, "Blood and Fire," 56.

64. LC.

65. Trulock, 157; Capt. Atherton W. Clark's Report, OR, ser. I, vol. 27, pt. 1, 627.

66. This appears to be a draft of Chamberlain's report to division commander General Barnes. Though it is undated, it appears to be a fairly early report, in that Chamberlain called it "unofficial," and wrote an official report later on July 6, "near Emmitsburg." Additionally, in the "Official Report," he writes that Colonel Rice referred to Big Round Top as "Wolf's Hill," something both Rice and Chamberlain did on July 6. By the time Rice's report came out on July 31, Rice had ceased calling it that. Finally, Chamberlain's figures for his dead are low in this report; in his other reports, which match, the figures are higher, probably closer to reality. This report, therefore, may be an early one.

The cover letter, although dated in September, seems to refer to a busier period. At the beginning of September, the brigade was encamped and not on active campaign. Perhaps Barnes requested a report he knew Chamberlain had already written. Regardless, this report to Barnes makes more sense alongside the Gettysburg reports.

3rd Brigade Sept 3d 1863

Gen Barnes,
Comdg Division,

I send the statement which is too long; but it takes time to be brief, & that I had not. If you will pardon the errors I shall be glad.

Chaplain Clark of the 83d Penna Vols. 3d Brigade can give valuable information in regard to localities.

very truly
J. L. Chamberlain
Col. 20th Maine

67. New York Historical Society, copy in files of GNMP.

68. UME, courtesy Tom Desjardin.

69. Since they are so similar, rather than print both the handwritten and published reports, the minor differences are noted.

70. The following paragraph appears at this point in the published version of Chamberlain's report, but not in the handwritten version: "Massed at first with the rest of the Division on the right of the road, we were moved several times farther towards the left. Although expecting every moment to be put into action, and held strictly in line of battle, yet the men were able to take some rest and make the most of their rations."

71. Underlined in original handwritten draft.

72. Bracketed initials were inserted into published version for clarity.

73. OR, ser. I, vol. 27, pt. 1, 622–26. Original draft (not in Chamberlain's hand), LC.

74. Rice's Report; Clark's Report; Maj. Robert T. Elliot's Report; Maj. William H. Lamont's Report, OR, ser. I, vol. 27, pt. 1, 621–33. Although some secondary sources disagree with these march dates, the dates from the regimental reports of the 3rd Brigade all agree and are used here.

75. MSA.

76. MSA.

77. OR, ser. I, vol. 27, pt. 1, 621–22, 627.

78. Trulock, 161. Strange as it may seem, the army has its own rules. Apparently, Rice was ordered to have his men sleep in an area that was unsuitable and, in kindness to them, allowed them to sleep upon more comfortable wheat sheaves. This was not the first time an officer got in trouble with his superiors for violating orders out of compassion for his men.

79. MSA.

80. LC.

81. MSA.

82. OR, ser. I, vol. 27, pt. 1, 622, 627; Trulock, 162–63, 167.

83. Original in NA. Copy courtesy PHS.

84. OR, ser. I, vol. 27, pt. 1, 622, 627.

85. Original in NA. Copy courtesy PHS.

86. MSA.

87. Trulock, 163.

88. MSA.

89. UME, rough draft at PHS.
90. Trulock, 164.
91. MSA.
92. A note, possibly written by Trulock, on the photocopied manuscript indicates that this letter was probably written in 1863.
93. LC.
94. LC.
95. Trulock, 167; Pullen, 159.
96. MSA.
97. Wallace, 118; Pullen, 159–60; Trulock, 170.
98. MSA.
99. MSA.
100. Pullen, 160–66; Wallace, 119; Trulock, 171–73.
101. Chamberlain Letterbook, PHS.
102. Wallace, 119–21; Pullen, 166; Trulock, 174.
103. Original in NA. Copy courtesy PHS.

1864

1. Trulock, 174; Pullen, 175.
2. LC.
3. NA, pension records of Isabella Fogg, Maine Civil War nurse. Courtesy Tom Desjardin.
4. MSA.
5. MSA.
6. Wallace, 121.
7. MSA.
8. Pullen, 176–94. Trudeau (p. 119) places Confederate casualties from the Wilderness fighting at 10,830 and Federal casualties at 17,666.
9. NA.
10. Trulock, 176.
11. Trudeau, 133–42; Cullen, 32–34; Pullen, 198.
12. Trudeau, 211.
13. Records as to the date Chamberlain returned to the army are sketchy, but Trulock (p. 177, n. 454) places him back on May 14, 1864.
14. Trulock, 177; Pullen, 202–3.
15. Trulock, 180–81.
16. MSA. Lines at the bottom say, "Let commissions [ill.] as requested. Cony, Gov."

17. Trulock, 181.

18. Wallace, 124; Trulock, 182.

19. Trulock, 182–83.

20. Trulock, 185.

21. Grant, vol. II, 279; Trulock, 185.

22. Trudeau, 264–98.

23. Grant, vol. II, 276.

24. Trulock, 186.

25. Pullen, 206.

26. Trulock, 188; Wallace, 125–26.

27. Trulock, 193. Chamberlain's files contain an overabundance of testimonials to his military ability from some highly regarded regular army officers, such as Generals Barnes, Griffin, and Bartlett. Retained by him over the years but tucked away, they may reveal both Chamberlain's pride and modesty.

28. Grant, 288–89; Trulock, 195.

29. Nesbitt, 117; Trulock, 195.

30. Trulock, 196.

31. Trulock, 196.

32. Trulock, 198.

33. Chamberlain, *"Bayonet! Forward,"* 46.

34. Chamberlain, *"Bayonet! Forward,"* 47.

35. Chamberlain Letterbook, PHS.

36. Sgt. Patrick DeLacy, statement and letter to Chamberlain, (n.d.), 3, LC.

37. Trulock, 201.

38. Chamberlain, *"Bayonet! Forward,"* 47.

39. Chamberlain, *"Bayonet! Forward,"* 47.

40. DeLacy, 3.

41. DeLacy, 4–5.

42. Chamberlain, *"Bayonet! Forward,"* 48. DeLacy thought he remembered the incident, but admitted not remembering all that was said. He quoted the staff officer: "The compliments of General Griffin to Col. Chamberlin [*sic*]. You are expected to charge from this point on the enemy's works. You have sixteen pieces of artillery in your immediate front together with the guns that can be trained on you from either flank, with two intrenched lines of infantry." Chamberlain returned the compliments and said that he would take care of his front but wanted his

flanks protected. In DeLacy's account, the staff officer simply knows too much about the enemy—seemingly more than Chamberlain knew who had been observing them for hours, and was telling Chamberlain something he already knew. DeLacy statement and letter, 5.

43. This note exists only in typewritten form, apparently dictated or typed by Chamberlain after the war. To the typescript were added several corrections and editing marks, which seem to be in Chamberlain's handwriting. A notation on the back in Chamberlain's hand says, "Copy of my note on receiving order to assault [ill.] works of Petersburg June 18, 1864." No doubt the original was lost or discarded like many of the field notes written and received during the war. Chamberlain's later editing may reflect corrections later remembered or polishing. Without the original handwritten copy, we'll never know. The version used herein includes his corrections.

44. MHS.

45. Trulock, 205.

46. DeLacy, 5.

47. Trulock, 205.

48. DeLacy, 4.

49. DeLacy, 6.

50. Chamberlain letter, October 26, 1862.

51. Trulock, 208.

52. DeLacy, 5–6.

53. DeLacy, 7.

54. Chamberlain letter, November 3, 1862.

55. Barnes, vol. II, part II, 363.

56. Trulock, 209.

57. Chamberlain letter, November 4, 1862.

58. DeLacy, 7.

59. Trulock, 209–12. Wallace, 131–32; quote from Chamberlain, *Armies,* 27.

60. DeLacy, 8.

61. DeLacy, 3.

62. Trulock (p. 214) says that is was 7:00 before the field surgeon, Dr. R. A. Everett, was able to look at Chamberlain. This estimate most certainly seems too early. If Chamberlain had been wounded about 3:15 P.M., lay in the mud until his aides reached him, sent them away, lay until Bigelow sent men to retrieve him, then was placed behind Bigelow's

guns to wait, he must not have even left the battlefield before 5:30 or 6:00. Considering Chamberlain's journey to the field hospital three miles to the rear (Trulock, 214): four men carrying a stretcher over unfamiliar roads must rest every so often, so traveling at a rate of one mile per hour would have taken them at least until 9:00 P.M. to reach the hospital. Even if they had used Bigelow's ambulance, an hour would have been incredibly good time. It took a while for Tom Chamberlain and surgeons Shaw and Townsend to find the hospital, and the operation lasted through the night (Trulock, 214; Pullen, 212). Before Chamberlain's ordeal was over, he must have suffered at least twelve hours.

63. Barnes, vol. II, pt. 2, 363. Included in Chamberlain's case history is a report from pension examiner O. Mitchell on September 18, 1873, which states, "The ball entered the right hip in front of and a little below the right trochanter major [the hip bone], passed diagonally backward, and made exit above and posteriorly to the left great trochanter. The bladder was involved in the wound at some portion, as the subsequent history of escape of urine from the track of the wound and its extravasation testified. He very often suffers severe pain in the pelvic region. The chief disability resulting indirectly from the wound is the existence of a fistulous opening of the urethra, half an inch or more in length, just anterior to the scrotum; this often becomes inflamed. The greater part of the urine is voided through the fistula, the fistula itself resulting from the too long or too continuous wearing of a catheter. No change has resulted since the last examination. Disability total." For this disability, Chamberlain was paid $30 per month.

64. Wallace, 134.

65. OR, vol. 46, pt. 3, 730–31.

66. BC.

67. Trulock, 215.

68. Charles D. Gilmore to Gen. John L. Hodsdon, July 5, 1864, MSA.

69. NA.

70. Gilmore to Hodsdon, July 5, 1864, MSA.

71. John C. Chamberlain to Hodsdon, July 22, 1864, MSA.

72. MSA.

73. A notation on the letter by Trulock indicates that Chamberlain was in the habit of writing annually to his mother on his birthday. Trulock surmised that this letter was written about that time, possibly September 8 or 9, 1864.

74. PHS (original notation, BC).

75. MSA.

76. Trulock, 219.

77. Trulock, 220; Wallace, 139.

78. Trulock, 221.

79. LC.

80. Trulock, 222–23.

81. Trulock, 223.

82. "Sae" was Chamberlain's younger sister, Sarah Brastow Chamberlain, who had become close friends with Fanny. Sae was twenty-seven years old in 1864, eleven years younger than her sister-in-law. Chamberlain seemed to use her often as a sounding board or as a go-between when affairs with Fanny grew stormy.

83. Notation by Trulock on photocopied manuscript dates this letter.

84. BC.

85. BC.

1865

1. Trulock, 224.

2. PHS.

3. Julia Oehmig, curator of the Pejepscot Historical Society, believes that Chamberlain's father had Southern sympathies. The fact that Chamberlain's younger brother was named after the great Southern orator John Calhoun certainly adds credence to this and perhaps was one reason Chamberlain's father wanted him out of the Federal army.

4. BC.

5. Not in Chamberlain's handwriting, but signed by him.

6. LC. An explanation on the reverse by Fowler, dated March 3, 1865, says that he calculated from the last report of the 1st Brigade, which placed the strength of the 198th Pennsylvania at 933 and the 185th New York at 628.

7. The book was finished by Chamberlain's daughter after his death.

8. Since his last few weeks in the army were so hectic, Chamberlain had little time to correspond, and so letters from the beginning of March 1865 to after the surrender at Appomattox are rare. But his recollections in *The Passing of the Armies* were vivid even after half a century and so are used liberally in this chapter to continue to reconstruct, in Chamberlain's words, what cannot be reconstructed using his letters.

9. BC.

10. OR, ser. I, vol. 46, pt. 1, 267–68.

11. Porter, 429.

12. Chamberlain, *"Bayonet! Forward,"* 68: "Military Operations on the White Oak Road."

13. Chamberlain, *Armies,* 47.

14. Chamberlain, *Armies,* 43–44.

15. Chamberlain to Sae, March 9, 1865, BC.

16. Chamberlain, *Armies,* 45–46.

17. Chamberlain, *Armies,* 45–46. From Chamberlain Letterbook, under heading "Wounded": "1865 March 29, Quaker Road, left breast & left forearm twice,—painfully." Apparently the bullet entered his forearm, then exited the arm to strike him in the chest.

18. Chamberlain Letterbook. Under heading <u>Horse shot under me:</u> "1865 Quaker Road—March 29. Charlemagne <u>neck</u> & then my breast."

19. Chamberlain, *Armies,* 46.

20. Chamberlain, *Armies,* 50.

21. Chamberlain, *Armies,* 44–54.

22. Chamberlain, *Armies,* 57.

23. Chamberlain, *Armies,* 59.

24. Porter, 427.

25. This letter is not in Chamberlain's handwriting, nor is it signed by him, but it no doubt was dictated by him.

26. LC (original manuscript). A slightly altered version appears in OR, ser. I, vol. 46, pt. 3, 308.

27. Chamberlain's later writing may reflect his opinion on a controversy that would emerge from the fighting at Five Forks. Sheridan, placed in overall field command, would relieve Warren of his command—unfairly, as Chamberlain and others believed. This would ruin Warren's reputation as a fine officer. The affair went to an official court of inquiry before it was settled, but to Chamberlain until his death, some, if not all, of the blame must have rested upon Sheridan's shoulders.

28. Chamberlain, *Armies,* 69–78.

29. Chamberlain, *Armies,* 87–106. Chamberlain spends quite a few pages explaining the confusing orders Warren received as a result of "too many chiefs" at Headquarters. Sheridan later used Warren's tardiness in reaching him—caused by these contradictory orders and the fact that he had just fought a battle—as part of the charges to relieve Warren of his command.

30. Chamberlain, *Armies,* 117–20.
31. Calkins and Bearss, 88.
32. Chamberlain, *Armies,* 123.
33. Chamberlain, *Armies,* 126.
34. Chamberlain, *Armies,* 126–27.
35. Chamberlain, *Armies,* 128–29.
36. Chamberlain, *Armies,* 130–33.
37. Chamberlain, *Armies,* 132–35. A receipt for the captured men showed how large the capture was: 2 colonels, 6 captains, 11 lieutenants, and 1,050 soldiers.
38. In *The Passing of the Armies,* (pp. 139–40), Chamberlain wrote about the incident: "What sharp sense of responsibility for those who have committed to them the issues of life and death! Why should I not have let this onset take its general course and men their natural chances? Why choose out him for his death, and so take on myself the awful decision into what home irreparable loss and measureless desolation should cast their unlifted burden?"
39. Chamberlain, *Armies,* 138–40.
40. Chamberlain, *Armies,* 142–44.
41. Chamberlain Letterbook, PHS.
42. Chamberlain, *Armies,* 145–50.
43. Calkins and Bearss, 108.
44. After a remarkable military career, Warren had to live with the disgrace of having been relieved of his command by Sheridan until 1879, when a court of inquiry was convened and he was cleared of Sheridan's accusations. Chamberlain was among numerous officers who testified at the hearing; his personal files at the Pejepscot Historical Society in Brunswick, Maine, and in the Library of Congress contain hundreds of pages pertaining to the Warren case.
45. Chamberlain, *Armies,* 201.
46. Chamberlain, *Armies,* 205–9.
47. Grant, *Memoirs,* 478–79.
48. Chamberlain, *Armies,* 218–29.
49. Chamberlain, *Armies,* 235.
50. Chamberlain, *Armies,* 235.
51. Chamberlain, *Armies,* 237–42.
52. Chamberlain, *Armies,* 246–47. Chamberlain apparently rode about during the time between Lee's arrival and Grant's, since they would have passed each other had Chamberlain remained in the same

place. Probably Chamberlain was at the right of his line when he "felt" Lee approaching from the Confederate lines; then he rode to the left to witness Grant's arrival from that direction.

53. Chamberlain, *Armies,* 247–48.

54. Chamberlain, *Armies,* 230–50.

55. Chamberlain, *Armies,* 251.

56. Chamberlain, *Armies,* 239. The letter referred to remains in a private collection but can be read in Chamberlain, *"Bayonet! Forward,"* 238–39.

57. LC (original manuscript). A slightly altered version appears in OR, ser. I, vol. 46, pt. 3, 707.

58. Chamberlain, *Armies,* 258.

59. Chamberlain, *Armies,* 258–61.

60. Chamberlain, *Armies,* 261–62.

61. Chamberlain, *Armies,* 262–63.

62. Chamberlain, *Armies,* 264.

63. Chamberlain, *Armies,* 265–66.

64. Chamberlain, *Armies,* 268.

65. Chamberlain, *Armies,* 270–71.

66. Chamberlain, *Armies,* 257–72.

67. OR, ser. I, vol. 46, pt. 3, 731.

68. BC.

69. Chamberlain, *Armies,* 284–86.

70. As he did with "Daisy" and "Daise," Chamberlain sometimes interchanged the spelling of his wife's name between "Fanny" and "Fannie."

71. When Chamberlain left Brunswick at the end of February, they had not yet named their daughter, and he left the naming up to his wife, who named her Gertrude Loraine. Sadly, she lived only seven months.

72. PHS.

73. Chamberlain, *Armies,* 287. If you drive west from Petersburg, Virginia, on Route 640, you can see the signs for Wilson's and Sutherland Station. Much of the area from Petersburg to Appomattox is relatively unchanged from 1865.

74. Chamberlain, *Armies,* 292.

75. LC.

76. OR, ser. I, vol. 46, pt. 3, 924.

77. "Ultimo" appears in many Civil War–era reports and correspondence and means in or of the previous month.

78. OR, ser. I, vol. 46, pt. 1, 847.

79. OR, ser. I, vol. 46, pt. 3, 970.

80. Chamberlain, *Armies,* 303.

81. Chamberlain, *Armies,* 308.

82. This letter remains in private hands but was published in Chamberlain, *"Bayonet! Forward,"* 220–21.

83. Chamberlain, *Armies,* 315.

84. Chamberlain, *Armies,* 317.

85. Chamberlain, *Armies,* 324.

86. Chamberlain, *Armies,* 339.

87. Chamberlain, *Armies,* 340.

88. Chamberlain, *Armies,* 343.

89. Chamberlain, *Armies,* 345–46.

90. Chamberlain, *Armies,* 353.

91. Chamberlain, *Armies,* 345–46.

92. BC.

93. Chamberlain, *Armies,* 391.

94. MSA.

95. PHS.

96. PHS.

CONCLUSION

1. Chamberlain, *Armies,* 343.

2. Chamberlain, *Armies,* 271.

3. Trulock, 208.

⊹⊱ BIBLIOGRAPHY ⊰⊹

MANUSCRIPTS
Bowdoin College Library, Special Collections
    Elisha Coan Manuscript
Gettysburg National Military Park Library
    William C. Oates Correspondence
Library of Congress
    Joshua L. Chamberlain Papers
    Patrick DeLacy Manuscript
Maine Historical Society
Maine State Archives
National Archives
Pejepscot Historical Society Archives
    Joshua L. Chamberlain Letterbook

BOOKS
Alleman, Tillie Pierce. *At Gettysburg, or What a Girl Saw and Heard of the Battle.* New York: W. Lake Borland, 1889. Reprint. Baltimore: Butternut and Blue, 1994.

Ames, John W. "In Front of the Stone Wall at Fredericksburg." *Battles and Leaders of the Civil War.* New York: Century Magazine, 1887–88, vol. 3, 122.

Barnes, Joseph K. *The Medical and Surgical History of the War of the Rebellion.* Washington, D.C.: Government Printing Office, 1877.

Calkins, Chris M. *The Battles of Appomattox Station and Appomattox Court House April 8–9, 1865.* 2d ed. Lynchburg, VA: H. E. Howard, 1987.

———. *The Final Bivouac: The Surrender Parade at Appomattox and the Disbanding of the Armies April 10–May 20, 1865.* 2d ed. Lynchburg, VA: H. E. Howard, 1988.

Calkins, Chris, and Ed Bearss. *The Battle of Five Forks.* Lynchburg, VA: H. E. Howard, 1985.

Chamberlain, Joshua L. *"Bayonet! Forward": My Civil War Reminiscences.* Edited by Stan Clark. Gettysburg, PA: Stan Clark Military Books, 1994.

————. *The Passing of the Armies.* Reprint. Dayton, OH: Morningside House, 1982.

Coddington, Edwin B. *The Gettysburg Campaign: A Study in Command.* New York: Charles Scribner's Sons, 1968.

Cullen, Joseph P. "Battle of Spotsylvania." *Wilderness and Spotsylvania.* Reprint. Harrisburg: Historical Times, 1971.

Frassanito, William A. *Gettysburg: A Journey in Time.* New York: Charles Scribner's Sons, 1975.

————. *Grant and Lee: The Virginia Campaigns 1864–1865.* New York: Charles Scribner's Sons, 1983.

Furgurson, Ernest B. *Chancellorsville 1863: The Souls of the Brave.* New York: Alfred A. Knopf, Inc., Reprint. New York: Vintage Books, 1993.

Grant, Ulysses S. *Personal Memoirs of U. S. Grant.* Volumes I and II. 1885. Reprint. New York: Bonanza Books, n.d.

Hardee, W. J. *Hardee's Rifle and Light Infantry Tactics.* New York. J. O. Kane, Publisher, 1862. Reprint. Cornith, MS: C & D Jarnagin.

Jomini, Baron Antoine Henri. *The Art of War.* Philadelphia: J. B. Lippincott & Co., 1862. Reprint. Westport, CT: Greenwood Press, n.d.

Judson, A. M. *History of the Eighty-third Regiment Pennsylvania Volunteers.* Erie, PA: B. F. H. Lynn, Publisher, n.d.

Luvaas, Jay, and Harold W. Nelson, eds. *The U.S. Army War College Guide to the Battle of Chancellorsville & Fredericksburg.* Carlisle, PA: South Mountain Press, 1988. Reprint. New York: Harper & Row, 1989.

McClellan, H. B. *The Campaigns of Stuart's Cavalry.* 1885. Reprint. Secaucus, NJ: The Blue & Grey Press, 1993.

Murfin, James V. *The Gleam of Bayonets: The Battle of Antietam and Robert E. Lee's Maryland Campaign, September 1862.* New York: Thomas Yoseloff, 1965.

Nesbitt, Mark. *Rebel Rivers: A Guide to Civil War Sites on the Potomac, Rappahannock, York, and James.* Mechanicsburg, PA: Stackpole Books, 1993.

Norton, Oliver Wilcox. *The Attack and Defense of Little Round Top, Gettysburg, July 2, 1863.* 1913. Reprint. Dayton, OH: Morningside Bookshop, 1983.

Oates, William C. *The War Between the Union and the Confederacy and its Lost Opportunities.* New York: The Neale Publishing Company, 1905.

Porter, Horace. *Campaigning with Grant.* 1897. Reprint. New York: Bonanza Books, 1961.

Priest, John Michael. *Antietam: The Soldier's Battle.* New York: Oxford University Press, 1989.

Pullen, John J. *The Twentieth Maine: A Volunteer Regiment in the Civil War.* New York: Fawcett World Library, 1962. Reprint. Dayton, OH: Morningside House.

Scott, Robert Garth. *Into the Wilderness with the Army of the Potomac.* Bloomington, IN: Indiana University Press, 1985.

Sheridan, Philip. *Civil War Memoirs.* New York: Bantam Books, 1991. Reprint of Civil War segment of *Personal Memoirs of P. H. Sheridan, General United States Army.* 2 vols. New York: Charles L. Webster & Co., 1888.

Styple, William B., ed. *With a Flash of His Sword: The Writings of Major Holman S. Melcher 20th Maine Infantry.* Kearny, NJ: Belle Grove Publishing Company, 1994.

Trudeau, Noah Andre. *Bloody Roads South: The Wilderness to Cold Harbor, May–June 1864.* Boston: Little Brown and Company, 1989.

Trulock, Alice Rains. *In the Hands of Providence: Joshua L. Chamberlain and the American Civil War.* Chapel Hill: The University of North Carolina Press, 1992.

United States War Department. *War of the Rebellion: Official Records of the Union and Confederate Armies.* 128 vols. Washington, D.C.: Government Printing Office, 1880–1901.

Wallace, Willard M. *Soul of the Lion.* New York: Thomas Nelson & Sons, 1960. Reprint. Gettysburg, PA: Stan Clark Military Books, 1991.

Wheeler, Richard. *On Fields of Fury from the Wilderness to the Crater: An Eyewitness to History.* New York: Harper Collins, 1991.

ARTICLES

Chamberlain, Joshua L. "Through Blood and Fire at Gettysburg." *The Gettysburg Magazine,* January 1992, 43–57. First published in *Hearst's Magazine,* June 1913.

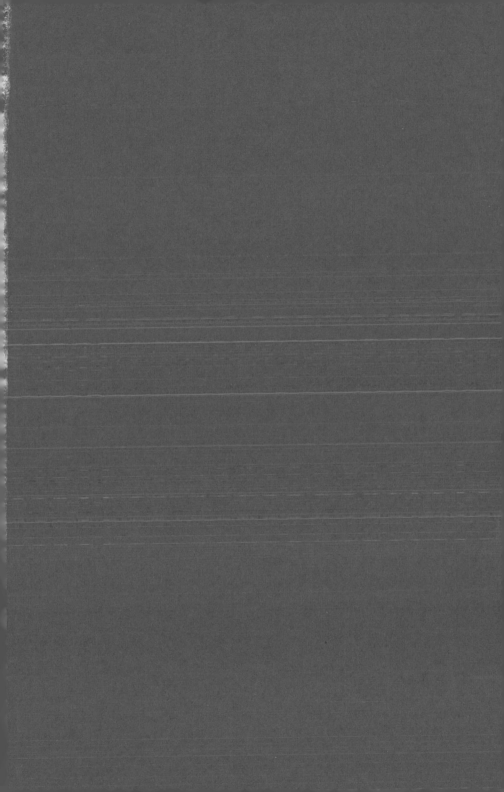